MULTICOMPUTER VISION

The published books from the Multicomputer Workshops series are:

Languages and Architectures for Image Processing
Michael J.B. Duff and Stefano Levialdi, eds., Academic Press, London, 1981.

Multicomputers and Image Processing, Algorithms and Programs
Kendall Preston, Jr., and Leonard Uhr, eds., Academic Press, New York, 1982.

Computing Structures for Image Processing
Michael J.B. Duff, ed., Academic Press, London, 1983.

Integrated Technology for Parallel Image Processing
Stefano Levialdi, ed., Academic Press, London, 1985.

Intermediate-Level Image Processing
Michael J.B. Duff, ed., Academic Press, London, 1986.

Evaluation of Multicomputers for Image Processing
Leonard Uhr, Kendall Preston, Jr., Stefano Levialdi, Michael J.B. Duff, Academic Press, New York, 1986.

MULTICOMPUTER VISION

Edited by

S. Levialdi
*Department of Mathematics, University of Rome,
Rome, Italy*

1988

ACADEMIC PRESS
Harcourt Brace Jovanovich, Publishers
London   San Diego   New York
Boston   Sydney   Tokyo   Toronto

ACADEMIC PRESS LIMITED
24/28 Oval Road, London NW1 7DX

United States. Edition published by
ACADEMIC PRESS INC.
San Diego, CA 92101

British Library Cataloguing in Publication Data

Multicomputer vision.
1. Computer systems. Parallel-processor systems
I. Levialdi, S.
004′.35

ISBN 0-12-444818-6

Filmset by Eta Services (Typesetters) Limited, Beccles, Suffolk
Printed in Great Britain by St Edmundsbury Press Limited
Bury St Edmunds, Suffolk

Contributors

GIANCARLO BONGIOVANNI, *Dipartimento di Matematica, Universita dell'Aquila, 67100, L'Aquila, Italy*

L. CARRIOLI, *I.A.N., C.N.R. Pavia, Italy*

MAN BUN CHU, *Department of Electrical and Computer Engineering, George Mason University, Fairfax, Virginia 22030, USA*

L. CINQUE, *Department of Mathematics, University of Rome, Rome, Italy*

S. CUNIOLO, *Dipartimento Informatica e Sistemistica, Università degli Studi, 27100 Pavia, Italy*

EDWARD DELP, *School of Electrical Engineering, Purdue University, West Lafayette, IN 47907, USA*

R.P.W. DUIN, *Department of Applied Physics, Delft University of Technology, Lorentzweg 1, 2628 CJ Delft, The Netherlands*

MARCO FERRETTI, *Dipartimento Informatica e Sistemistica, Università degli Studi, 27100 Pavia, Italy*

LEAH H. JAMIESON, *School of Electrical Engineering, Purdue University, West Lafayette, Indiana 47907, USA*

PIETER P. JONKER, *Pattern Recognition Group, Department of Applied Physics, Delft University of Technology, The Netherlands*

ANARGYROS KRIKELIS, *Department of Electrical Engineering and Electronics, Brunel University, Uxbridge, UB8 39H*

MARK LAVIN, *IBM T.J. Watson Res. Center, PO Box 218, Yorktown Heights, NY 10598, USA*

STEFANO LEVIALDI, *Dipartimento Matematica, Universita di Roma, Ple. Aldo Moro 2, 00185 Rome, Italy*

R.M. LEA, *Department of Electrical Engineering and Electronics, Brunel University, Uxbridge, Middlesex UB8 3PH*

HUNGWEN LI, *IBM T.J. Watson Research Center, Yorktown Heights, New York 10598, USA*

MASSIMO MARESCA, *D.I.S.T.—University of Genova, Via Opera Pia 11A, 16145 Genova, Italy*

ALAIN MERIGOT, *Universite Paris I, Institut d'Electronique Fondamentale, Lab Associe au CNRS, Batiment 220, F-91405 Orsay Cedex, France*

ANTHONY P. REEVES, *Department of Electrical Engineering, Cornell University, Ithaca, NY 98195, USA*

G. ROBBINS, *Intelligent Systems Division, Information Sciences Institute, 4676 Admiralty Way, Marina Del Rey, CA90292-6695, USA*

AZRIEL ROSENFELD, *Center for Automation Research, University of Maryland, College Park, MD 20742, USA*

D.H. SCHAEFER, *Department of Electrical and Computer Engineering, George Mason University, Fairfax, Virginia 22030, USA*

L. UHR, *Computer Science Department, 1210 West Dayton Street, University of Madison-Wisconsin, Madison, Wisconsin 53706, USA*

FRANK WEIL, *School of Electrical Engineering, Purdue University, West Lafayette, IN 47907, USA*

STEVEN WILSON, *Applied Intelligent Systems Inc, 110 Parkland Plaza, Ann Arbor, Michigan 48103, USA*

Preface

This book contains most of the papers and discussions presented at the 8th Workshop on Multicomputers, held at Rome (Italy) on June 2–5, 1987. As some researchers, in the area of multiprocessor systems for image analysis, may remember, the previous seven Workshops were held at Windsor (1979), Ischia (1980), Madison (1981), Abingdon (1982), Polignano (1983), Tucson (1984), Bonas (1985) and, finally in 1987 in Rome.

The animating principle of these Workshops has always been to provide an informal frame of reference: more than reporting on current work participants have always spoken out their doubts and problems in the design and development of algorithms, architectures or languages aimed at the best exploitation of multiprocessor systems. The typical problems that have been considered are: evaluation of systems and algorithms by means of cleverly thought benchmarks, representation of pictorial data and definition of the different levels of abstraction (from the pixel level to the symbolic one), definitions of the borderlines between low level and high level vision tasks, primitive functions that should necessarily be embedded in the elementary processing unit, ways to disseminate, reuse and expand existing software for image analysis.

In particular, the Rome meeting was aimed at a clarification on the contents and extent of the high level vision tasks. The contributions contained in this book fall into three areas: 1) new multicomputer algorithms for image processing, 2) evaluation and suggestions on multicomputer systems and 3) new designs in advanced architectures for computer vision.

The first area in the book contains four papers: the first one by G. Bongiovanni et al. *Bimodality Analysis Using Pyramids*, describes a pyramidal algorithm for image segmentation based on the definition of the "bimean" of a population, showing preliminary results on artificially generated data. The second one, by M. Maresca et al. *Parallel Hough Transform Algorithms on Polymorphic Torus Architecture* uses the Polymorphic Torus architecture to yield positive results when computing the Hough Transform by executing mesh and tree algorithms without communication overhead; it is shown that the implementation of several parallelization techniques (in the image space, in the feature point space, in the parameter space) may be adequately performed on the suggested architecture. The third paper is by David H. Schaefer et al. *Pyramids and "End"*, here objects are recognized by means of the five-level quad-tree pyramid (GAM) based on chips from the MPP machine. Simple objects are considered and the examples contained in the paper generalize the concept of "end" or terminus in regions, fingers and characters. The fourth and last paper of this group is by Frank Weil et al. *An Algorithm Database for an Image Understanding Task Execution Environment.* The idea of an intelligent operating system for matching the system configuration to the requirements of the computation is brought forward with particular reference to the databases required for scheduling and reconfiguration decisions based on the user's task definition.

The second area, oriented towards the evaluation of multicomputer systems contains five papers: a first one by L. Uhr, *The Coordinated Evaluation of Parallel Architectures for Perceptual Tasks*; addresses the issue of the general evaluation of multi-processor architectures oriented towards perceptual tasks. A methodology is suggested by which a specification procedure should describe and assign costs. The underlying topologies should also be classified, special purpose algorithms should be developed for object recognition and computer vision and, finally, a performance measurement in terms of time and hardware should be estimated. A second paper by A. Krikelis et al. *An Associative Approach to Computer Vision* presents a fine grain associative string structure showing its advantages when used for a general purpose computer vision system. A simulation of the VLSI implementation of the architecture enables the evaluation of the system on a set of image processing tasks. A third paper is by A. Reeves, *Meshes and Hypercubes for Computer Vision.* Although many novel architectures have been suggested for computer vision few have been built and very few possess good programming facilities: the topics of algorithm design and coding with comfortable programming environments are considered together with the presentation of performance meaures for the evaluation of the mesh and hypercube architectures. A fourth paper is by R.P.W. Duin et al. *Processor Arrays Compared to Pipelines for Cellular Image Operations* where a comparison between processor arrays and pipeline computers is performed using identical single processor elements: pipelines are slower, smaller and more flexible than processor arrays and are also independent from image size. The last paper by L. Carrioli et al. *Image Processing Experiments on a Commercial MIMD System*, is an evaluation of a commercial MIMD machine (Sequent Balance 8000) on a typical set of low level tasks: thresholding, mathematical closing and distance transform computation.

The third area, on the design features of new multiprocessor architectures, starts with a paper by A. Mérigot, *Designing Memories for Cellular Processors*, where the memory limitations of parallel machines are discussed and a new design for a unified multi media memory is presented showing the organization of cellular processors with a hybrid memory and an efficient indirect access to it. The second paper, by Stephen S. Wilson, *One Dimensional SIMD Architectures*, presents a physical realization of a one-dimensional array of 128 to 1024 identical processors where the individual memory can hold an entire column of the image to be processed with further storage space to store intermediate results. A particular commercial system is described (the AIS-5000) where truth tables in hardware may enhance neighborhood and logic operations apart from having instantaneous vertical communication of data. Moreover, to further enhance performance, a pipeline of one-dimensional arrays may be operated in multi-SIMD mode. To conclude this group and the book, a paper by G. Robins, *The ISI Grapher: a Portable Tool for Displaying Graphs Pictorially* shows how a portable program for displaying graphs in a visual manner (using windows, menus and icons), may be constructed so introducing the concept of "grapher"; such a program codes a linear-time algorithm for laying out graphs.

The near future of multicomputer systems for artificial vision looks promising in terms of real working systems, much may be gained by studies on parallel algorithms, high level languages to code those algorithms and new, comfortable, environments with man-machine interfaces to visualize, test and re-program the computations on real images. I hope that the friendly and informal exchange of information on current research in this area (including negative results) may be still active along those international channels which have been available during all the Multicomputer Workshops we have held until now.

University of Rome   *Stefano Levialdi*
1987

Contents

Contributors   v

Preface   vii

NEW MULTICOMPUTER ALGORITHMS FOR IMAGE PROCESSING

Chapter One   1
Bimodality Analysis Using Pyramids
G. BONGIOVANNI, L. CINQUE, S. LEVIALDI and A. ROSENFELD

Chapter Two   9
Parallel Hough Transform Algorithms on Polymorphic Torus Architecture
M. MARESCA, M. LAVIN and H. LI

Chapter Three   23
Pyramids and "End"
D.H. SCHAEFER and MAN BUN CHU

Chapter Four   35
An Algorithm Database for an Image Understanding Task Execution Environment
F. WEIL, L. JAMIESON and E. DELP

EVALUATION AND SUGGESTIONS ON MULTICOMPUTER SYSTEMS

Chapter Five   53
The Coordinated Evaluation of Parallel Architectures for Perceptual Tasks
L. UHR

Chapter Six   75
An Associative Approach to Computer Vision
A. KRIKELIS and R.M. LEA

Chapter Seven   97
Meshes and Hypercubes for Computer Vision
    A.P. REEVES

Chapter Eight   117
Image Processing Experiments on a Commercial MIMD System
    L. CARRIOLI, S. CUNIOLO and M. FERRETTI

NEW DESIGNS IN ADVANCED ARCHITECTURES FOR COMPUTER VISION

Chapter Nine   131
One Dimensional SIMD Architectures—The AIS-5000
    S.S. WILSON

Chapter Ten   151
Processor Arrays Compared to Pipelines for Cellular Image
Operations
    R.P.W. DUIN and P.P. JONKER

Chapter Eleven   171
Designing Memories for Cellular Processors
    A. MÉRIGOT

Chapter Twelve   185
The ISI Grapher: a Portable Tool for Displaying Graphs Pictorially
    G. ROBINS

Chapter One

Bimodality Analysis Using Pyramids

G. Bongiovanni, Luigi Cinque and Stefano Levialdi

Department of Mathematics, University of Rome, Rome, Italy

Azriel Rosenfeld

Center for Automation Research, University of Maryland, College Park, MD 20742

ABSTRACT

We call a population bimodal if it can be divided into two subpopulations whose variances are small relative to the population variance. We show in this paper that a pyramid computer can detect the bimodality of a population of pixels in a number of computational steps on the order of the log of the population size. We also present an iterative pyramid technique that segments a bimodal population by mapping its values into two constants, which are approximately the means of the subpopulations.

1 INTRODUCTION

Bimodality of a population—for example, of the gray levels in a digital image—is an indication that the population may be a mixture of two subpopulations. Bimodality detection on an image's histogram is the basis for segmenting the image by thresholding its gray levels so as to separate the two histogram peaks. Thus it is of interest to develop efficient computational techniques for detecting bimodality and determining the locations of the peaks.

In this paper, we call a population bimodal if it can be divided into two subpopulations whose variances are small relative to the population variance. Specifically, let the population size be n and its variance σ^2. Let us divide the population into two subpopulations of sizes n_1 and n_2, with variances σ_1^2 and σ_2^2. We find the subdivision that minimizes the statistic

$$\frac{n_1\sigma_1^2 + n_2\sigma_2^2}{n\sigma^2} \qquad (*)$$

This minimum value of $(*)$ is a measure of the bimodality of the population.

We show in this paper that a pyramid computer can be used to rapidly detect bimodality of the gray levels in a digital image input to the base of the pyramid. We use the standard nonoverlapped pyramid in which the successive levels $l, l - 1, \ldots, 1, 0$ have sizes $2^l \times 2^l, 2^{l-1} \times 2^{l-1}, \ldots, 2 \times 2$, 1×1, and each cell on level k is connected to a 2×2 block of "children" on level $k + 1$. In our experiments, we used $l = 4$, with input images of size 128×128. For a collection of papers on pyramid computers see [1].

The basic bimodality detection algorithm is described in Section 2. In Section 3 we describe an iterative version of the algorithm that produces improved results.

2 BIMODALITY DETECTION

The basic idea of our method of bimodality detection is as follows: Initially, we divide the image into blocks, say of size 8×8 (so that a 128×128 image consists of $16 \times 16 = 256$ blocks). For each of these blocks, we consider all possible partitions of its gray levels into two intervals, and compute ($*$) for each partition. We call the block bimodal if the minimum value of ($*$) does not exceed some threshold t_1 (to be discussed below); otherwise, we call it nonbimodal.

If a block is determined to be bimodal, we record the sizes n_1 and n_2 of its two gray level subpopulations, their means μ_1 and μ_2, and their variances σ_1^2 and σ_2^2. If it is nonbimodal, we record only its total population size ($n = 64$), its mean μ, and its variance σ^2. These values are computed at level 4 of the pyramid, i.e. at the level whose cells represent 8×8 blocks of the image.

We now use a recursive computation in the pyramid to estimate the bimodalities of larger image blocks. Each cell at level 3 receives inputs from its four children at level 4. Each of these inputs is either of the form $(n_1, n_2, \mu_1, \mu_2, \sigma_1^2, \sigma_2^2)$ or of the form $(n = 64, \mu, \sigma^2)$, depending on whether or not the child was determined to be bimodal. Thus the cell receives between 4 and 8 μ values from its children, depending on how many of them were called bimodal. It arranges these values in order of size and divides them into two intervals in all possible ways. For each such division, the cell computes the sizes and variances of the two subpopulations, and from them computes ($*$). We call the cell bimodal if the minimum value of ($*$), computed in this way, does not exceed some threshold t_2 (see below); otherwise, we call it nonbimodal.

The process is now repeated for levels 2, 1, and 0. If a cell at level 3 is called bimodal, it records two population sizes, two means, and two variances; if it is called nonbimodal, it records only one size, mean, and variance. Each cell at level 2 receives the resulting data from its four children at level 3, and carries out the computation described in the previous paragraph, and similarly for the cells at levels 1 and 0. If the (sole) cell at level 0 is determined to be bimodal, we call the entire input image bimodal.

The entire process involves only a bounded amount of computation to process the blocks (whose size does not grow with the image size), followed by a bounded amount of computation at each level of the pyramid above the level corresponding to the block size. In this sense we can say that the total amount of computation is proportional to the number of pyramid levels, which is the logarithm of the image size.

How should the thresholds used in this process be chosen? One way to do this is to observe that if the input image has uniformly distributed gray levels, we should not call it bimodal; thus the thresholds should be chosen so as to ensure that a uniform image is never called bimodal. It can be shown that the theoretical (*) for a uniform distribution is 0.25, which suggests that any threshold <0.25 could be used; but if we use small blocks (e.g. 8 × 8) of a uniformly distributed image, we may find that 0.25 is not a safe threshold. To verify this, we computed (*) for each block of a randomly generated 128 × 128 image having uniformly distributed gray levels. Table 1 shows the resulting (*) values when we used blocks of sizes 4 × 4, 8 × 8, 16 × 16, and 32 × 32. For each case we show the smallest (*) obtained for any block, the average (*), and the largest (*). We see that a safe threshold must be considerably smaller than 0.25 when we use small blocks.

At higher levels of the pyramid, on the other hand, the threshold can be larger than 0.25. This is because a cell at a higher level is dealing with between 4 and 8 subpopulations (1 or 2 from each of its four children), and if the input image is uniform, each of these subpopulations is a sample of the same uniform population. For example, if there are four subpopulations (as there should be), they all have equal sizes, say m, and all have about the same variance σ^2, so that if they are subdivided with i of them in one interval and $4 - i$ in the other, (*) becomes

$$\frac{im\,\sigma^2 + (4 - i)m\,\sigma^2}{4m\,\sigma^2} = 1.$$

(This is confirmed by our computational experiments; the values of (*) rapidly approach 1 as we move upward in the pyramid.) Thus at the higher levels we can use a threshold much closer to 1, and a threshold such as 0.5 would be very safe.

To test the ability of our method to detect bimodality, we used images whose gray level populations were an equal mixture of two Gaussians. The

Table 1

Block size	Value of (*)		
	Min	Mean	Max
4 × 4	0.068	0.251	0.478
8 × 8	0.152	0.255	0.368
16 × 16	0.217	0.260	0.307
32 × 32	0.236	0.253	0.269

Table 2

Standard deviation	Value of (∗)		
	Min	Mean	Max
3	0.0053	0.0099	0.0162
6	0.0185	0.0388	0.0670
9	0.0380	0.0820	0.1320
12	0.0690	0.1350	0.2530
18	0.1230	0.2270	0.3390
24	0.1430	0.2850	0.3960

means of the Gaussians were 100 and 160 (recall that the gray scale is 0, ..., 255), and their standard deviations (both equal) were 3, 6, 9, 12, 18, or 24. Table 2 shows the smallest, average, and largest (∗) values obtained for these images (at level 4 of the pyramid) when we divided them into 8×8 blocks. We see that a threshold of $t_1 = 0.25$ would work for most of the blocks, but a safer threshold would only work for the cases having small standard deviations.

If we always call a block bimodal (i.e. we use $t_1 = 1$), and carry out the pyramid computation as described above, calling every cell bimodal (i.e. also using $t_2 = 1$), we find that the values of (∗) remain about the same as we go up the pyramid; thus a safe threshold of $t_2 = 0.5$ would work very well at the higher levels. The difficulty is at the lowest level (the initial image blocks), where the choice of threshold is more critical.

3 AN ITERATIVE SCHEME

Some improvement in bimodality detection performance can be obtained by using an iterative scheme, involving several computational passes through the pyramid. The basic idea is as follows: Suppose a cell has a below-threshold value of (∗), so that we regard it as bimodal, but its father (on the level above it) has an above-threshold value (this might happen, for example, if the other children of that father were not recognized as bimodal). Let us call such a cell a "root cell". We can improve the father's (∗) score by "thresholding" the root cell's population; instead of treating it as composed of two subpopulations of sizes n_1, n_2 with means and variances μ_1, μ_2 and σ_1^2, σ_2^2, we regard it as composed of n_1 μ_1's and n_2 μ_2's, so that its two subpopulations now have variances of zero. (This is equivalent to "thresholding" the cell's image block, and setting every pixel's gray level to either μ_1 or μ_2 depending on whether it belongs to the first or second subpopulation.) When this is done, the father's (∗) score may no longer be above threshold, so that the father is now called bimodal; and the process can be iterated (in our experiments, we used only two iterations).

Figures 1 and 2 illustrate the effect of applying this iterative method to two input images, one having uniformly distributed gray levels and the other having a gray level distribution that is a mixture of two Gaussians (means 100 and 160, standard deviations 18). In both cases we started with 8×8 image blocks and used the threshold $t_1 = 0.4$. (Note that this is a high threshold and forces us to call many of the uniformly distributed blocks bimodal.) At the higher level cells we used $t_2 = 0.07$ (i.e. accepting only very strong bimodality) at the first iteration, and 0.04 (an even stronger criterion) at the second iteration. We show, in each case, the original histogram and the histograms that result when we "threshold" the subpopulations of the root cells at the first and second iterations. (Note that the histograms only show gray level values having a number of pixels different from zero.) We see that when the two-Gaussian image is treated in this way, after the second iteration it becomes completely "thresholded" into the two gray levels 98 and 160 (essentially the means of the two Gaussians); but when the same process is applied to the uniform image, it is not perfectly thresholded, although its histogram does become strongly bimodal (with peaks approximately at the $\frac{1}{4}$ and $\frac{3}{4}$ points of the grayscale). The ability of the two-pass method to yield a

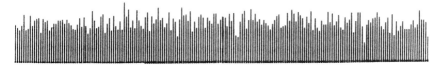

(*a*) *Central portion of the histogram of the artificially generated image*

(*b*) *Histogram of the image resulting from the first computational pass*

(*c*) *Histogram of the image resulting from the second pass*

Fig. 1. Segmentation of a uniformly distributed image.

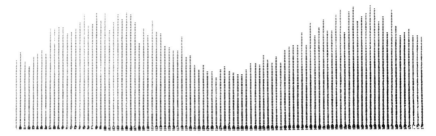

(a) *Central portion of the histogram of the artificially generated image (with means 100 and 160 and standard deviations 18)*

(b) *Histogram of the image resulting from the first computational pass*

(c) *Histogram of the image resulting from the second pass*

Fig. 2. Segmentation of a bimodal image.

"thresholding" of the two-Gaussian image suggests that it may be useful in detecting bimodality in cases where the one-pass method cannot readily do so.

4 CONCLUDING REMARKS

We have shown that a pyramid computer can detect the bimodality of a population of pixels in a number of computational steps on the order of the log of the population size. We have also presented an iterative pyramid technique that segments a bimodal population by mapping its values into two constants, which are approximately the means of the subpopulations.

It should be mentioned that other measures of bimodality could have been used in place of the statistic (∗). For example, in [2] the reciprocal of the squared *Fisher distance*, $\dfrac{n_1\sigma_1^2 + n_2\sigma_2^2}{n(\mu_1 - \mu_2)^2}$, is used in place of (∗), with very good results.

REFERENCES

[1] V. Cantoni and S. Levialdi, eds. (1986). *Pyramidal Systems for Computer Vision,* Springer, Berlin.
[2] T.Y. Phillips, A. Rosenfeld and A.C. Sher. (1987). *O(log n) bimodality analysis,* TR-1900, Center for Automation Research, University of Maryland, College Park, August 1987.

Chapter Two

Parallel Hough Transform Algorithms on Polymorphic Torus Architecture

Massimo Maresca[1], Mark Lavin[1] and Hungwen Li[2]

[1]*DIST-University of Genova, Via Opera Pia* 11*A,*
16145 *Genova, Italy*
[2]*IBM T.J. Watson Res. Center, P.O. Box* 218,
Yorktown Heights, N Y 10598, *USA*

ABSTRACT

The Hough transform is a powerful technique for curve detection and parameter extraction in digital images. The number of operations required to carry it out is proportional to the number of feature points in the original image and to the quantization of the parameter space. Von Neumann computers show themselves unable to efficiently compute the Hough transform when real time constraints have to be met. Parallelization techniques for the Hough transform computation on fine grain parallel computers have been proposed which take advantage of mesh and tree interconnection networks. This paper shows how a newly proposed architecture, the Polymorphic-Torus, is able to execute both mesh and tree algorithms for the Hough transform computation without any communication overhead. The flexibility of the Polymorphic-Torus allows for the implementation of several parallelization techniques which may be convenient depending on the characteristics of the input image and on the desired quantization of the parameter space.

1 INTRODUCTION

The Hough transform is a powerful technique for curve detection and parameter extraction in digital images [1]. Given a set of curves, represented by an equation and a set of parameters, each image feature point "votes" for all the curves which it could belong to. For each curve a counter is incremented at each vote. At the end of the voting process either a thresholding process on the counters is applied or the maxima among the counters are found. The Hough transform is an intermediate level vision task since it converts an iconic representation of an image into a symbolic one.

MULTICOMPUTER VISION
ISBN 0-12-444818-6

The computational complexity and storage requirements of the Hough transform grow exponentially with the quantization and the dimensionality of the parameter space. Von Neumann computers show themselves unable to efficiently compute the Hough transform when real time constraints are expected. Techniques have been developed for sequential processors to reduce both the memory requirements and the computational complexity [2]. However further improvements can be obtained by exploring the use of parallel computers.

Mesh Connected Computers (MCC) and pipeline architectures have been proposed to compute the Hough transform for straight line detection [3–5]. Augmented mesh networks, with independent addressing capabilities or additional tree connections, have also been advocated [6] for the same task. Furthermore tree architectures were proposed for the Hough transform computation for any kind of curve [7].

Several techniques of parallelization of the Hough transform are possible, each of which performs well on a particular architecture and poorly on another. Furthermore the performance of each technique depends on the characteristics of the image (e.g. number of feature points vs. quantization of the parameter space) which in general cannot be determined a priori. As a result there lacks the flexibility of pairing parallel algorithms with parallel architectures.

How to provide such a flexibility and remove the restriction on architectures are the themes of this paper. We show how different techniques of parallelizing the Hough transform can be implemented on a Polymorphic-Torus architecture [8, 9], with performance as good as in the architectures specifically proposed for each individual technique. Section 2 introduces the Hough transform and outlines four parallelization techniques for mesh and tree connected computers. Section 3 describes the Polymorphic-Torus architecture and Section 4 shows how the four parallelization techniques can be implemented in the Polymorphic-Torus. Section 5 discusses the advantages of the four techniques and their performance on the Polymorphic-Torus architecture. Finally Section 6 provides a concluding remark.

2 HOUGH TRANSFORM PARALLELIZATION TECHNIQUES

In the usual formulation of the Hough transform the *image space*, a two-dimensional array of pixels, is mapped into the *parameter space*, that is a k-dimensional array of values. Parameter space points correspond to curves in the image space and vice versa. Curves are detected by having each point in the image space vote for all the curves it could belong to. Usually a feature extraction phase precedes the Hough transformation; in this case only a few elements of the image array are feature points and contribute in the voting process.

The complexity of the Hough transform is proportional to the number of feature points and to the quantization of the parameter space. For example in the straight line detection problem, each feature point (f_x, f_y) votes for all the pairs (ρ, θ) which are a solution of the equation $\rho = f_x \cos \theta + f_y \sin \theta$. The total complexity of the voting process is $O(fK_\theta)$, where K_θ is the quantization of the parameter space in the direction θ. After the votes have been computed either local maxima are extracted or only the lines with a number of votes greater than a given threshold are considered. We will restrict our analysis to the vote computation phase.

A reduction in the computational complexity can be obtained by combining the thresholding process, which usually comes after the vote collection, and the Hough transform computation. If the threshold t is known in advance, then hierarchical techniques can be applied. The Fast Hough Transform algorithm (FHT) [2] hierarchically subdivides the parameter square (or more in general the k-dimensional hypercube where k is the dimensionality of the parameter space) into four sub-squares (or 2^k sub-hypercubes). The number of points voting for each square is computed and only the squares which have received at least t votes are further analyzed. In this case the complexity depends on the distribution of the feature points in the original image and on the threshold used and therefore cannot be determined a priori.

We will now present four parallelization techniques for the Hough transform suitable for fine grain parallel computers. We suppose we have an array of N × N bit-serial Processing Elements (PE) associated with a N × N image array. A central controller broadcasts instructions and memory addresses to the array and executes regular instructions on its private data. Data communication among PEs is implemented through a mesh or tree interconnection network. In a mesh each PE is connected to its four nearest neighbors (N, E, W, S) whereas in a tree-augmented mesh each PE is also connected to its father and to its two sons (F, LS, RS). Programs are partially executed by the processor array, when the instructions deal with the data allocated into the array memory, and partially executed by the central controller, which operates on scalar variables like counters and indexes.

2.1 Parallelization in the image space

In the first parallelization technique the image array is traversed by a set of counters, which follow the curves to be detected. At each step of the algorithm each counter visits a different PE and increments its value if the PE contains a feature point. Then each PE computes the coordinates of the next PE which the counter is supposed to visit and sends it there. In order to carry out this computation the counters must be accompanied by the k parameters identifying the particular curve they are following. Of course conflicts may arise when several packets meet at some node, since they can be processed only one at a time.

2.2 Parallelization in the feature point space

In the second parallelization technique each PE is associated to a pixel in the
image space and the PEs not associated to feature points are turned off. The
parameter space is scanned sequentially by the central controller and each
point in the parameter space (which is a curve in the image space) is
broadcast to the processor array. All the PEs associated to feature points give
their votes if they belong to the curve broadcast. Since the parameter space is
sequentially scanned this technique lends itself to an hierarchical decomposition of the parameter space as in the FHT algorithm, in order to reduce the
number of steps to be executed.

2.3 Parallelization in the parameter space

In the third parallelization technique each PE is associated to a curve, that is
a point in the parameter space, or to a (k-2)-dimensional array of curves if the
dimensionality k of the parameter space is greater than two. The feature
points are pulled out of the processor array one at a time and broadcast back
to it, so that at each step of the algorithm all the PEs simultaneously process
the same feature point. Each PE checks whether the currently broadcast
feature point belongs to the curve the PE is associated to and conditionally
increments a counter. No data communication is involved in this technique
except for extracting and broadcasting the feature points.

2.4 Parallelization in the feature point and parameter space

In the fourth parallelization technique the PEs are grouped into sets and each
set is associated to a feature point. Inside each set the PEs correspond to
different values of one of the parameters. Therefore each PE is identified by a
feature point and by a parameter. The voting process proceeds as follows.
The parameter space is scanned along (k-2) dimensions (because one
dimension has been assigned to the processor array) and for each set of (k-1)
parameters all the PEs compute the k-th parameter. When the dimensionality
of the parameter space is two, say in the (ρ, θ) space, each PE is identified by a
feature point and by a value of θ. In one step all the PEs simultaneously solve
the line equation and compute the corresponding ρ.

3 2-D POLYMORPHIC-TORUS NETWORK

In this section we briefly present the basic architecture of the Polymorphic-
Torus interconnection network, and the communication mechanisms it
implements. The Polymorphic-Torus is a new interconnection network
which allows emulating small diameter topologies like tree and hypercube on

a two-dimensional torus network. Since the architecture is based on a two-dimensional torus, all mesh algorithms can be executed without any communication overhead. Furthermore each node can be dynamically excluded by the computation and in this case its four ports (N, E, S, W) can be interconnected under program control. The resulting network is able to mimic different topologies, by combining reconfiguration policy with clock control, in order to allow for long distance communication.

3.1 Composite physical and internal network

The Polymorphic-Torus consists of a global, fixed physical network (PNET) and a programmable internal network (INET) at each node of the PNET. In a Polymorphic-Torus consisting of $N \times N$ processors, the PNET is an $N \times N$ mesh with its boundary connected in either torus mode or spiral mode (Fig. 1). A processor $P(i, j)$ is situated at the mesh junction with coordinate (i, j) and is equipped with four ports $N(i, j)$, $E(i, j)$, $W(i, j)$ and $S(i, j)$. These four ports connect themselves to both PNET and INET, and are the interface between the PNET and the INET. The wiring of these ports to

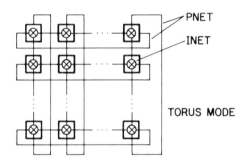

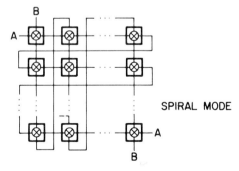

Fig. 1. Composite physical and internal network of Polymorphic-Torus.

$$
\begin{array}{c}
\begin{array}{cccc} N & E & W & S \end{array} \\
\begin{array}{c} N \\ E \\ W \\ S \end{array}
\left[
\begin{array}{cccc}
I & X & X & X \\
  & I & X & X \\
  &   & I & X \\
  &   &   & I
\end{array}
\right]
\end{array}
$$

$$
X = \begin{cases} I & \text{Connected} \\ O & \text{Non-connected} \end{cases}
$$

Fig. 2. Matrix representation of the INET correction.

PNET are shown in Fig. 1. Except for the selection of "torus" or "spiral" mode, the PNET is a hard-wired, fixed, non-programmable network.

While the PNET is fixed, the INET is totally programmable. At the (i, j) junction of the PNET, there resides an INET(i, j) which is a complete graph of four ports $(N(i, j), E(i, j), W(i, j)$ and $S(i, j))$. By "complete", we mean that each port can be connected to every other port. In the matrix representation in Fig. 2, a "1" in the entry (port(s), port(t)) of the matrix means that port(s) and port(t) are connected where port(s) and port(t) can be $N(i, j)$, $E(i, j)$, $W(i, j)$ or $S(i, j)$. The insertion of "1" into the matrix is controlled by program, furthermore, each INET can be programmed differently. By default, the diagonal entries of the matrix are all "1". Note that only the upper or lower triangle of the matrix is needed to express the connection.

The processor connection of the Polymorphic-Torus is programmable by inserting an "INET control pattern" into the entries of the matrix. Subject to the "INET control pattern" local to each processor, two pairs of ports can be connected (e.g. N connected to S and E connected to W), a triple of ports can be connected (e.g. N connected to both E and W) or all four ports are connected together. By synthesizing a concerted set of "INET control patterns" according to processor identification, one can derive out of the Polymorphic-Torus a network matching the task graph. We call the composite graph approach and the synthesis of the INET control pattern the polymorphic concept. A switch function, the SHORTPORT, is needed to support the programmability. This is discussed next.

3.2 The SHORTPORT switch function

The SHORTPORT function is a textual notation for the "INET control pattern". The format is SHORTPORT {g1}, {g2}. The parameters g1 and g2 are group of ports that are connected (or "short-circuited"). For example, {E, W} can be in the same group or three ports can be in the same group (e.g. {N, E, W}). In the extreme case, all four ports can be in the same group (i.e. {N, E, W, S}).

The effect of the SHORTPORT is to equate the logical level of the ports.

For example, SHORTPORT {E, W}; will make the signals on port E and port W be at the same logical level so that they are in effect "short-circuited", a phenomenon from which the switch function receives its name. The "short-circuit" phenomenon is an efficient mechanism for communication between two processors that are far apart physically in the PNET. Such a long-distance communication can be done by SHORTPORT along with two other traditional communication protocols: SEND (value, port) and RECEIVE (port); the former sends "value" to the prescribed port while the latter receives "value" from the prescribed port.

For example, the communication between P(1) and P(N) in a row of N processors can be established by the following commands simultaneously executed:

where (address= = 1) SEND (variable, East);

where (address= = N) variable = RECEIVE (West);

where ((address != 1) && (address != N)) SHORTPORT (East, West);

Under the command, P(1) sends "value" to port E, then the signal "value" ripples through P(2), P(3), ..., P(N-1) because of their port E and port W are all "short-circuited". Finally, "value" arrives port W of P(N) and is received by P(N).

4 HOUGH TRANSFORM ON POLYMORPHIC TORUS

The Polymorphic-Torus architecture can be efficiently programmed to execute the Hough transform using the four parallelization techniques introduced in Section 2. The performance obtained for each technique is as good as it is in the particular architecture for which the technique was designed, i.e. mesh or tree. By using the Polymorphic-Torus architecture one can choose the best suited parallelization technique for its environment, depending on the number of feature points and on the quantization of the parameter space. We present four algorithms corresponding to the four techniques for a two-dimensional parameter space. The extension to a k-dimensional parameter space is straightforward.

4.1 Parallelization in the image space

Two algorithms [4, 6] have been proposed for straight line detection through the Hough transform on mesh connected computers. The two algorithms share a basic idea, which is to inject computation waves into one side of the processor array (e.g. West) and let them propagate in a pipeline fashion along the array (e.g. from West to East). Each wave corresponds to a value of θ and traces N parallel lines in the image space shifting horizontally and/or vertically depending on θ and on the actual position. After the last wave reaches the opposite side of the processor array (e.g. the East-most column) the process is over. Conflicts are avoided by dividing the θ dimension into four sections, namely $(0, \pi/4)$, $(\pi/4, \pi/2)$, $(\pi/2, 3\pi/4)$ and $(3\pi/4, \pi)$. Each section is examined separately so that only lines with not too different slope simultaneously traverse the array. This is shown to prevent conflicts [4].

The computational complexity of this parallelization technique is $O(N + K_\theta)$, where N is the number of steps to traverse the array and K_θ is the number of waves injected into the array. Since the Polymorphic-Torus physical network can emulate a mesh without any communication overhead, it is able to optimally implement this parallelization technique without making use of any reconfiguration.

4.2 Parallelization in the feature point space

Parallelization in the feature point space was recently proposed by Li [10]. Such an approach consists of examining each point of the parameter space, corresponding to a curve, and computing the votes in parallel by summing up the contributions of the PEs belonging to the curve. The scanning of the parameter space can be performed hierarchically as suggested by Li et al. [2], through the Fast Hough Transform (FHT) algorithm. The interconnection requirements of this technique include a tree network to carry out the summation of the feature point votes in $O(\log f)$ steps. The Polymorphic-Torus capability of embedding a tree lends itself to such a task and therefore even this kind of parallelization can be effectively executed by a Polymorphic-Torus. The details of tree embedding in the Polymorphic-Torus are described in [9].

The computational complexity of this technique can be evaluated only partially because it depends on the distribution of the feature points in the original image. In [2] this subject is discussed for the sequential algorithm. The parallelization in the feature space leads to a linear to logarithmic $(f -> \log f)$ performance improvement over the sequential algorithm.

4.3 Parallelization in the parameter space

Ibrahim et al. [7] proposed an algorithm to detect straight lines using parallelization in the parameter space for a tree connected computer. The algorithm can be easily generalized for a k-dimensional parameter space and can be implemented in the Polymorphic-Torus network with the same performance as in tree connected computers. The processor array is made to correspond to the parameter space so that each PE can be identified by a pair (ρ, θ) (considering $K_\rho = K_\theta = N$). The coordinates of each feature point, which is a curve in the parameter space, are extracted from the processor array one at a time and broadcast back to all the PEs. Each PE selectively increments a counter depending on whether its coordinates (that are ρ and θ) and the feature point coordinates just received are a solution of the line equation. The algorithm is implemented by the following loop:

```
main(){
        fp_addr = 0;
        while ( fp_addr = get_next( fp_addr)) {
        broadcast ( fp_addr);
        if (line_eq (ρ(i), θ(j), fp_addr)) + + count;
        }
}
```

The procedure *get_next* (*fp_addr*) returns the coordinates of the next feature point in the array (in snake order) starting from the position *fp_addr*. If the address *fp_addr* in the processor array corresponds to a feature point, then that address is returned by the procedure. If not, the address of the next PE associated with a feature point (if any) is returned. The pseudo code of the *get_next*() procedure is given below.

```
get_next ( fp_addr) {
        where ( fp_addr) if ( feature_point) return (PE_addr);
        where (not feature_point) {
                SHORTPORT (West, East)
                disable ();
        }
        where ( fp_addr) SEND (Enquire, East);
        where ( feature_point && (Enquire = RECEIVE(West)))
                return (PE_address);
}
```

The procedure *get_next* () embeds a data dependent segmentable ring into the Polymorphic-Torus. It takes advantage of the Polymorphic-Torus capability of propagating signals along a chain of short-circuited processors. The Polymorphic-Torus borders are connected in spiral mode and a token propagates in snake order from the North-West corner. The PEs which do not contain feature points let the token pass whereas the PEs associated to feature points open the circuit and stop it. So the only PE receiving the token is the next feature point.

The computational complexity of parallelization in the parameter space is $O(f)$, meaning that for each feature point the curve equation has to be solved. We may neglect the delay related to the search for the next feature point, because such a search and the equation computation can be executed in parallel, since the latter does not require any communication.

4.4 Parallelization in the feature point and parameter space

Ibrahim et al. [7] also proposed a line detection algorithm exploiting parallelization in the feature point and parameter space on a tree connected computer. The basic idea is to parallelize the process by assigning a set of PEs to each feature point and assigning each member of each set a different θ. We implement that in the Polymorphic-Torus by assigning one dimension of the processor array, say the columns, to the feature points and the other dimension, the rows, to one of the parameters, say θ. So we have N columns associated to at most N feature points (if there are more than N then several planes have to be stacked on top of each other) and N rows associated to N values of θ ($K_\theta = N$). Both computation and collection can be done in parallel. The vote computation can be carried out in parallel on each PE, since the processor array maps the (f, θ) space. $PE_{i,j}$ computes the value of the ρ generated by the feature point fp_i at $\theta = \theta_j$. The collection process exploits the tree emulation capability of the Polymorphic-Torus. For each ρ all the rows are summed up so that N pairs (ρ, θ) are computed in parallel.

The algorithm consists of three procedures, as shown below:

main () {

        distribute_fp();

        compute_votes();

        collect_votes();

}

The procedure *distribute_fp()* spreads the feature points on the processor array so that each of them is associated to a column of the processor array. If the feature points are more than the number of columns (N), feature point planes can be stacked on top of the processor array, so that each PE contains at most $\lceil f/N \rceil$ feature points. The procedure *distribute_fp* () is implemented by iteratively calling the procedure *get_next()*, presented in the previous section. The procedure *compute_votes()* computes the ρ values in each PE, given the feature point (i.e. the column number) and the θ, i.e. the row number. The code is shown below.

compute_votes() {

        $\rho = line\_eq\,(\theta(i), fp(j));$

}

The procedure *collect_votes()* scans the two-dimensional parameter space and for each interval considered collects the votes. This is done by sequentially broadcasting all the ρ intervals to the processor array. For each ρ interval broadcast each PE sets a variable if its ρ falls in that interval. Then such variables are summed up by taking advantage of the tree interconnection strategy which can be embedded in a Polymorphic-Torus [9].

The computational complexity of parallelization in the feature point and parameter space is given by the sum of the complexities of the three procedures. The procedure *distribute_fp()* takes $O(f)$ steps, since it extracts the feature point from the processor array one at a time. The procedure *compute_fp()* takes $O(1)$ steps because all the ρ's are computed in parallel for each θ and for each feature point. The procedure *collect_fp()* takes $O(K_\rho \log N)$ steps. If the number of feature points f exceeds the number of columns N then several planes have to be stacked. The multi-plane algorithm computational complexity is $O(f + \lceil f/N \rceil K_\rho \log N)$.

5 DISCUSSION

Each of the four techniques presented may be convenient depending on the characteristics of the original image and on the quantization of the parameter space. The first technique can only detect straight lines, because it takes advantage of the straightness of the lines to avoid conflicts while traversing the array. Its complexity does not depend on the number of feature points since the image array is completely traversed even when few PEs actually contribute in the voting process. At the limit, if pixel values are directly used instead of feature points, the algorithm takes the same time and computes the projections of the image along straight lines.

The second technique has no constraints about the dimensionality of the parameter space. The sequential scanning of the parameter space obviously has a very high complexity ($O(K_\theta K_\rho)$) but, when a threshold is known in advance, a hierarchical decomposition of the parameter space may be applied, so that the complexity turns out to be much lower. The performance improvement of the parallel implementation of the FHT algorithm on a Polymorphic-Torus architecture over the sequential implementation can be computed. For a given image and a given threshold the FHT algorithm consists of H iterations (where H depends on the image and on the threshold). Each iteration takes $O(f)$ steps, since the feature point space must be completely examined. Therefore the total complexity is $O(H f)$. By making use of a tree architecture, which can be embedded in a Polymorphic-Torus, the complexity of each iteration goes down to $O(\log N)$ and the total complexity becomes $O(H \log N)$. Therefore the second parallelization technique is more efficient when the number of feature points is high.

In the complexity of the third and fourth techniques there is a factor proportional to f. Therefore both are convenient when the number of feature points is low. The third technique must solve the curve equation at each step, so that the complexity $O(f)$ must be weighted with a very high constant, whereas the fourth technique complexity depends on f linearly but with a very low constant only due to the feature point distribution phase. However, the fourth technique also depends on the quantization of the parameter space so that, depending on the precision required, the number of operations required may be larger than in the third technique.

The Polymorphic-Torus interconnection network is able to carry out the four parallel techniques for the Hough transform computation with the same performance as either mesh or tree interconnection networks whichever performs better. Specifically, the ability of Polymorphic-Torus to embed a tree, a mesh and a data dependent segmentable ring substantiates such a result.

The mesh, needed in the first technique, can be embedded in a Polymorphic-Torus without any transmission overhead because the INET is not used and only local communication is involved. Therefore all the mesh algorithms can be optimally executed.

The tree, needed in the second and fourth techniques, can be embedded in a Polymorphic-Torus architecture by selectively bypassing some PEs depending on their address. Embedding a tree allows reducing the complexity of vote accumulation from linear to logarithmic.

The data dependent segmentable ring can be embedded in a Polymorphic-Torus by having a token asynchronously propagate through the PEs. The token either crosses a PE or stops depending on the PE status. The data dependent segmentable ring allows for the fast enumeration of feature points, which is used in the third and fourth techniques.

6 CONCLUSION

Four parallelization techniques for the Hough transform computation have been presented. The efficiency of each technique depends on the number of feature points in the original image and on the desired quantization of the parameter space. Techniques with complexity independent of the number of feature points are used after a scarcely selective feature extraction whereas techniques with complexity linearly dependent on the number of feature points are used when a few feature points are to be analyzed. However, each of the four techniques has some interconnection requirements that make either a mesh or a tree interconnection network best suited for its implementation. Therefore the availability of a certain architecture constrains the choice of the parallelization technique even when it would not be the best suited.

In this paper we have shown that the Polymorphic-Torus architecture is able to implement the four parallelization techniques without any communication overhead. We have analyzed the complexity of the four approaches and in particular their dependence on the number of feature points and on the quantization of the parameter space. We have also analyzed what capabilities of the Polymorphic-Torus have been used to implement the four parallelization techniques and outlined the structure of the corresponding algorithms.

REFERENCES

[1] D.H. Ballard and C.M. Brown. (1982). *Computer Vision*. Prentice-Hall.
[2] H. Li, M.A. Lavin, and R.J. Le Master. (1986). Fast Hough Transform: A

Hierarchical Approach. *Computer Vision, Graphics and Image Processing*, **36:** 139–161.

[3] T.M. Silberberg. (1985). The Hough Transform on the Geometric Arithmetic Parallel Processor. *Proc. IEEE CAPAIDM*, Miami Beach (FL), November 1985.

[4] C. Guerra and S. Hambrusch. (1987). Parallel Algorithms for Line Detection on a Mesh. *Proc. IEEE CAPAMI*, Seattle (WA), October 1987.

[5] J.L.C. Sanz and E.B. Hinkle. (1987). Computing Projections of Digital Images in Image Processing Pipeline Architectures. *IEEE Trans. on Acoustic, Speech and Signal Processing*, ASSP-35(2), February 1987.

[6] R.E. Cipher, J.L.C. Sanz, and L. Snyder. (1987). The Hough Transform has O(N) Complexity on SIMD N × N Mesh Array Architectures. *Proc. IEEE CAPAMI*, Seattle (WA), October 1987.

[7] H.A.H. Ibrahim, J.R. Kender, and D.E. Shaw (1986). On the Application of Massively Parallel SIMD Tree Machine to Certain Intermediate-Level Vision Tasks. *Computer Vision, Graphics and Image Processing*, **36:** 53–75.

[8] H. Li and M. Maresca. (1987). Polymorphic-Torus Network. *Proc. Int. Conf. on Parallel Processing*, Chicago (IL), August 1987.

[9] H. Li and M. Maresca. (1987). Polymorphic-Torus: a new Architecture for Vision Computation. *Proc. IEEE CAPAMI*, Seattle (WA), October 1987.

[10] H. Li. (1986). Fast Hough Transform for Multidimensional Signal Processing. *Proc. IEEE ICASSP*.

Chapter Three

Pyramids and ''End''

David H. Schaefer and Man Bun Chu

Department of Electrical and Computer Engineering,
George Mason University, Fairfax, Virginia 22030

1 INTRODUCTION

The word "end" has an ominous feel about it. Websters Dictionary gives the following definitions:

(1) A limit or boundary; especially a limiting region or part;
(2) Death; destruction;
(3) The extremity or conclusion of any event or series of events;
(4) The extreme or last point or part; extremity; tip;
(5) The object being aimed at in any effort; purpose;
(6) Conclusion; issue; consequence; also, ultimate state;
(7) That which is left; a remnant; as, odds and ends.

Definitions one, four and seven relate to object recognition, the subject of this article. Definition number two, the most ominous meaning, can be ignored as this paper discusses algorithms being run on the GAM Pyramid [1], and pyramids are known to bring good luck. Definitions three, five and six will be referred to later.

The purpose of this paper (definition five) is to examine the concept of "end" in describing and identifying objects, and to demonstrate its use in recognition algorithms being run on the GAM Pyramid.

The GAM Pyramid is a five-level quad tree structure containing 341 processing elements (Fig. 1). Each processing element has a direct connection to its parent on the level directly above its own level, to its four children on the level directly below, and to its four nearest neighbors on its own level (Fig. 2). The four children have the labels, "V", "X", "Y" and "Z", as shown in the figure. The binary value of any child can be "sent up" to its parent in one clock cycle, while any Booleian function of the four children can be delivered to their parent in four cycles. A parent's value can be "moved down" to all four children in one cycle.

The philosophy that is being pursued in our laboratory is to identify

MULTICOMPUTER VISION
ISBN 0-12-444818-6

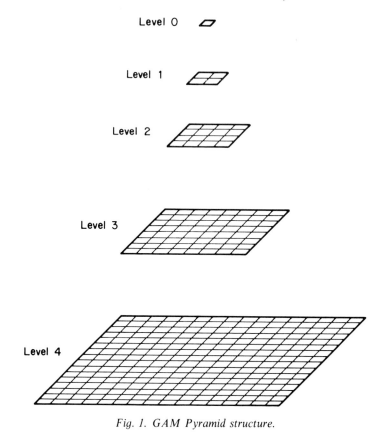

Fig. 1. GAM Pyramid structure.

objects from descriptions. Using generalized descriptions, identification of generic objects is possible. By "generic" is meant the identification of any object type, such as a fork. Such a fork might even have a different number of prongs than any that have been previously sensed. These descriptions depend on the extraction of "primary" and "supporting" features.

2 IMAGE FEATURES

Primary features extracted from an input image of an unknown object are: the number of holes, the number of end regions, the number of fingers, the number of vertices, and the number of long lines.

These primary features are supplemented by supporting features. One supporting feature is the determination of the position of end regions with respect to the object by determining whether a straight line that joins two end

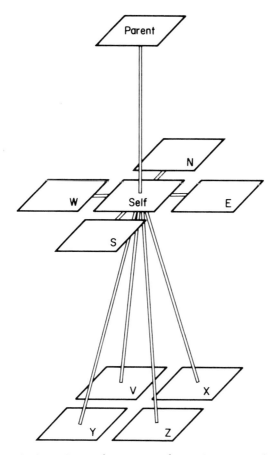

Fig. 2. GAM Pyramid processing element interconnections.

regions forms a hole. Other supporting features supply information about the position of holes and fingers with respect to the object. They also provide information about the existence and alignment to each other of long straight runs of object pixels, and furnish a measure of how well certain objects match a generated triangle. A final supporting feature yields information about whether certain objects are wide or narrow.

These features have successfully described a set of thirteen objects (generally paper cutouts of the objects) irrespective of their orientation, size, amount of closure in the case of objects such as scissors and pliers, and amount of curling in the case of snakes.

The most unsophisticated features mentioned above are holes and end regions. Holes are intuitively obvious, and the number of holes is easily calculated using the Euler Characteristic Number.

The meaning of "end regions" is not so intuitive. A knife and a snake both have two readily identifiable end regions. A square, however, either has no end regions, or possibly four. Connecting the end regions of a knife with a straight line does not form a hole. Connecting the end regions of an L with a straight line does form a hole.

2.1 End region extraction procedure

Establishing the number of end regions is more difficult than determining the number of holes. An algorithm that makes use of two levels of the pyramid has been employed. In this algorithm the patterns:

```
0  0  0      0  0  0      0  0  0      0  0  0  X
0  1  0      0  1  0      0  1  0      0  1  0  X
0  0  0      0  1  0      0  0  1      0  1  1  0
             X  0  0  0
             X  0  1  0      (X = don't care)
             0  1  1  0
```

and their ninety degree rotations are located. These configurations of object pixels (including the ninety degree rotations) are called "tail points".

Figure 3 shows images generated during execution of the end region algorithm. The input image on the base of the pyramid is shown in Fig. 3a. Initially, tail points of this image are located and stored. These points, known as "base tail points", constitute a first set of end regions (Fig. 3b).

The "V" children alone are now treated as a new image (Fig. 3c). The formation of this new image is easily generated on the pyramid by simply sending the V children up to level three. Tail points in this new image are located and the image showing their locations (Fig. 3d) is stored on level three. It should be noted that the location and storing operations are identical to those carried out on the base to obtain the base tail points, except that the operations are performed on level three, rather than on level four. Tail points are then found in the level three images formed from the "X", "Y", and "Z" children (Figs. 3f, 3h and 3j).

Four sets of tail point images have now been obtained and stored on level three. Next, a fifth image is generated on level three where a pixel is "one" only if all of its level four children are "ones", that is, the parent assumes the value of the AND of its children (Fig. 3k). The tail points in this AND image are located, providing a fifth level-three tail point image (Fig. 3l).

The five images that have been generated on level three are now compared. If at least three tail points are either touching, or on top of each other, when the five images are superimposed, then that region is considered to be a "level-three end region" (Fig. 3m). These regions generally consist of more than one pixel.

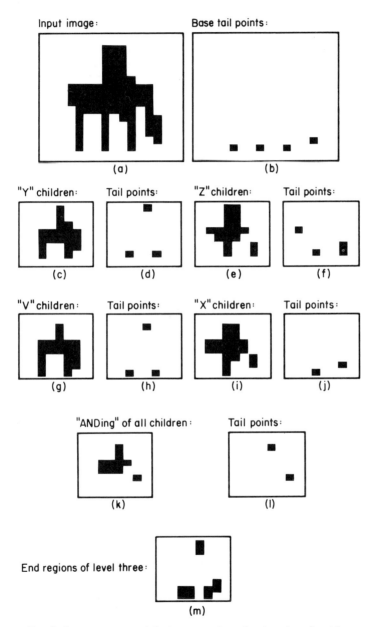

Fig. 3. Images generated during execution of end region algorithm.

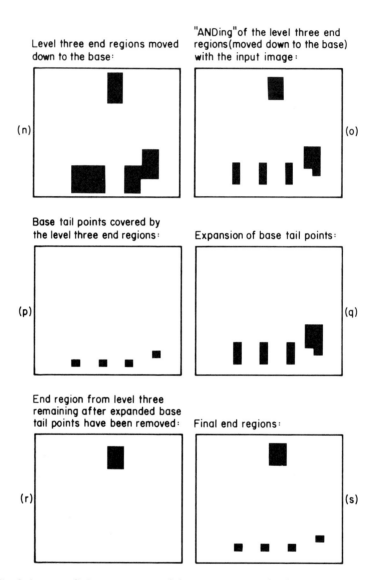

Fig. 3. (continued) Images generated during execution of end region algorithm.

To locate all end regions, the level-three end regions are moved down to the base (Fig. 3n), ANDed with the original image (Fig. 3o), and then compared with the base tail point image. All level-three end regions that cover a base tail point are discarded. This discarding process involves the locating of the base tail points covered (Fig. 3p), their expansion into the shapes of the covering level-three regions (Fig. 3q), and the extraction of the remaining level-three regions (Fig. 3r). Therefore, the final end regions (Fig. 3s) consist of the base tail points and end regions found on level three that are not in the same location as the base tail points.

After the end regions are extracted, they are counted by an algorithm that utilizes the Euler Characteristic Number.

The algorithm can be generalized for use on a pyramid of any size by considering the AND image at any level as the input, and repeating the algorithm at this level and the level directly above. The "coming down" procedure is identical to that described above, except that it is repeated several times.

2.2 Algorithm results

Figure 4 shows the end regions extracted from a set of representative image inputs. For each pair of images the input image is on the left, the end regions image on the right. Figure 4a shows end regions extracted from an image of a fork. Four end regions are produced for this three-pronged fork, the expected result. Results for a four-pronged fork are shown in the following illustration. A knife at an angle (Fig. 4c) shows the expected two end regions, even though the lower one is a bit eccentric. As can be seen from the illustration, the L-squares (Figs. 4d and 4e) produce two end regions, while a T-square (Fig. 4g) generates three. One would expect a spoon to have two end regions, but the algorithm consistently ignores the large end (Figs. 4h and 4i). This is both an aid in recognizing spoons, and is consistent with the result that a square or a rectangle close to a square has no end regions (Fig. 4j).

How many end regions should a triangle have? It should have three vertices, and the definition of vertices is tailored for triangles. But how many end regions? The illustration shows a case of obtaining none, and of obtaining one.

The closed scissors of Fig. 4m produces two end regions, while an open one produces three (Fig. 4n). The end region image of a pair of pliers in Fig. 4o exhibits three end regions, one of which, surprisingly, is the whole handle. The snake of Fig. 4p has the expected two end regions, but the snake of Fig. 4q produces a false end region, while ignoring the true one.

A summary of the results of end region determination on a training set of 231 images of objects is shown in Table 1. From this chart it can be seen that if an unknown object has five or more end regions, its chance of being a fork is 76%. If it has two end regions, and if a connection linking these end regions forms a hole, then there is a 40% chance that the unknown object is an L-

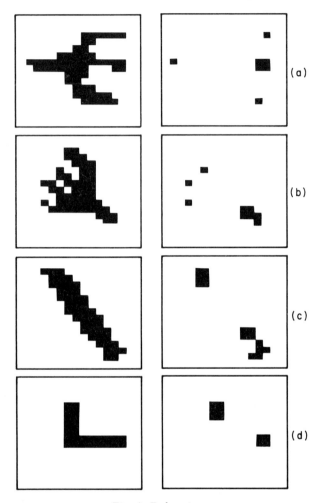

Fig. 4. End regions.

square. If the unknown object has two end regions and connecting these end regions does not form a hole, then it has a 37% chance of being a knife and a 12% chance of being a snake. An object with three end regions has a 42% chance of being T-shaped, while an object that has only one end region has a 33% chance of being a spoon. Cups and rectangles in the training set have no end regions.

For the other objects in the object vocabulary, the end region feature gives only a small amount of identifying information. For instance, an unknown object has a 20% chance of being a triangle if it has one end region, but this

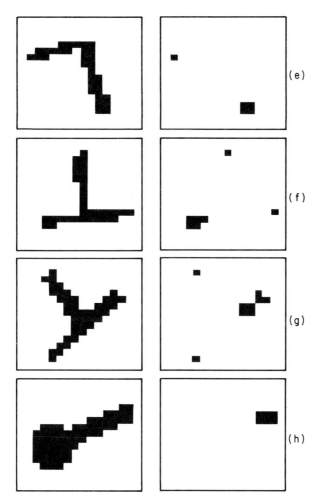

Fig. 4 (continued) End regions.

same object has close to a 60% chance of being a triangle if it has three vertices. All features and probabilities, both large and small, are taken into account in the recognition procedure.

Definition 7, which defines an end as a remnant, or something that is left, interestingly meets the definition of "finger", as fingers remain when a "palm area" is removed. A palm area is formed by locating those pixels surrounded by eight neighbors, and then expanding the resulting image. Figure 5 shows an example of the difference between end regions and fingers. In general the number of end regions is not equal to the number of fingers.

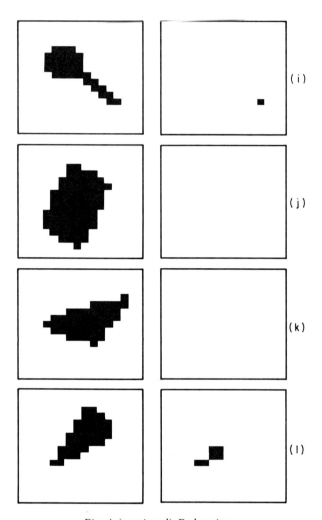

Fig. 4. (continued) End regions.

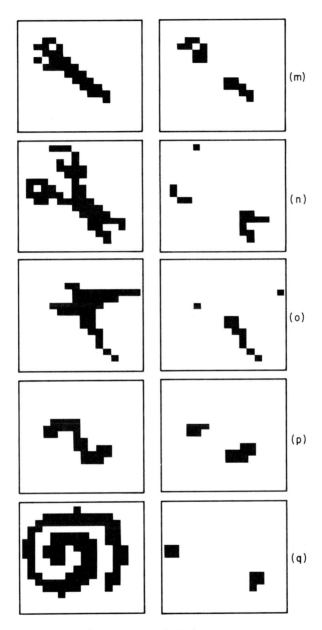

Fig. 4. (continued) End regions.

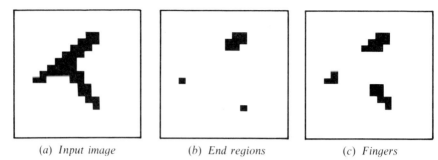

(a) *Input image*   (b) *End regions*   (c) *Fingers*

Fig. 5. *End regions and fingers of a T-square.*

Table 1

Probability of an unknown object being the object in left hand column, given number of end regions in top row

| | End Regions | | | | | | |
	0	1	2	2*	3	4	⩾ 5
Pliers	0.00	0.00	0.03	0.13	0.22	0.28	0.06
Forks	0.00	0.00	0.03	0.00	0.11	0.43	0.76
Knives	0.00	0.02	0.37	0.00	0.00	0.00	0.00
L-squares	0.00	0.00	0.14	0.40	0.05	0.00	0.00
T-squares	0.00	0.01	0.05	0.03	0.42	0.00	0.00
Rectangles	0.36	0.00	0.00	0.00	0.00	0.00	0.00
Triangles	0.03	0.20	0.13	0.00	0.00	0.00	0.00
Drafting Triangles	0.11	0.20	0.04	0.00	0.00	0.00	0.00
Wrenches	0.15	0.12	0.03	0.05	0.04	0.00	0.00
Cups	0.36	0.00	0.00	0.00	0.00	0.00	0.00
Scissors	0.00	0.04	0.07	0.09	0.10	0.29	0.18
Spoons	0.00	0.33	0.00	0.00	0.00	0.00	0.00
Snakes	0.00	0.07	0.12	0.29	0.05	0.00	0.00

* Holes are formed when the two end regions are joined together with a straight line.

2.3 Ending (per definitions 3 and 6)

Recognition of real world objects with all their variability is impossible unless one is able to easily extract meaningful features. This paper has shown that a pyramid structure provides an excellent architecture for the rapid extraction of end regions, a fundamental feature of objects.

REFERENCES

[1] Schaefer, D.H., Ho, P., Boyd, J. and Vallejos, C. (1987). The GAM Pyramid. In L. Uhr (Ed.): *Parallel Computer Vision*, Academic Press, Boston, pp. 15–42.

Chapter Four

An Algorithm Database for an Image Understanding Task Execution Environment

Frank Weil, Leah Jamieson and Edward Delp

School of Electrical Engineering, Purdue University,
West Lafayette, IN 47907

ABSTRACT

A partitionable parallel processing system requires a method for matching the system configuration to the requirements of the routines to be executed. One approach is to use an Intelligent Operating System to manage the system's resources. In this paper, we discuss some of the components of an Intelligent Operating System used for executing image understanding tasks on a partitionable parallel processor. The databases required to make scheduling and reconfiguration decisions based on the user's task specification are detailed and two examples are developed.

1 INTRODUCTION

The general purpose of an image understanding task is to produce a scene description from an input image. The user's task specification indicates what the description should detail and what form it should take. For example, one task might be to produce a list of objects and their descriptions contained in an outdoor natural color scene. Another task might produce a graph of that same scene where the nodes are the objects in that scene and the arcs represent the relations among the objects. Both tasks produce a *high-level* description of the input image and require approximately the same processing steps. The final form of the output is structured to meet the needs of the user that initiated the task.

This research was supported in part by the Air Force Office of Scientific Research under Grant F49620-86-K-006.

Image understanding tasks tend to be computationally intensive and therefore execute relatively slowly on a conventional, non-parallel (Von Neumann) processing system. There are a number of ways to use parallel processing to increase execution speed. One method is to split the task into smaller units, or subtasks, and distribute the processing load across a number of processors by assigning different subtasks to different processors. Another method of achieving speedup is to assign a number of processors to a single subtask so that the subtask can be finished quickly. The use of a partitionable parallel processing system that implements both of these strategies can greatly reduce the overall execution time of image understanding tasks.

A partitionable parallel processing system is one that can have several simultaneous partitions (or subsets of the processor's resources), each executing a different process. Each partition has a varying amount of the system's resources depending on the needs of the job it is currently executing and the needs of the other partitions. Examples of such systems include RP3 [1], the Butterfly [2], the Cosmic Cube [3], and PASM [4]. In the PASM (*Pa*rtitionable *SI*MD/*M*IMD) system, each of the partitions has 2^N processing elements (for some integer N), can operate in either SIMD or MIMD mode, and can switch dynamically between modes. Each PASM processing element consists of a processor/memory pair and various communication controllers; when fully implemented, the system will have 1024 separate processing elements. For a particular task, the system might be running with four partitions: two with 128 processing elements each in MIMD mode, one with 256 processing elements in MIMD mode, and one with 512 processing elements in SIMD mode. At a later time, the system might be configured to run 32 MIMD processes, each in a partition of 32 processing elements. If all available processing elements are not needed for the current task, the unused ones will simply remain idle.

Using a parallel processing system requires that the user's task be broken down, or decomposed, into appropriately sized subtasks. The appropriate size is a balance of three factors:

(1) a large number of small subtasks allows a greater opportunity for parallelism than a small number of large subtasks;
(2) more subtasks require more interprocess communication and synchronization and therefore entail a greater amount of system overhead;
(3) many subtasks have an inherent or "natural" degree of parallelism and may experience a degradation if too few processors (loss of speed) or too many processors (waste of system resources) are assigned to the subtask.

Once the task has been written in terms of properly sized subtasks, both the parallelized code for each individual subtask and a schedule for the subtasks to be run is needed. For image understanding tasks, neither one is trivial. Therefore, in an effort to isolate the user from the underlying parallel processing system, we are developing an environment for the execution of image understanding tasks [5, 6]. This environment consists of two major parts: an Image Understanding System and an Intelligent Operating System. Both of these components are constructed based on a library of prewritten image processing algorithms. The image understanding task is specified in terms of these algorithms (or subtasks). The user, then, does not need to be aware of the details of the underlying parallel processor, understand how to write (efficient) parallel code, or spend time debugging the code. The user can also execute the task on any parallel processor that is running the Intelligent Operating System.

Throughout the text, the terms *database* and *knowledge base* appear. It would be useful at this point to define them. A database contains information about pertinent objects and possibly the objects themselves. If the database detailed information about auto parts, it obviously could not contain the actual parts, only their descriptions. However, in the case of computer code, the object itself is an abstract entity stored on some magnetic media and is therefore capable of being included in the database. In our system, the database objects are image processing routines and the information is the image analysis performance characteristics and the execution characteristics of each stored routine. A knowledge base contains procedural information detailing specific functions or activities. The knowledge base used in our system contains information about what processing is required to complete a given task and also scheduling and reconfiguration methodologies.

The Image Understanding System (IUS) consists of a user interface, a knowledge base of task processing requirements, and a database of algorithm templates and image analysis performance characteristics. The main function of the IUS is to provide the specification of the task (see Fig. 1). This may be done via interaction with a user, by retrieving stored fixed task processing schemes, or by the execution of an image understanding expert system. When used interactively, the IUS aids the user in the choice of exactly how to decompose the task. This aspect will be discussed in greater detail later. The IUS then provides the Intelligent Operating System with a data dependency graph that lists the algorithms needed to be run to complete the given task. No specific execution order is given by the IUS. The Intelligent Operating System can infer such constraints from the parameter lists of the named algorithms and from the data dependency graph.

As was seen in Fig. 1, the Intelligent Operating System (IOS) is intended to serve as an interface between the Image Understanding System and the underlying parallel processor's low-level operating system. It also relies on a knowledge base and a database to complete its scheduling and reconfiguration tasks. The knowledge base contains such information as scheduling schemes and the capabilities of the underlying parallel processing system. This information allows the IOS to make intelligent use of the parallel processor's resources. The database contains information about the execution characteristics of specific implementations of an algorithm as a function of the system resources allocated to the routine. The IOS uses the data dependency graph to determine an initial configuration and list of routines to be run by the parallel processor. The IOS then waits for one of the

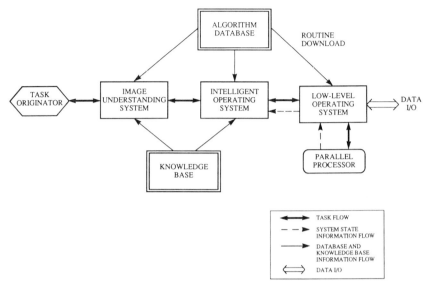

Fig. 1. Image understanding environment overview.

processes (a subtask in a partition) to complete execution so that it may decide which routine should be run next and in what configuration.

The IOS supplies two different types of information to the low-level operating system. First, the low-level operating system must be supplied with the initial set of routines to be executed and the configuration in which they are to be run. The low-level operating system then places the parallel processor in the required configuration and loads these routines from the library of algorithm implementations. The low-level operating system subsequently monitors the progress of the routines in each partition and supplies run-time information back to the IOS. Once supplied with this information, the IOS may then decide how best to fit the next routine to be run into the processor's available resources. As routines finish executing and different amounts of resources become available, the IOS will determine how to schedule the routines awaiting execution. The scheduling, then, is a dynamic process dependent on the task, the underlying parallel processor, and the input image.

One can think of the image understanding environment as a series of layers over the parallel processor. At the lowest layer, or level, exists the low-level operating system. It handles the details of the parallel processor such as reconfiguration, process loading, mass storage interface, network communication, and process monitoring. Since the user should not need to be aware of these details when a task is to be run, the IOS is provided as the next layer. It makes the scheduling and reconfiguration decisions necessary to execute a task. This layer transforms the specification of the user's task into directives to the low-level operating system. When several versions of an algorithm to be run exist, the IOS selects an implementation of that algorithm that will fit in well with the other routines to be run. At the next layer, the IUS, the relatively abstract task specification consisting of general algorithm names is translated into a definite set of algorithms to be run. By using this layering scheme, tasks are portable among machines running the IUS/IOS and the user is isolated from the details of the underlying parallel processing system.

To further illustrate this image understanding environment, two examples will be developed throughout the text. The first example shows the information used by the Image Understanding System when it translates a user's task specification into a representation that provides the precedence information needed by the IOS scheduler. The second example uses edge linking algorithms to illustrate how individual routines will be chosen by the Intelligent Operating System.

2 OVERVIEW OF THE ALGORITHM DATABASE

The algorithm database described here consists of three parts (see Fig. 2): the Image Understanding System database, the Intelligent Operating System database, and the algorithm library. Note that each of the three components used in executing image understanding tasks uses a part of the algorithm database. This common thread among the levels follows the flow of the task from the user to the parallel processor itself. It is one of the features of this image processing environment that allows a natural progression from the abstract user's view of the specified task to the specific code and configuration needed to execute a routine required by that task.

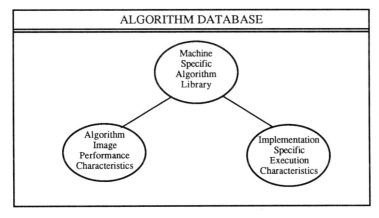

Fig. 2. Algorithm database overview.

2.1 Algorithm library

The algorithms in the database will contain low-, mid-, and high-level image processing routines. The low- and mid-level algorithms are general purpose routines that serve as the basic building blocks for the user's task specification. They are commonly used as preprocessing steps for the high-level routines. Most high-level routines are specific to the given task. An example high-level routine is an expert system designed for object recognition based on region and edge information and a generic scene model.

The algorithm library is the most machine-specific component of the algorithm database. The library consists of different implementations of image processing algorithms. Examples of algorithms to be included in the library are listed in Table 1. For each given algorithm, a number of different implementations of that algorithm will be included in the database. The different implementations might be based on varying the data allocation schemes (such as splitting up the data per processing element by rows, columns, or regions), the number of processing elements required, the format of the data produced, etc. As more implementations of algorithms are included in the database, the IOS has the possibility of constructing more time-efficient schedules since there will be more chances to effectively match

Table 1
Example library algorithms

$\nabla^2 G$	Hilbert Transform
Algebraic Reconstruction Algorithms	Histograms
Blackboard-based Segmentation	Homomorphic Filtering
Block Truncation Coding	Hough Transform
Canny Edge Detector [Can86]	Huffman Coding
Constrained Deconvolution	Huffman Shift Coding
Contour Tracing	Inverse Filtering
Correlation	Kalman Filtering
Cosine Transform	Karhunen-Loeve Transform
Covariance	Laplace Filtering
Differentiation	Maximum Likelihood Classification
Edge Linking	Medial Axis Transform
Edge Thinning	Median Filtering
Filtered-backprojection Reconstruction	Min-max Filtering
Fourier Shape Descriptors	Predictive Compression
Fourier Transform	Rank-order Filtering
Gaussian Smoothing	Region Growing
Gray Level Correction	Region Linking
Gray Scale Modification	Rule-based Object Recognition
Hadamard Transform	Run-length Coding
Hankel Transform	Sobel Operator
High-emphasis Filtering	Thresholding

processes and partitions. This time savings generally occurs when task migration, data reformatting, and processor reconfiguration are kept to a minimum. Of course, the overall savings are heavily dependent on routine execution times which are often dependent on the input data.

2.2 Image Understanding System database

The Image Understanding System database contains information on each database algorithm's image analysis performance characteristics. For example, there might be three different edge linking algorithms: one that works well for low noise images, one that works well in noisy images, and one that can deal with badly broken edges. The Image Understanding System uses this data, possibly in conjunction with interaction with the user, in selecting exactly which algorithms will be used to complete a specified task. The Image Understanding System database information, together with the data from the execution characteristics database, is also useful in optimizing the overall task processing time. In some processing scenarios, it may be acceptable to sacrifice resultant analysis performance for a decrease in execution time. For example, an object recognition algorithm may not need a complete set of connected line segments to determine if an object is a building or not. In this case, a faster but less robust edge linking algorithm may be used. However, it may be important to use the most complete set of edges possible (e.g. recognizing aircraft type from outlines) so that it becomes preferable to use a slower but better edge linker.

Also contained in this database is an algorithm template detailing what the inputs and outputs are for each of the library algorithms. For example, the algorithm $ALG1$ might be listed as $ALG1(X, Y, Z)$ with X as an **input**, Y as a **modified input**, and Z as an **output**. An **input** is data that is used by the routine but is not changed in any way. A **modified input** is data that is used by the routine and, upon exit from the routine, has had one or more of its values changed. An **output** is data that is produced by the routine but is not a **modified input**. The distinction between these three types of parameters is important for the scheduling of the routines. A given routine cannot be executed before the data for each of its inputs and modified inputs is

Table 2
Database algorithm classification parameters

Algorithm mode (SIMD or MIMD)
Number of processing elements required
Expected execution time
Input data format
Output data format
Input data allocation
Output data allocation

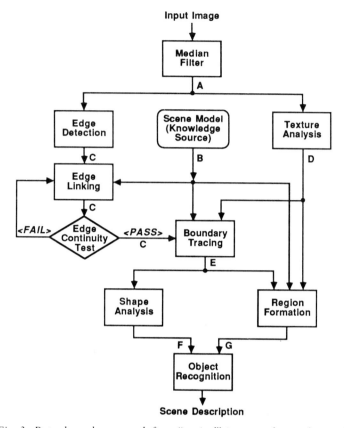

Fig. 3. Data dependency graph for a "typical" image understanding task.

available. If the data is produced by another routine (i.e. it is an output of some routine), a time constraint has been placed on the execution order of those two routines. That is, the producer of the data has to execute before the consumer.

For the first example, Fig. 3 presents a data dependency graph for a "typical" image understanding task. The Image Understanding System might initially represent this task as follows:

```
Median_filter (INPUT-IMAGE, A)
Scene_model ("TANKS-FLIR DATA", B)
Edge_detect (A, C)
Edge_link (B, C)
while (Edge_continuity (C) < 0.9)
        {Edge_link (B, C)}
Texture_analysis (A, D)
```

Boundary_trace (B, C, D, E)
Shape_analysis (E, F)
Region_Formation (B, D, E, G)
Object_recognition (F, G)

The Image Understanding System database contains input and output parameter information for each of these routines. Conceptually, this information is stored as a template for each routine:

Boundary_trace (INPUT, INPUT, INPUT, OUTPUT)
Edge_continuity (INPUT) : FLOAT
Edge_detect (INPUT, OUTPUT)
Edge_link (INPUT, MODIFIED INPUT)
Median_filter (INPUT, OUTPUT)
Object_recognition (INPUT, INPUT)
Region_Formation (INPUT, INPUT, INPUT, OUTPUT)
Scene_model (INPUT, OUTPUT)
Shape_analysis (INPUT, OUTPUT)
Texture_analysis (INPUT, OUTPUT)

The Image Understanding System now has enough information to construct a data dependency graph for the task. This data dependency graph is passed to the Intelligent Operating System for processing. The IOS then interacts with the low-level operating system to control the actual execution of the task.

For the second example, we will look at edge detection algorithms. Assume that there are three different edge detection algorithms: version A, which is fast but only works on non-noisy images; version B, which has intermediate speed but has good performance in the presence of noise; and version C, which is slow but can detect badly fragmented edges. Table 3 summarizes the example information contained in the database about these three versions. If the edge detection algorithm is required by the task specification (indicated by a line of the form $EDGE\_DETECT(X, Y)$ where X is the input image and Y is the edge detector output), the decision of which version of the algorithm to use has to be made. The Image Understanding System, possibly

Table 3
Example IUS database information

Algorithm Name I/O Template	EDGE_DETECT (INPUT, OUTPUT)	
Version	Relative Speed	Noise Threshold
A	fast	low
B	medium	medium
C	slow	high

in consultation with the user, will decide on the algorithm version based on the input image characteristics (i.e. noisy or non-noisy) and the overall task specification (i.e. whether or not degraded performance is acceptable). This decision will be indicated by a branching point in the task specification based on the appropriate image characteristic. This example is continued at the end of Section 2.3.2.

2.3 Intelligent Operating System database

2.3.1 Overview

The Intelligent Operating System's function of determining a set of routines to be used to achieve a good execution time for a given task can be compared to the bin packing problem. The basic idea is to find a mapping of the necessary routines onto the parallel processor's resources that gives good performance and makes efficient use of those resources. The scheduling problem here is actually more complicated than "classical" bin packing in that the routines to be scheduled (i.e. the pieces to be packed) are, quite often, of unknown size. Although routines that are not data dependent, such as a 9 by 9 edge mask in SIMD mode, have well defined execution times, data driven routines such as an MIMD edge linking algorithm have an execution time that cannot be predicted *a priori*. Instead of attempting to adapt one of the current and time-expensive bin packing methods to our needs (bin packing in itself is NP-hard [7]), we will use heuristics to choose the specific implementation by taking into account the overall processing scenario. In order to select an implementation, the Intelligent Operating System will use specific information stored about each routine. A discussion of a bin-packing approach to processor allocation is presented in [8].

In addition to the database information on each routine, the selection of the specific implementation also depends on the current configuration of the system. Reconfiguring the parallel processing system involves changing the size and/or number of partitions. In general, reconfiguration should be minimized since it uses system time that cannot be used for executing the desired task. There are several factors which influence the decision of whether or not to reconfigure. If there are jobs currently running in some of the partitions, those partitions will either have to be preserved or the jobs will have to be migrated to new partitions [9]. Even if no jobs are currently executing, the system will have some overhead associated with setting up the new partitions. Reconfiguration may be advantageous, however, when a job that needs to be run requires more processing elements than are available in any current partition. This possibility can occur when either the routine needs the processing elements due to its implementation or the routine has a high priority and all available processing elements need to be assigned to it in order to decrease its execution time.

2.3.2 Algorithm parameters

Each database routine will be classified by seven general parameters (see Table 2). Additional candidate parameters are discussed in [10]. The first parameter is the mode of the algorithm (either SIMD or MIMD). The mode determines whether or not the partition has to be switched from SIMD mode to MIMD mode (or vice versa) for the given routine. Switching the partition mode takes time that cannot be used for processing and therefore should be minimized. This factor may or may not be significant in terms of the task's execution time depending on the amount of system overhead associated with the change. In the PASM system, for example, the system overhead for the switch is insignificant (only a few instructions) compared to a typical routine execution time.

The second parameter is the number of processing elements that are required (or desired) for the routine. In general, the more processing elements used by the routine, the faster the execution time up to some maximum value for the routine. However, processing elements used by one routine are obviously not available for use by another. Some compromise must be made between concurrent execution of routines and execution speed for individual routines. If more processing elements are required than exist in some idle partition, the system will have to be reconfigured which will increase the overall processing time of the task.

The third parameter is the expected execution time. This parameter is a function of the number of processing elements used, the size of the data set being operated on, the format of the data (binary, integer, floating point, or symbolic), the mode that the routine is operating in (SIMD or MIMD), and the amount of communication between processing elements. This information is important since it may be more efficient to run a slower routine without reconfiguring the system and/or reallocating the data per processing element than it is to run a faster routine that requires a system reconfiguration.

The fourth parameter is the format of the input data used by the routine and the fifth parameter is the format of the output data produced by the routine. These parameters state the type of data used and produced. Binary and integer operations are generally faster than floating point operation and therefore should be used whenever possible. Other formats of data include character, double precision, strings of symbolic data, etc.

The sixth and seventh parameters are, respectively, the input and output allocation of data among the processing elements. Typical allocations of data are by rows, columns, and rectangular regions. These two parameters help determine whether or not reconfiguration is necessary. When one routine finishes and the next routine to be executed needs data in the same allocation as that produced by the first routine, it is advantageous not to store the data when the first routine finishes and then reload it when the next routine starts. In this way, overhead from large data transfers can be reduced. The algorithm database may also contain specialized routines to perform common reallocation and reformatting functions such as by-row to by-column reallocating and integer to floating point casting. For a speech analysis task, examples of such routines are presented in [11].

To continue with example 2, assume that version B of the edge detection algorithm has been selected. Therefore, the node of the form *EDGE_DETECT_B*(*X*, *Y*) in the data dependency graph is to be executed. Assume that there are four implementations of that algorithm in the algorithm library. The four implementations might be

I1) a SIMD version with an edge list output
I2) a MIMD version with an edge list output
I3) a SIMD version with a binary image output
I4) a MIMD version with a binary image output.

The Intelligent Operating System must now choose which of the four implementations of *EDGE_DETECT_B* will give the minimum execution time taking into account the overall processing plan. To make this decision, the classification information in the Intelligent Operating System database will be used. Table 4 summarizes example information contained in the database about these four implementations. Suppose that the routine which creates the intermediate image *X* used by the *EDGE_DETECT_B* routine was run in SIMD mode in a partition of 16 processing elements and left its data in the appropriate form (i.e. split up by regions). The Intelligent Operating System must make its choice of which algorithm implementation to use by weighing the relative advantages and disadvantages of 1) changing mode or staying in SIMD mode, 2) reconfiguring (and therefore moving the intermediate image) or using the current 16 processing element partition, and 3) optimizing this step versus possibly causing a slowdown in subsequent steps.

Once an implementation for this algorithm has been chosen and placed in the data dependency graph, the IOS interacts with the low-level operating system to control the execution of the code.

2.3.3 Heuristics

The Intelligent Operating System is comprised of expert systems to do the algorithm implementation selection and the task scheduling. The expert systems make use of heuristics which are written in the form of rules understood by the inference engine. These heuristics embody a "rule of thumb" type of knowledge about scheduling.

As an example, suppose that two implementations of algorithm Alg exist in the library. If algorithm Alg is part of the task being scheduled, then both implementations are candidates to be included in the processing and one of them must be chosen. For the purpose of this example, assume that both implementations are basically the same and will execute in the same amount of time, but that the first implementation needs its data allocated among the

Table 4
EDGE_DETECT_B implementation data

Parameter	Implementation			
	I1	I2	I3	I4
Mode	SIMD	MIMD	SIMD	MIMD
# PE's	$\leq \dfrac{\#\,pixels}{64}$	no bound	$\leq \dfrac{\#\,pixels}{64}$	no bound
Time	$\dfrac{6*image\_size}{\#\,PE's} + 4*\#\,PE's$	$\dfrac{4*image\_size}{\#\,PE's} + \dfrac{image\_size}{64}$	$\dfrac{6*image\_size}{\#\,PE's}$	$\dfrac{4*image\_size}{\#\,PE's} + \dfrac{image\_size}{64}$
Input format	1 byte/pixel	1 byte/pixel	1 byte/pixel	1 byte/pixel
Output format	edge list	edge list	binary image	binary image
Input allocation	regions	regions	regions	regions
Output allocation	regions	regions	regions	regions

processing elements by rows and the second implementation needs its data allocated among the processing elements by regions. A heuristic that would probably be used in deciding which implementation would be chosen is:

"If two implementations could be used and they both take the same amount of time to execute, then choose the one that requires the least system overhead."

This heuristic is stated in a much too abstract way to be implemented directly. A more concise and detailed statement of the rule might be:

"If two implementations of the algorithm to be scheduled exist, the expected execution times of the implementations are the same for the number of processing elements being used in the partition, and the output allocation of the routine currently being executed is the same as the input allocation of one of the candidate implementations, then choose that implementation."

Stating the rule in this form gives more of the details that are implied by the heuristic. For the sake of simplicity, it is assumed in this example that the only factor affecting the system overhead is the matching of output to input data allocation.

Exactly how this statement is translated into a rule depends on the syntax of the expert system being used. In CLIPS (C Language Integrated Production System) [12, 13], a forward chaining expert system shell, the rule might be translated as follows:

```
(defrule schedule_1
    ; The next algorithm to schedule is Alg.
    (next_algorithm ?Alg)

    ; See if an implementation I1 of algorithm Alg exists in the
    ; database and a different implementation, I2, also exists there.
    (DB ?Alg ?I1)
    (DB ?Alg ?I2 &: (neq ?I1 ?I2))

    ; The current data output allocation of the routine in the partition
    ; is outalloc and the current number of processing elements in
    ; the partition is numpe.
    (current output_allocation ?outalloc)
    (current number_of_pe ?numpe)

    ; The expected execution times for implementations I1 and I2
    ; given the number of processing elements in the current
    ; partition are time1 and time2 respectively.
    (DB ?I1 execution_time ?numpe ?time1)
    (DB ?I2 execution_time ?numpe ?time2)

    ; See if the execution times are the same.
    (test (eq ?time1 ?time2))
```

```
; The data output allocation for implementation I1 is
; outalloc1. See if it is the same allocation as the
; that of the current routine.
(DB ?I1 output_allocation ?outalloc1)
(test (eq ?outalloc ?outalloc1))

= >

; Given that the facts listed above are all true,
; (and they must be for this conclusion to be executed)
; then implementation I1 is the better of the two choices.
(printout "I would use implementation " ?I1))
```

2.4 Use of the system

When an image understanding task is run on the parallel processing system, the algorithm database is used in the process of expressing the task in a form usable by the low-level operating system. The first step is to translate the user's task specification into a set of algorithms that need to be run to complete the task. This set will be generated in the form of a data dependency graph. This step makes use of the Image Understanding System database when selecting which algorithms will be used. Speed/performance tradeoffs can be made to tailor the algorithm selection to the current application.

Once the algorithm selection is complete, one of the implementations of each algorithm must be chosen by using the stored database information about each routine and by taking into account the current operating environment. These routines are then passed, again in the form of a data dependency graph, to the scheduler so that an appropriate schedule and configuration can be generated. Exactly which implementation of an algorithm is chosen is based on trying to minimize the overall execution time of the specified task. The data contained in the Intelligent Operating System database (i.e. algorithm execution characteristics) allows the system to fit the best implementation of the specified algorithm into the overall processing scenario. Factors to be taken into account in the routine selection include the current partitioning of the parallel processor, the routine executed prior to the current one, the routines that will be executed after the current one, reconfiguration overhead, and task migration overhead.

From the data dependency graph, the scheduler determines a partitioning of the parallel processor and which routine will be run in each partition. Assuming that all the algorithms for a given task cannot be run concurrently on the parallel processor, this scheduling process is dynamic. Although it is advantageous for the Intelligent Operating System to look as far ahead in the task as possible when scheduling, it can do so only as far in advance as the nearest decision point. Since the results of the conditional cannot be determined *a priori*, the branch that the execution takes cannot be predicted. That branch is not worked into the overall schedule until it has been determined. In this manner, inefficient processing due to selecting routines in anticipation of a given branch and then having that branch not be taken is avoided. An alternative is the inclusion of probabilistic information analogous to that used in handling branches in some optimizing compilers. As processes finish executing and intermediate information becomes available, the scheduler must determine the next configuration and set routines to be run.

The system configuration and set of routines to be run are passed to the low-level operating system. The parallel processor is then repartitioned (if necessary) and the code for the routines is loaded from the algorithm library and placed in the appropriate partitions.

One advantage of using this system is the ability to have machine-independent task specifications. The user and the Image Understanding System need not be aware of the specifics of the underlying parallel processing system. Once the task is specified, the Image Understanding System database (which is also machine independent) is used to construct a data dependency graph. No user intervention is necessary from this point on. The routine execution characteristics and the routines themselves are, in part, machine dependent. When the algorithm library is created, the routine characteristics will be tabulated and recorded in the Intelligent Operating System database. In this manner, an image understanding system that uses algorithms as primitives is achieved.

3 CONCLUSION

The current research involves constructing an algorithm database for a partitionable parallel processing system. The Intelligent Operating System will use this database to efficiently map image understanding tasks onto the processor's architecture. The three parts of the algorithm database (the algorithm image analysis performance database, the routine implementation execution characteristics database, and the algorithm library) will be employed to give minimized execution time for the specified tasks.

By reducing the task execution time, efficient and rapid prototyping of image understanding tasks becomes possible. The algorithm database also allows task specifications that are independent of the underlying parallel processing system.

The research currently being done on the Intelligent Operating System is aimed at integrating it into PASM's operating system where it is logically a companion to the system control unit. The scheduling heuristics are being implemented using the CLIPS expert system shell developed at NASA [12]. Verification and testing will make use of the image understanding task described by Ohta [14] since it supplies a complex, time intensive, and realistic task.

REFERENCES

[1] G.F. Pfister et al. (1985). The IBM Research Parallel Processor Prototype (RP3): Introduction and Architecture, *1985 International Conference on Parallel Processing*, August 1985, pp. 764–771.

[2] W. Crother et al. (1985). Performance Measures on a 128-Node Butterfly Parallel Processor, *1985 International Conference on Parallel Processing*, August 1985, pp. 531–540.

[3] C. Seitz. (1985). The Cosmic Cube, *Communications of the ACM*, Vol. 28, January 1985, pp. 22–33.

[4] H.J. Siegel et al. (1981). PASM: a Partitionable Multimicrocomputer SIMD/MIMD System for Image Processing and Pattern Recognition, *IEEE Transactions on Computers*, Vol. C-30, December 1981, pp. 934–947.

[5] H. Chu, E.J. Delp, and H.J. Siegel. (1987). Image Understanding on PASM: A User's Perspective, *2nd International Conference on Supercomputing*, May 1987, pp. 440–449.

[6] E.J. Delp, H.J. Siegel, A. Whinston, and L.H. Jamieson. (1985). An Intelligent Operating System for Executing Image Understanding Tasks on a Reconfigurable Parallel Architecture, *IEEE Computer Society Workshop on Computer Architecture for Pattern Analysis and Image Database Management*, November 1985, pp. 217–224.

[7] E. Horowitz and S. Sahni. (1978). *Fundamentals of Computer Algorithms*, Computer Science Press, Maryland, 1978.

[8] D.L. Tuomenoksa and H.J. Siegel. (1981). Application of Two-dimensional Bin Packing to Task Scheduling in PASM, *Allerton Conference on Communication, Control, and Computing*, University of Illinois, October 1981, p. 542.

[9] T. Schwederski, T.L. Casavant, and H.J. Siegel. (1987). Task Migration in Partitionable Parallel Processing Systems, *Internal Documentation*, January 1987.

[10] L.H. Jamieson. (1987). Characterizing Parallel Algorithms, *The Characteristics of Parallel Algorithms*, L.H. Jamieson, D.B. Gannon, and R.J. Douglass, editors, MIT Press, Massachusetts, 1987, pp. 65–100.

[11] E.C. Bronson and L.J. Siegel. (1982). A Parallel Architecture for Acoustic Processing in Speech Understanding, *1982 International Conference on Parallel Processing*, August 1982, pp. 307–312.

[12] F.M. Lopez. (1986). *CLIPS Reference Manual*, Artificial Intelligence Section, Mission Planning and Development Division, NASA, July 1986.

[13] J.C. Giarratano. (1986). *CLIPS User's Guide*, Artificial Intelligence Section, NASA-Johnson Space Center, October 2, 1986.

[14] Y. Ohta. (1985). *Knowledge-based Interpretation of Outdoor Natural Color Scenes*, Pitman Publishing, Massachusetts, 1985.

Chapter Five

The Coordinated Evaluation of Parallel Architectures for Perceptual Tasks

Leonard Uhr

Department of Computer Sciences, University of Wisconsin-Madison

ABSTRACT

This paper explores how research might in a coordinated way develop new multi-computers by examining and assessing a variety of parallel architectures for their capabilities on a range of perceptual tasks.

(1) A specification procedure should be developed to describe and assign costs to multi-computers in terms of their basic components, and from this assess hardware complexity and total costs.
(2) Underlying topologies should be categorized, and generic, generalized structures and specific multi-computers chosen from each for further examination.
(3) Algorithms should be developed (consulting architects, to get balance) for a range of perceptual tasks, from image enhancement to object recognition and computer vision.
(4) For each architecture, the performance (time and hardware needed) of each algorithm should be analyzed and estimated; for a selected set, the algorithm should be programmed and run.

The results of such an enterprise would give a systematic set of comparisons between topologies, and between particular multi-computers within each topology. Selected comparisons would show how closely actual performance is predicted by estimated performance, and indicate where and how to improve upon the specifications of basic components and their costs. Thus tools would be developed for relatively quickly estimating architectures' capabilities.

1 INTRODUCTION

The development of good multi-computers for image processing, pattern recognition, and computer vision is an extremely important, and difficult, task. It requires careful examination, analysis, and development of both hardware architectures and software algorithms and programs. This paper

MULTICOMPUTER VISION
ISBN 0-12-444818-6

examines how this might best be done. Ideally, every promising architecture should be thoroughly tested on a good representative sample of algorithms. But unless large numbers of researchers worked on this task in a coordinated manner, it would be necessary to examine, analyze, and simulate, to choose a much smaller manageable number of the most promising.

A carefully selected sample of parallel architectures should be evaluated for how well they perform on a range of algorithms and programs for perceptual tasks. Architectures should be chosen and grouped in terms of their underlying topologies; they should be assigned costs in terms of their basic resources. Tasks should range from simple to complex. For each task, as fast and efficient as possible an algorithm should be developed for each architecture.

A system should be developed that can be used to do the following:

(1) Describe parallel computers in terms of their basic resources (processors, memories, controllers, switches, and the wires that link them).
(2) Describe each basic resource in terms of primitive devices (transistors, or chip area).
(3) Assign costs in terms of these resources. (Dollar costs should also be used where available and they do not reflect market forces, for overall comparison.)

The various graph topologies of the multi-computer architectures that have been built, designed, or suggested to date should be surveyed, and their similarities and differences explored. This entails examining the actual multi-computers and specifying the underlying topology of each, and also searching for promising topologies that have not yet been embodied in hardware. A tentative taxonomy should be developed, and used to help choose a good set of topologies to evaluate and compare. The generalized topology should be specified, and also specific examples (including, where possible, several multi-computers on which programs can actually be run). Costs should be assigned to each topology, and to each of its resources, using counts of underlying devices and estimates of chip area.

A representative sample of tasks, and the algorithms and programs that handle them, should be developed for image processing, pattern recognition and computer vision. Architects' judgments should be used to help give a balanced set. These should be of three general types:

(1) Basic well-formed tasks for which simple algorithms are known (e.g. compute mean, median, histogram, convolutions, connected components).
(2) Relatively simple, solvable tasks that can be handled by clear-cut combinations of a few basic algorithms (e.g. skeletonize the Abingdon Cross, get Hough transforms, find blobs).
(3) Complex tasks (e.g. recognizing objects) for which large programs are needed. Here behavior must be evaluated and compared across systems, since these are not-yet-solved tasks.

For each task, as efficient as possible an algorithm should be developed for each architecture, and evaluated as to its performance and its complexity (in terms of time), with respect to the space complexity and cost estimates of the architecture's hardware. The attempt should be made to discover a proved-optimal algorithm; but in general to find as efficient an algorithm as possible.

This should result in a set of performance estimates for a set of architectures that can be used to assess, and also to suggest additional architectures worthy of study, improved tools for specifying architectures and assigning costs, and additional tasks with which to evaluate. Thus this should be a continuing, cycling, process.

2 MULTI-COMPUTER ARCHITECTURES—TOPOLOGIES AND SPECIFICATIONS

The following is a brief survey of what presently appear to be the most promising multi-computers and topologies, focussing on perceptual tasks. The ones actually examined, specified, and tested should be chosen as part of a continuing study. (See [1, 2, 3, 4, 5, 6, 7] for fuller and more detailed examinations.)

Stars (Bus-based systems) The recently developed commercial systems defined by Bell, 1985 [8], as "multis" use a common bus to link a number of processors along with other resources, including memories, i-o devices, and controllers. Thus the bus serves as the node at the root of a 1-ply tree (the root is the center of what is often called a star) whose leaves are the processors and the other resources. Examples are the Aliant, Concept, Elexsi, and Sequent.

Lines (Pipelines, and 1-Dimensional Arrays) These systems have L nodes, n = 1, 2, ..., L, each linked to n − 1 and n + 1 (its 2 adjacent nodes). This gives a pipeline—e.g. WARP [9], Cytocomputers [10, 11]—when data flows into node 1, moving through to node L. When each processor has its own controller, this becomes Flynn's, 1972, [12] classical MISD (multiple instructions single data-stream) system. It gives a 1-dimensional array—e.g. CLIP7 [13], AIS-5000 [14], when each processor continues to work on local data, passing results to adjacent processors as needed. When all processors have one controller, arrays become classical SIMD (single instruction multiple data-stream) systems.

Polygons and Rings The two ends of a line can be linked, to form a polygon, and a bus can similarly be turned into a ring. Examples of such systems include [15], which links 256 simple 8-bit computers via a shift register that cycles messages, and [16], which links 20 more powerful 32-bit computers via a high-speed bus/ring.

Trees, and Slightly Augmented Trees Shaw's 1982 [17], 1984 Non-Von [18], Mago's 1980 reduction machine [19], and Stolfo's 1984 Dado [20] are good examples of tree-linked multi-computers (with a single root from which successive plies of processors fan out, possibly with a few extra links).

2-Dimensional Arrays Each node is linked to its 4 square, 8 square + diagonal, or 6 hexagonal near neighbors, that is to its adjacent nodes in each dimension. Examples are Duff's 1976 96-by-96 CLIP4 [21], Reddaway's 1978 64-by-64 DAP [22] and Batcher's 1980 128-by-128 MPP [23] along with designs that link transputer chips (Whitby-Stevens, 1985 [24]) into arrays.

Binary N-Cubes N-dimensional cubes with all nodes vertices are among today's most popular topologies (e.g. [25]). Commercial systems are being sold by Intel, N-Cube, and Floating Point Systems. Hillis' 1985 connection machine [26] links 1-bit processors via both N-Cube and 2-dimensional array.

NlogN Reconfiguring Network-Based Systems LogN banks of switches linking N processors give most of the capabilities of N × N crossbars, at substantially lower cost [27, 28]. They are used in the BBN Butterfly [29], IBM RP3 [30], NYU Ultracomputer [31], and PASM [32].

2.1 Several more complex candidate architectures

There are several additional architectures that appear to have desirable properties. These include hybrids that combine several of the basic structures described above, several variants on trees that are augmented with additional links (usually at their leaves)—including x-trees [33], hyper-trees [34] and de Bruijn graphs [35, 36], several graphs that are optimal [37] in terms of density (the closeness of nodes to one another), and several compounds of structures that pull nodes closer together [38].

(i) *Clusters of Clusters.* These are chiefly bus- or crossbar-based clusters linked via buses. They include Swan et al.'s 1977 Cm* [39], larger models of systems like the Aliant and Sequent that link several basic multis, and Kuck et al.'s 1983 Cedar [40].

(ii) *Pyramids.* Pyramids that tree-link successively smaller arrays, to give parallel-hierarchical structures with logarithmic global distances, are being developed by Cantoni et al. [41, 42], Schaefer [43], Schaefer et al. [44], and Tanimoto [45], and Tanimoto et al. [46].

(iii) *Denser Graphs and Compounding Operations.* A large number of optimally or relatively dense graphs have been discovered, along with a number of procedures for building larger graphs (see [38]). Examples are the Petersen and Singleton graphs, and good small N-node graphs embedded in the $N + 1$-node complete or $N \times N$ complete bipartite graphs.

2.2 Augmented hybrid systems presently being built, or designed

Several systems that have not yet been built, or even designed in detail, appear to be among the most promising. This kind of system should test the usefulness of specification/evaluation procedures in suggesting design alternatives. Here Schaefer, Tanimoto, and Uhr have been developing designs for augmented pyramids. Li, [48], is designing a polymorphic array that can be reconfigured (by short-circuiting processors) into a large number of topologies. Levitan et al. [49], are beginning to construct CAAPP, a 3-layered structure that combines an SIMD array with successively smaller MIMD networks of microprocessors and Lisp machines.

3 EVALUATING ARCHITECTURES AND ALGORITHMS

After a thorough examination of the perceptual recognition problem and of multi-computer topologies, representative tasks should be chosen, and estimates made as to how well algorithms and programs that accomplish these tasks can be executed by representative architectures. Each architecture should be specified, and costs assigned to its components, with enough detail and precision to estimate cost-effectiveness.

3.1 A system for describing, and assigning costs to, parallel architectures

The topologies of different architectures can be represented as graphs, at any of several levels of detail. Then appropriate costs can be assigned to each node in terms of basic resources used.

3.2 Representing multi-computer topologies

A multi-computer's underlying topology can be described as a graph whose edges are the wires linking nodes, and whose nodes represent components, at whatever level of detail one wants to examine. At a high level, each node might represent an entire computer, or even a cluster of computers. At the lowest level, each node might represent a single primitive device—a logic gate, or transistor. Still another representation is the area on the planar chip or wafer (usually treated as a grid) into which is embedded the graph whose nodes represent components.

Probably the most informative level has nodes which represent the processors, memories, controllers, and switches (plus input and output transducers) from which computers are built. Since these can vary greatly in size (e.g. from a simple 1-bit processor built from 50–500 devices to a powerful 64-bit processor built from hundreds of thousands of devices; from a 1-bit memory register to a 16 megabyte memory), in order to describe multi-computers with reasonable precision one must assign values to them in terms of smaller components.

There are several different types of each resource (e.g. pins, off-chip wires, special-purpose processors) that must be treated separately in assigning costs. There are also several structures (e.g. crossbars, NlogN switching networks, polymorphic capabilities) that are best treated as separate modules to which costs are assigned.

3.3 Assigning costs to an architecture's nodes and links

Architectures are best described as graphs, and costs assigned to nodes and links. These costs should typically be gate or transistor counts and where possible exact counts extracted from papers or discussions with the architects, otherwise informed estimates. When possible, costs should also be assigned in terms of chip area. This is probably the best assignment—to the extent one can assume that the chip has been packed densely and efficiently. A third type of estimate should be made using the actual dollar costs of architectures that have been built. But these depend strongly on economic forces, and can mislead. Where indicated, corrected estimates should be made that attempt to take into account sales volume, overhead costs, and similar factors. Roughly, the attempt should be made to estimate dollar costs if sales volume and competition were great enough to drive design, overhead, and profit margin to minima. Overall dollar costs include a variety of factors (e.g. problems in packaging and wiring off the chip) that are not captured by the other types of estimates.

Several different assignments of costs should be made, in enough cases where this can be done, so that the alternate approaches to estimating cost can be compared. This should throw very useful light on the validity of the different types of cost estimates.

Estimates should be of the following sort (adjusted, as needed, for special situations):

A processor's size is a function of complexity, p, and the number of bits, b, processed in parallel, plus (as needed) features of the VLSI implementation, v, and details of special resources, s.

* A b-bit processor needs bp devices (typically, $p = 1000$).
* Where VLSI considerations dictate (e.g. gate arrays are used, or microcode chosen to implement much of the processor), an additional multiplicative constant, v, should be used (typically, $v = 10$–100).

   * A processor with special resources (e.g. special-purpose processors), s, for particular purposes needs s times more devices.

Memory size should be a function of the number of bits, b, in a word, the number of words, w, and the type and speed of memory, t. For example:
   * A high-speed static memory might need 12 transistors per bit.
   * A low-speed static memory might need 4 per bit.
   * A low-speed dynamic memory might need 1 per bit.

Switches should in general be analyzed in terms of their basic components.
   * A 2-by-2 switch needs 4 devices per bit.

Controllers can vary so much that they should typically be estimated separately in each case. But the generic controller should often best be considered equivalent to one full chip (e.g. the transputer chip).

In addition, where indicated, adjustments should be made in terms of expected packing densities, p. A primary example is memory, where it should be assumed that $4 < p < 20$ times as many devices can be packed into the same chip area as can be packed for processors.

More generally, the more micro-modular and planar the design, the better the expected packing density. Therefore a 2-dimensional array of 1-bit processors should pack appreciably better ($2 < p < 10$) than the random logic used in more complex processors. This is not true for actual chips fabricated to date; but it seems likely that the far greater total design effort put into chips for memory and for traditional 32-bit processors means they are far better understood, hence better packed.

3.4 Combining the description of the topology with cost estimates

Consider the following examples:
   A 1-dimensional array can be represented by the graph:

$$\ldots \text{O-O-O-O-O-O-O-O} \ldots$$

Each component might be:

(a) A separate powerful computer, as in the CMU WARP systolic pipeline.
(b) A specialized 8-bit processor with a minimum of (memory) registers, as in the Cytocomputers.
(c) A specialized processor with a number of image memories, as in the NBS PIPE.
(d) A 1-bit PE (processor, data-collection network, and a relatively large memory of thousands of 1-bit registers, but without a controller), as in a 1-dimensional version of the CLIP4 array.

A 2-dimensional array can similarly be represented. Here each component might be:

(a) A separate transputer.
(b) A CLIP4 array's PE (see above).
(c) A polymorphic processor (i.e. with switches that allow short-circuiting).

To bring out these distinctions, a graph can be drawn at the appropriate level of detail, to specify the components that make a difference, and each component's size/cost assigned.

Usually the most informative level will have nodes that represent memories, processors, controllers, and switches with values (indicating either gate/transistor counts or chip area) assigned to each. Costs should be modified or added for special situations (e.g. high-speed registers, or NlogN switching networks to reconfigure topologies).

The individual members in a related family of architectures can thus be identified by starting with a graph at a high enough level to represent all family members, then moving down to a level of detail that distinguishes between them. Now the generic graph for the whole family and the individual graph for each member can all be assigned costs, and compared with one another.

Consider the following assignments of some of the costs for the above examples:

(a) WARP uses 15MFLOP 64-bit Weitek processor chips that each cost roughly $1,000, and have several hundred thousand transistors.
(b) A simple 1-bit CLIP processor has roughly 300 gates/transistors, plus 250 for the data-collection network.
(c) Each 1-bit polymorphic processor needs roughly 30 additional devices to handle short-circuiting.

These kinds of specifications will frequently be incomplete and include rough estimates. Therefore an additional architecture should be specified—a generalized/generic version that makes estimates based on a single technology and packing density, as corrected for expected densities for different types of nodes.

Specifying topologies and assigning costs are only the first steps. Once algorithms are specified, and evaluated for how well (in terms of complexity and performance) they execute on each architecture, the results are estimates giving performance/cost profiles and comparisons.

3.5 Categorizing multi-computer topologies, and choosing a range of examples

The different parallel computers already built and designed should be surveyed and examined. Ultimately even more important, the much larger set of possible topologies (all possible graphs) should be surveyed and explored. The attempt should be made to categorize, and build a taxonomy of, parallel structures.

This can only be a tentative first attack at what is a very difficult problem, since a good taxonomy can be achieved only after the realm being categorized is well understood; the taxonomy reflects and expresses the highlights of this understanding. But the attempt to categorize should throw light on the problem, and help to choose a better set of topologies (to then examine for how well they execute different algorithms) than could be got using other criteria—for example, those that are widely publicized, or commercially successful.

3.6 Complexity and actual cost estimates, of generic architectures

Stout [50, 51] has specified a generic 2-dimensional array and a generic pyramid. He points out that from the standpoint of traditional complexity measures many details (e.g. number of links to each component, and even power of each processor) can be ignored. Thus a complexity analysis' characterization of an algorithm on an array might be O(N), and of an equivalent algorithm on a pyramid O(logN). This is most informative when considering arbitrarily large problems. But perceptual problems, though large, are still small enough so that factors (e.g. number of ports to a node; size of a processor) that can be ignored in analyses of complexity drastically affect cost estimates. (These issues of space complexity for architectures are similar to those of time complexity for algorithms.)

The intricacies of point-to-point linked systems, where each processor has direct access to relatively small sub-parts of the total memory, and information must be passed among processors, make it preferable to specify, and assign costs to, each architecture's component resources, including the linking wires, to develop a measure of overall cost.

3.7 Basic topologies, and representative architectures for each

It already seems clear (see [52]) that the topology underlying almost all multi-computers built or designed to date is either a star, line, polygon, tree, 2-dimensional array, binary N-cube, or NlogN shuffle-exchange based reconfiguring network. From one perspective this seems reasonable, since these are the most simple and basic topologies. From another it is surprising, since there is such an overwhelming number of other possibilities—all possible graphs. It is also encouraging, since it indicates the importance of the underlying topology, and means that architectures can be categorized and compared relatively easily.

Each of these underlying topologies should be considered a family, and should be specified generically. In addition, several specific architectures should be chosen, for comparison both within the family and with other families.

3.8 Tentative choice of a test set from among all the possibilities

The important point to note for the long run is that, although the list of prime candidates that follows (a list that results from rather extensive examinations of the field—see [3, 53, 52], is already long, it is a miniscule sample of the possibilities. But if from the practical point of view it is too large to handle, a smaller set should be specified and assessed for algorithm performance, and an even smaller set actually programmed and timed exactly.

If this were to be done today, prime candidates would include the following:

Stars: Aliant, Sequent.
Lines: Pipe, Warp; CLIP7, AIS-5000.
Rings: Crystal, Z-Mob.
2-Dimensional arrays: CLIP4, DAP, MPP.
Trees: Dado, Non-Von.
Augmented trees: de Bruijn graphs, Hypertrees.
Binary N-cubes: N-cube, connection machine.
Dense graphs: Petersen, Singleton.
NlogN networks: Butterfly, RP3.
Pyramids, including new designs: Schaefer, Tanimoto, Uhr.
Hybrid systems: CAAPP, polymorphic arrays.
Augmented pyramids: Fattened, Multi-apex, Dense-graph embedded.
Clusters of clusters: Cedar, Complete-graph embedded Singleton.

As new topologies worth examining are discovered, and new systems built, this list should be augmented.

4 TASKS, AND THE ALGORITHMS AND PROGRAMS THAT REALIZE THEM

A representative set of tasks should be chosen, by examining the processes typically used, the sets the community of researchers have developed, abstract underlying characteristics, and the choices of the multi-computer and program designers themselves. There appear to be enough simple, widely used tasks for a reasonably representative sample to be got.

Researchers developing architectures should be urged to suggest tasks, as well as to run tasks from the current list. This should give an important kind of representative sampling [5A]. When each group suggests tasks their systems handle well, the total set becomes balanced.

Traditionally, people have developed algorithms to be run on a serial computer, whose topology is a single-node graph. But as soon as parallel computers with differing topologies must be compared, one must develop the best algorithm for each topology. So one must start anew, examining the underlying task, from which the specific algorithm is then developed.

This raises several complex new problems:

(a) Do the different algorithms give identical results, and if not, how can roughly equivalent results be compared?

(b) Can tasks and algorithms be posed so that slight or irrelevant differences in architecture do not override. For example, how compare two arrays of processors, one 96 × 96 the other 128 × 128 if the job is to process a 512 × 512 image array?

(c) Since different topologies are best suited to different processes, how can a balanced set of tasks be built?

(d) If a particular multi-computer has a particular capability suited to a particular task, when should that be discounted, or be compensated for by estimated extensions to other architectures?

There are currently two major efforts to develop sets of tasks with which to evaluate and compare parallel architectures for perceptual tasks.

One was initiated during a series of workshops in which many of the people developing architectures, languages, algorithms, and programs for image processing have participated (e.g. [55, 56]). The preface to the volume edited by Uhr et al. [5], describes this group and presents the results of their first attempt at specifying a set of tasks and algorithms. Coordinated with this, Preston, [57], presents results of his efforts to collect benchmarks on what has become known as the "Abingdon Cross" (named for the town where the meeting that decided on and specified it was held—[58]).

The second is being carried out by the researchers involved in the DARPA-funded Autonomous Land Vehicle (ALV) project, who are trying to establish a set of benchmarks [59]. This appears to be growing into a large project, but it focuses on only those architectures (primarily ones funded by DARPA) that are being considered for the ALV. This project will focus on navigation through different kinds of terrain, rather than object recognition or other aspects of the vision problem.

There have been a number of developments of simple single benchmarks, and several researchers have used sets of benchmarks to evaluate a single multi-computer. For example, Kopp, [60], developed a very simple benchmark to input-compare (by convolving) an image with a reference image. Verghese et al. [61], used a set of benchmarks to estimate performance of the PIPE.

Tasks can (somewhat arbitrarily) be grouped into three major categories, and a representative sample chosen from each. These include:

(1) Very simple well-specified and clear-cut problems.

(2) Well-understood tasks that can be solved using relatively small programs that combine several simple algorithms.

(3) Complex recognition problems that at best are only partially handled by the largest and most powerful systems built to date.

4.1 Simple basic tasks and algorithms

A large number of algorithms have been developed over the years. But a rather small number of these appear to be widely used and generally considered useful for evaluation purposes. A small sample of this kind of simple task should be chosen.

Among the most likely candidates are:

(a) Mean
(b) Median (local, and global)
(c) Histogram
(d) Component linking and labelling
(e) Local window operations
(f) Window operations using larger, or global, windows
(g) Relaxation

4.2 Toward categorizing tasks and algorithms in terms of underlying characteristics

There has been some progress in developing more abstract criteria for categorizing algorithms. Thus Stout [50, 62] has defined three general classes:

(a) mesh-local
(b) perimeter-bound
(c) globally-dense

These are functions of two underlying factors: the amount of information that the algorithm must examine, and the distance over which this information must be passed. Thus mesh-local algorithms pass only small amounts of information only small distances; globally dense algorithms pass arbitrarily large amounts of information arbitrarily large distances.

The cost of the functions processors use to actually assess and combine this information will also have a major effect on execution time. For complexity analyses this is usually treated as a constant (since they remain the same no matter how many processors) hence ignored. But to determine actual performance in perceptual problems of interest it quickly becomes a constant that is large enough to play a major role. For example, if large 4,096-by-4,096 image arrays are processed using $O(\log N)$ algorithms, the constant number of processes used, and each process's constant cost quickly becomes far greater than $\log N$.

4.3 Tasks that combine several simple tasks and algorithms

The Abingdon Cross [57, 63] is probably the best example of a relatively simple but common task that makes use of a structure of several basic, reasonably well understood algorithms. The problem is: Given a $512 \times 512 \times 8$ image of a cross (each arm 424×64; basic intensity $= 160$ except the center $64 \times 64 = 192$); on a background (basic intensity $= 128$); with Gaussian noise (mean $= 0$, standard deviation $= 32$)—recover a good skeleton (that is, a thin-line cross). This has been successfully run on, or estimated for, over 40 different architectures.

A typical parallel program should first average, difference, expand, shrink to eliminate noise, get edges and strong borders; then skeletonize, by shrinking from the borders. But there appears to be no exact structure of specific algorithms that could be specified for all possible architectures, and details of implementations have varied considerably.

It is important to note that although this was agreed to by the group at Abingdon, who felt they had posed a clear-cut problem, when one begins to implement a program for a particular computer, or to estimate performance on a particular topology, problems arise. For example: How can things be standardized over multi-computers that are designed to handle different-sized image arrays (e.g. larger arrays give better resolution, but may take longer); Each architecture's program has been considered to have succeeded, although some give better results than others. That is, it is hard to evaluate the quality of the result.

One or two similarly complex tasks of the following sort should be chosen:

(a) Hough transform to get sloped edges of some object
(b) Locate and count blobs
(c) Match stereo images

4.4 Complex, relatively ill-formed tasks

The ultimate goal of perception systems is to recognize and describe complex real-world objects. Very large and powerful programs must be developed to handle such tasks. Today one can at best develop programs for very limited domains, to handle only a few relatively clean examples of a few different objects. [This is much like the situation for other problems of comparable difficulty. There is nothing approaching a good general-purpose game player; with a great deal of work programs have been developed to play one particular game—usually chess—with reasonable skill. Nor is there anything like a generally-expert system; on the contrary, each "knowledge-based expert system" is carefully designed to handle a very limited well-formed domain.]

The recognition problem is so difficult, that the following kinds of simplifications should be made: Each image contains only one object; the program's task is to name it; only "good" examples of each object should be used, with relatively firm contours, clear lighting, and not-unusual features. (Since this probably can't be objectified, human judges should be asked to eliminate obscure examples). Otherwise, examples should not be constrained—for example, they should not be chosen to "look alike". And to guard against biases, examples should be chosen by people who know nothing about the architectures that should be compared.

Here several tasks should be specified, of the following sort: Recognize instances of 3 to 10 different objects from:

(a) Hand-printed letters (e.g. B, D, P, R, etc.)
(b) Simple hand-drawn symbols (e.g. cross, arrow, star)
(c) Outdoor objects (e.g. house, tree, bicycle)
(d) Indoor objects (e.g. chair, table, floorlamp)

5 EVALUATING DIFFERENT ARCHITECTURES' PERFORMANCE ON DIFFERENT ALGORITHMS

Algorithms should be developed for each task for each architecture. The component costs and (space) complexity of the architecture, and the (time) complexity of the algorithm as it runs on that architecture, will give power and cost-effectiveness estimates. Actual runs should be made for selected tasks on available hardware.

5.1 Handling the difficult problems in evaluating performance on complex recognition tasks

The recognition of complex objects poses special problems, that should be handled as follows. To start, a system of the sort developed at Wisconsin that applies parallel-hierarchical structures of micro-modular feature detectors [64, 65] can be used. Actual runs should be made using small sets of feature detectors for small problems; from these, estimates should be made as to how large a structure of feature detectors is needed to handle larger problems. This should be used to estimate performance of equivalent systems for different architectures (see [1, 66] for examples of previous work of this sort). These should include topologies (e.g. serial computers, arrays, pyramids, N-cubes) into which it is known how to embed parallel-hierarchical structures, and any other topologies that can be given comparable algorithms. The resulting estimates would be rough, but complex recognition is the ultimate goal of perception systems, and they should throw important light beyond that got from the much simpler tasks. Ideally, several researchers should cooperate in developing systems for, and making runs on, still other architectures.

5.2 Evaluating architectures on tasks—A few examples

The following gives some of the details for evaluating serial computers, arrays, pyramids, and the connection machine, on histogramming and assessing hierarchies of local features.

The tasks are: $[31 < B < 1,025; \ 127 < N < 4,097; \ 7 < F < 2,049; \ 1 < W < 8]$

(1) Compute a B-bin histogram on an $N \times N$ image array.
(2) Apply a hierarchical structure of operations to an $N \times N$ image: Assess F features using $W \times W$ windows of information, and output results to an $N/2 \times N/2$ array; now assess features in this transformed image, and continue to converge and assess through logN layers.

The following specifies the generalized architectures:

(A) Serial computer: 1 32-bit processor, F $N \times N$ memories, 1 controller, $O(FN \times N)$ wires in the network that links memories to processor, 32 input-output wires.

(B) Array: $N \times N$ 1-bit processors, each with F memories, 1 controller, $O(F)$ wires from its memories to each processor, N input-output wires, $2N \times N$ wires (to 4 neighbors; toroidal wires at borders).

(C) Pyramid: $((4/3) - 1)(N \times N)$ 1-bit processors, each with F memories, logN controllers, $O(F)$ wires from its memories to each processor, $(4N/3) - 1$ input-output wires, $9/2((4/3) - 1)(N \times N) - 4N \times N$ wires (to 4 neighbors, 4 children, 1 parent; toroidal links at borders, except $N \times N$ array processors have no children).

(D) Connection machine: The array as specified above, plus $\log_2 N/2(N \times N)$ wires linking processors over the additional N-cube network.

Several details are missing, and adjustments are needed, before actual costs are assigned; e.g.:

(a) Since pyramids rarely if ever fetch simultaneously from children and siblings, to link between chips only 1 pin (plus a switch) may suffice.
(b) To input-output images in parallel with processing (as in the MPP), an array's N input-output wires must be replaced by the $2N \times N$ wires plus $N \times N$ registers needed to shift images in and out at the same time that processors use their $2N \times N$ array of connecting wires.
(c) Since the number of ports each connection machine processor needs continues to increase, and this becomes an increasingly expensive commodity, extra costs must be included.
(d) The connection machine, although all processors work in simple SIMD mode, needs an elaborate system to handle message routing through the N-cube (as indicated by the fact that the N-cube network is its most costly part (a 256×256 connection machine costs $3,000,000).

The following sketches out, for a few cases, how for a particular architecture an algorithm can be specified for each task, and its costs estimated.

A histogram algorithm for a serial computer: Fetch each of the $N \times N$ image values, compute what bin-interval it is in, and add 1 to the count for that bin. This needs $O(N \times N)$ time. Computing total costs more exactly, about 4–8 instructions are needed to increment indexes, test for borders, and fetch each value, $\log N$ comparisons to find its bin, and 2 instructions to increment that bin's count. So it needs $O((\log N + 10)(N \times N))$ time.

To apply a hierarchical structure of F $W \times W$ window features, using a serial computer, FW^2N^2 instructions are needed to assess F $W \times W$ features everywhere in the original $N \times N$ array—giving $O((4/3 - 1)FW^2N^2)$ time needed. This should be multiplied by roughly 100, to handle the nested For-loops through the large array, and through the window around each cell.

To histogram on a pyramid: starting with the first bin, each cell in the base passes 1 to its parent if its value falls in that bin; all parents total their children's values and pass this total to their parents. At each step, the cells at the base start processing the next bin. Thus each bin is accumulated in $\log N$ steps, and it takes $B + \log N$ steps to process all bins. This needs $O(\log N)$ time, if B is considered a constant. But since $\log N$, even for the largest of images, will never exceed 10 or 20, while B might sometimes be several hundred or thousand, it is important when estimating costs to take B into account.

To assess a hierarchy of features on a pyramid needs $O(\log N)$ time: Each feature is assessed in parallel at each cell in the base; parents examine the results in applying each feature at the next level; this continues up the pyramid. Thus $FW \times W \log N$ steps are needed (but F and W can be considered constants, and W can always be kept small, by decomposing larger windows into hierarchies of small windows). Depending upon more details of wires and gates to allow parallel examinations of windows, assessing a feature in a 3×3 window might need anywhere from 1 to roughly 20 steps.

There is space to only touch upon array and connection machine: An array can accumulate histogram bins or converge features only by shifting through the array. So (except for mesh-local) most algorithms need at least $O(N)$ time. The connection machine's N-cube routing network, in common with specific global capabilities that have been given actual arrays (e.g. CLIP4's fast propagation, DAP's row and column highways), can improve on this.

These kinds of examinations should be made more detailed, especially where needed to compare different variant architectures. For example, CLIP4 and DAP global capabilities should be specified, for comparisons with connection machines. And they should be expanded to include other architectures and other tasks.

5.3 Using and improving architecture specifications and cost estimates

Comparing estimates with results of actual runs will throw light on how to improve these kinds of descriptive models and cost estimates. Good estimates, once achievable, not only make comparisons far simpler; they can also be used to help decide which architectures to simulate in more detail, or to build.

The final goal of this kind of research enterprise is to develop tools with which to evaluate the cost and speed of multi-computer architectures on a range of perceptual tasks. To achieve this, both multi-computers and perceptual tasks must be examined and categorized. Tools must be developed with which to specify topologies precisely enough to estimate hardware costs (space complexity, and actual total component costs). The speed (time complexity, and actual execution timings) of algorithms and programs for a range of tasks on each architecture will indicate comparative suitability and cost effectiveness.

6 SUMMARIZING COMMENTS AND RESULTS TO BE EXPECTED

This kind of research is best carried out as a continuing enterprise by a closely interacting, cooperating and competing research, community. It would produce a representative set of tasks for which algorithms and programs have been developed for a representative range of multi-computer architectures. The analyses in terms of component costs and space complexity (hardware) and time complexity (speed) of each algorithm for each architecture would thus make possible the specification of a set of algorithms with which to benchmark and evaluate for particular purposes.

A generalized specification should be developed for each topology, and performance compared with performance of particular multi-computer architectures of that type. This would indicate how important the particular variation is with respect to any additional costs for additional hardware. It would also make possible general as well as specific comparisons between different types of architectures.

Where actual hardware is available, algorithms should be programmed and run. In this way exact performance as well as estimated performance can be got, and compared. This also serves as a check for how accurate the estimates are. To the extent that estimates prove good, this becomes a simple but powerful way to choose the most promising architectures to use, buy, or build. Where actual architectures differ from estimates, because of additional resources or design details that were not handled, the attempt can be made to develop more detailed and precise specification techniques.

In addition to the development of tools for describing and evaluating architectures and algorithms, and actual evaluations and comparisons of important and representative architectures and algorithms, this kind of research would point to and help develop new architectures and algorithms. Being able to estimate and observe what an architecture does well and what it does poorly, and juxtaposing this with other architectures that do what it does poorly well, should be a powerful tool for discovering what kinds of improvements to make.

REFERENCES

[1] Uhr, L. (1982). Comparing serial computers, arrays and networks using measures of "active resources," *IEEE Trans. Computers*, **30**, pp. 1022–1025.

[2] Uhr, L. (1983). Augmenting pyramids and arrays by compounding them with networks, *Proc. Workshop on Computer Architecture for Pattern Analysis and Image Data Base Management*, IEEE Computer Society Press, pp. 162–169.

[3] Uhr, L. (1984). *Algorithm-Structured Computer Arrays and Networks*, Academic Press, New York.

[4] Uhr, L. (1985(b)). Pyramid Multi-Computers, and Extensions and Augmentations. In *Algorithmically Specialized Computer Organizations*, D. Gannon, H.J. Siegel, L. Siegel and L. Snyder (Eds.), Academic Press, New York, pp. 177–186.

[5] Uhr, L. (1986(c)). Multiple image and multi-modal augmented pyramid networks. In *Architectures and Algorithms for Image Processing*, M.J.B. Duff (Ed.), Academic Press, London.

[6] Parallel, hierarchical software/hardware pyramid architectures. In *Pyramidal Image Processing Systems*, V. Contoni and S. Levialdi (Eds.), Springer-Verlag, Berlin.

[7] Hwang, K. and Briggs, F.A. (1984). *Computer Architecture and Parallel Processing*, McGraw-Hill, New York.

[8] Bell, G.C. (1985). Multis: A new class of multiprocessor computers, *Science*, **228**, pp. 462–467.

[9] Dohi, Y., Fisher, A.L., Kung, H.T. and Monier, L.M. (1985). The programmable systolic chip: project overview. In *Algorithmically Specialized Parallel Computers*. (Ed. L. Snyder, L.H. Jamieson, D.B. Gannon, H.J. Siegel), pp. 47–53. Academic Press, New York.

[10] Sternberg, S.R. (1978). Cytocomputer real-time pattern recognition. Paper presented at *Eighth Pattern Recognition Symp.*, National Bureau of Standards.

[11] Lougheed, R.M. and McCubbrey, D.L. (1985). Multiprocessor architectures for machine vision and image analysis, *Proc. Int. Conf. Parallel Proc.*, pp. 493–497.

[12] Flynn, M. (1972). Some computer organizations and their effectiveness, *IEEE Trans. Comput.*, **21**, pp. 948–960.

[13] Fountain, T.J. (1983). The development of the CLIP7 image processing system, *Pattern Recognition Letters*, **1**, pp. 331–339.

[14] Wilson, S.S. (1985). The PIXIE-5000—a systolic array processor. *Proc. Workshop on Computer Architecture for Pattern Analysis and Image Database Management*, IEEE Computer Society Press, pp. 477–483.

[15] Rieger, C., Bane, J. and Trigg, R. (1980). A highly parallel multiprocessor, *Proc. IEEE Workshop on Picture Data Description and Management*, pp. 298–304.

[16] DeWitt, D.J., Finkel, R., and Solomon, M. (1984). The CRYSTAL multicomputer: Design and implementation experience. *Univ. of Wisconsin Computer Sci. Dept. Tech. Rept.*

[17] Shaw, D.W. (1982). The NON-VON Supercomputer, *Comp. Sci. Dept. Tech. Rept.*, Columbia University, August.

[18] Shaw, D. (1984). SIMD and MSIMD variants of the NON-VON supercomputer, *COMPCON Spring 84.*

[19] Mago, G.A. (1980). A cellular computer architecture for functional programming, *Proc. COMPCON*, pp. 179–187.

[20] Stolfo, S.J. (1984). Five parallel algorithms for production system execution on the DADO machine, *Proc. Nat. Conf. on Artif. Intell.*

[21] Duff, M.J.B. (1976). CLIP4: a large scale integrated circuit array parallel processor. *Proc. IJCPR-3*, **4**, pp. 728–733.

[22] Reddaway, S.F. (1978). DAP—a flexible number cruncher, *Proc. 1978 LASL Workshop on Vector and Parallel Processors*, Los Alamos, pp. 233–234.

[23] Batcher, K.E. (1980). Design of a massively parallel processor, *IEEE Trans. Computers*, **29**, pp. 836–840.

[24] Whitby-Stevens, C. (1985). The transputer, *12th Ann. Int. Symp. on Comput. Arch.*, pp. 292–300.

[25] Fox, G.C. and Otto, S.W. (1984). Algorithms for concurrent processors, *Physics Today, AR-370*, May, pp. 13–20.

[26] Hillis, W.D. (1985). *The Connection Machine*, MIT Press, Cambridge.

[27] Benes, V.E. (1965). *Mathematical Theory of Connecting Networks and Telephone Traffic*, Academic Press, New York.

[28] Siegel, H.J. (1984). *Interconnection Networks for Large Scale Parallel Processing.* Lexington, Mass: Lexington.

[29] Crowther, W., Goodhue, J., Starr, E., Thomas, R., Milliken, W. and Blackadar, T. (1985). Performance measurements on a 128-node butterfly parallel processor. *Proc. Int. Conf. Parallel Proc.*, pp. 531–540.

[30] Pfister, G.F., Brantley, W.C., George, D.A., Harvey, S.L., Kleinfelder, W.J., McAuliffe, K.P., Melton, E.A., Norton, V.A., and Weiss, J. (1985). The IBM research parallel processor prototype (RP3), *Proc. Int. Conf. Parallel Proc.*, pp. 764–771.

[31] Gottlieb, A.B., et al. (1983). The NYU ultra-computer—designing an MIMD shared memory parallel computer, *IEEE Trans. Computers*, **C-32**, pp. 175–189.

[32] Siegel, H.J. (1981). PASM: a reconfigurable multimicrocomputer system for image processing. In *Languages and Architectures for Image Processing*, M.J.B. Duff and S. Levialdi (Eds.), Academic Press, London.

[33] Despain, A.M. and Patterson, D.A. (1978). X-tree: a tree structured multiprocessor computer architecture. *Proc. Fifth Ann. Symp. on Computer Arch.*, pp. 144–151.

[34] Goodman, J.R. and Sequin, C.H. (1981). Hypertree: a multiprocessor interconnection topology, *IEEE Trans. Computers*, **C-30**, pp. 923–933.

[35] de Bruijn, D.G. (1946). A combinatorial problem. *Koninklijke Nederlandsche Academie van wetenschappen et Amsterdam, Proc. Section of Sciences* **49**, **7**, pp. 758–764.

[36] Imase, M. and Itoh, M. (1981). Design to minimize diameter on building-block network, *IEEE Trans. Computers*, **30**, pp. 439–442.

[37] Hoffman, A.J. and Singleton, R.R. (1960). On Moore graphs with diameter 2 and 3, *IBM J. Res. Devel.*, **4**, pp. 497–504.

[38] Bermond, J.-C., Delorme, C. and Quisquater, J.-J. (1983). Strategies for interconnection networks: some methods from graph theory, *Manuscript M58, Phillips Research Lab.*, Brussels.

[39] Swan, R.J., Fuller, S.H. and Siewiorek, D.P. (1977). Cm*—A modular, multi-microprocessor, *Proc. AFIPS NCC*, pp. 637–663.

[40] Kuck, D.J., Lawrie, D., Cytron, R., Sameh, A. and Gajski, D. (1983). The architecture and programming of the Cedar system, *Proc. 1983 LASL Workshop on Vector and Parallel Processing.*

[41] Cantoni, V., Ferretti, S., Levialdi, S. and Maloberti, F. (1985). A pyramid project using integrated technology. In *Integrated Technology for Image Processing* (ed. S. Levialdi), pp. 121–133. Academic Press, London.

[42] Cantoni, V., and Levialdi, S. (1987). PAPIA: A case history. In *Parallel Computer Vision* (L. Uhr, ed.), pp. 3–13. Academic Press, Boston.

[43] Schaefer, D. (1985). A three-dimensional MPP—The MPP pyramid. A pyramid implementation using a reconfigurable array of processors, *Proc. Workshop on Computer Architecture for Pattern Analysis and Image Data Base Management*, IEEE Computer Society Press.

[44] Schaefer, D., Ho, P., Boyd, J., and Vallejos, C. (1987). The GAM pyramid. In *Parallel Computer Vision* (L. Uhr, Ed.), Academic Press, Boston, pp. 15–42.

[44] Tanimoto, S.L. (1983). A pyramidal approach to parallel processing. *Proc. 10th Annual Int. Symposium on Computer Architecture*, Stockholm, pp. 372–378.

[45] Tonimoto, S.L., A pyramidol approach to parallel processing. In *Proc. 10th Int. Symp. on Computer Architecture*, Stockholm, 1983, 372–378.

[46] Tanimoto, S.L., Ligocki, T.J., and Ling, R. (1987). In *Parallel Computer Vision* (L. Uhr, Ed.), Academic Press, Boston, pp. 43–83.

[47] Uhr, L., Schmitt, L. and Hanrahan, P. (1982). Cone/pyramid perception programs for arrays and networks. In *Multi-Computers and Image Processing*, K. Preston, Jr. and L. Uhr (Eds.), Academic Press, New York, pp. 180–191.

[48] Li, H.W. (1987). Polymorphic Arrays, *IBM Watson Research Center Tech. Rept.*

[49] Levitan, S.P., Weems, C.C., Hanson, A.R. and Riseman, E.M. (1987). The UMASS Image Understanding Architecture. In *Parallel Computer Vision* (L. Uhr, Ed.), Academic Press, Boston, pp. 215–248.

[50] Stout, Q. (1986(a)). Algorithm-guided design considerations for meshes and pyramids. In *Intermediate-Level Image Processing*, (M.J.B. Duff, Ed.), Academic Press, London, pp. 149–165.

[51] Stout, Q. (1986(b)). An algorithmic comparison of meshes and pyramids. In *Evaluation of Multicomputers for Image Processing* (L. Uhr, K. Preston, S. Levialdi, M.J.B. Duff, Eds.), Academic Press, London, pp. 107–121.

[52] Uhr, L. (1987). *Multi-computers for Artificial Intelligence.* Wiley, New York.

[53] Uhr, L. (1986(a)). Parallel multi-computer architectures for image processing, computer vision and pattern perception. In *Handbook of Pattern Recognition and Image Processing*, T. Young and K.S. Fu (Eds.), Academic Press, New York, pp. 438–469.

[54] Uhr, L. (1986(b)). On benchmarks: dynamically improving experimental comparisons. In *Evaluation of Multi-Computers for Image Processing*, L. Uhr, K. Preston, S. Levialdi, and M.J.B. Duff (Eds.), Academic Press, New York, pp. 123–138, 13–21.

[55] Duff, M.J.B. and Levialdi, S. (Eds.) (1981). *Languages and Architectures for Image Processing.* Academic Press, London.

[56] Preston, K. and Uhr, L. (Eds.) (1982). *Multicomputers and Image Processing*, Academic Press, New York.

[57] Preston, K. (1986). Benchmark results: the Abingdon Cross. In *Evaluation of Multi-Computers for Image Processing*, L. Uhr, K. Preston, S. Levialdi, and M.J.B. Duff (Eds.), Academic Press, New York, pp. 23–54.

[58] Duff, M.J.B. (Ed.) (1983). *Computing Structures for Image Processing*. Academic Press, London.

[59] Rosenfeld, A. (1987). A Report on the DARPA Image Understanding Architectures Workshop, *Proc. DARPA Image Understanding Workshop*.

[60] Kopp, H. (1981). Intel standard assembly language benchmarks. In *8086 16 bit Microprocessor Benchmark Report*, Intel Corp.

[61] Verghese, G., Mehta, S., and Dyer, C.R. (1986). Image processing algorithms for the Pipelined Image-Processing Engine, *University of Wisconsin Comp. Sci. Dept. Technical Report 668*.

[62] Stout, Q. (1987). Pyramid algorithms optimal in the worst case. In *Parallel Computer Vision* (L. Uhr, Ed.), Academic Press, Boston, pp. 147–165.

[63] Preston, K. (1987). Benchmarking PRIP systems, *Computer*, in press.

[64] Li, Z.N. and Uhr, L. (1986). A pyramidal approach for the recognition of neurons using key features, *Pat. Recog.*, **19**, pp. 55–62.

[65] Li, Z.N. and Uhr, L. (1987). Pyramidal Algorithms for Analysis of House Images, *IEEE Trans. Syst., Man, Cyber.*, **16**, in press.

[66] Li, Z.N. and Uhr, L. (1985). Comparative Timings for a Neuron Recognition Program on Serial and Pyramid Computers, *Proc. Workshop on Computer Arch. for Pat. Anal. and Image Data Base Management*, IEEE Computer Society Press, pp. 99–106.

Chapter Six

An Associative Approach to Computer Vision

A. Krikelis and R.M. Lea

Department of Electrical Engineering and Electronics,
Brunel University, Uxbridge, Middlesex, United Kingdom, UB8 3PH

1 INTRODUCTION

The field of computer vision, also referred to as image processing, has developed considerably during the last decade, with growing applications in the fields of industrial production, medicine, space exploration, military, robotics and the discovery of natural resources. Image processing generally involves very large amounts of data (e.g. $512 \times 512 \times 8$ bits) and modern applications require rapid computation (usually in the range of 33–40 ms per image) of image sequences.

Computer vision systems accept as inputs images which have been digitised to an array of points called pixels and their outputs are some type of description of the input image. The output description includes details for the properties of the image regions and their relationships (e.g. sizes, shapes, visual textures etc.). Therefore, computer vision systems must be capable of "number crunching" the image pixels and processing the symbols representing the properties and relationships of the image areas. If systems must be kept small in size and reliable, as it is required in many computer vision applications, they must contain units capable of performing adequately numerical and symbolic computations.

This paper describes a novel parallel computer architecture, a fine grain associative string structure, and discusses the issues related to the use of the architecture for the implementation of general purpose computer vision systems. In addition, performance indications (based on simulations) are given of a VLSI implementation of the architecture for a range of image processing tasks.

MULTICOMPUTER VISION
ISBN 0-12-444818-6

© 1988 Academic Press Limited
All rights of reproduction in any form reserved

2 THE ASSOCIATIVE STRING PROCESSOR (ASP)

The Associative String Processor (ASP) [1, 2] is a SIMD parallel processing computational structure. Although the acronym ASP was used in the past [3], for Association-Storing Processor the structures differ considerably. The Association-Storing Processor was specially designed for the parallel storage and retrieval of semantic data structures. The Associative String Processor, as the name suggests, is a string of identical Associative Processing Elements (APEs), as shown in Fig. 1, having local content-addressable memory and using associative techniques to process data. From the above description it is clear that a greater degree of autonomy characterises the cells of the Associative String Processor.

The ASP in fact belongs to the category of Distributed Logic Memories (DLMs) [4], and it has many features in common with the usual DLMs. For instance, in its memory cells data as well as various flags are stored. The cells can be identified by global content-addressing, and they are locally connected for inter-communication. Synchronous and asynchronous communication between the Associative Processing Elements is achieved with signals being transferred in the ASP using the Inter-APE Communication Network running in parallel with the associative string.

Associative Processing Elements (APEs) are connected along the Inter-APE Communication Network; all the APEs share common Data, Activity and Control Busses and a single feedback line MR (Match Reply), which are maintained by an external ASP controller. An ASP controller comprises the standard bit-slice microprocessor components of typical high-speed micro-program controllers. The ASP controller also buffers data transmitted between the ASP modules and the host environment. The two end-ports LAP (Left Activity Port) and RAP (Right Activity Ports) of the Inter-APE Communic-ation Network allow activation signals to be injected and sensed by the

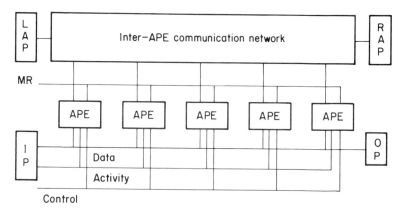

Fig. 1. The Associative String Processor (ASP).

external ASP controller; they also act as the left neighbor of the left-most APE and the right neighbor of the right-most APE in the ASP.

Each APE comprises a Data Register, an Activity Register, a Comparator and logic for local processing and interface with the Inter-APE Communication Network as it is shown in Fig. 2. The specifications of the Data Register and the processing element logic are application dependent; ASP is a generic concept for associative parallel processors, with a great range of options. A single-bit ALU will be sufficient for high performance arithmetic computation. The processing power of the parallel architectures is the result of many processors working simultaneously. A more powerful ALU will reduce the number of processing elements placed on a given hardware design. It is another characteristic feature of the ASP that the same memory array can be used to store "memorized" data and data structures, as well as descriptions of the searching criteria; the latter, named activity structures, usually are used as flags to denote a relation between data stored in different APEs. The activity structure of each APE is stored in the respective Activity Register. There are many applications of parallel processing where the activity structure is quite useful. For example, in image processing, local window operations are applied simultaneously on different parts of the image array and the functions being performed are independent of the "memorized" data but depend on

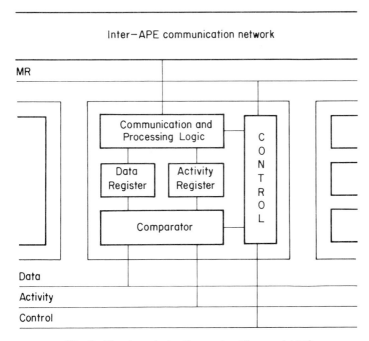

Fig. 2. The Associative Processing Element (APE).

the relative position of the pixel to the applied window. The relative position can be stored in the Activity Register, in a coded form, of the respective APE and the functions will be executed on the set of the APEs satisfying the activity criteria.

ASP modules can be linked together to configure a chain increasing linearly the processing power of the system; the modules' interconnection strategy is user transparent. In addition to a single chain of linked ASP modules, multiple channels of linked ASP modules can support computational configurations such as:

(1) SIMSIMD (Single Instruction control of Multiple SIMDs);
(2) MIMSIMD (Multiple Instruction control of Multiple SIMDs).

The term MSIMD is also used to describe MIMSIMD configurations [5]. An ASP based MIMSIMD configuration is depicted in Fig. 3. Such MIMSIMD structures offer higher application flexibility than the SIMD structures, especially in knowledge processing applications.

The APE data registers can be formatted to support a variety of different data structures. Moreover, if the situation demands, the data work-space can easily be extended by concatenating the data registers of neighboring APEs. However, such configurations reduce the number of effective APEs per ASP module; e.g. $N/2$ instead of N APEs if the registers of two neighboring APEs are concatenated.

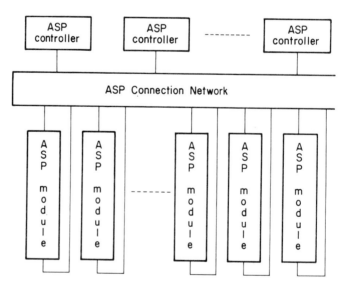

Fig. 3. ASP-based computational configurations.

2.1 ASP operations

The ASP structure can operate in one of the following two modes: bit-serial/word-parallel, bit-parallel/word-parallel. In both modes the ASP structure executes Associative Processing Instructions (APIs). Each API is divided to four basic phases: *content-search, clear, activate, read/write.*

content-search. During the content-search phase, selected bits of the Data Register (when in bit-serial/word-parallel mode) or a group of bits (e.g. a byte) of the Data Register (when in bit-parallel/word-parallel mode) are compared with the content of the Data Bus, and the content of the Activity Register is compared with the content of the Activity Bus. The result of the content-search is a set of "matching APEs". Bit-serial arithmetic operations are also supported during that phase. The flexibility of the associative processing of the ASP is used during that phase instead of the complicated and hardware demanding address decoding.

clear. During the clear phase, selected bits of the Data and Activity Registers are cleared.

activation. During the activation phase the inter-APE Communication Network is employed to provide an activation mapping between "matching APEs" and the domain of the ASP. Such activation mapping are:

(1) Symbol activation: "Matching APEs" activate single individual, neighbouring or remote APEs, and
(2) String activation: "Matching APEs" activate a contiguous group of APEs.

read/write. The content of the Data Register of activated APEs can be read onto the Data Bus during the read phase. If different data are read onto the Data Bus from a number of activated APEs, a bus contention will result to loss of meaningful data. Also, individual bits or a group of the Data Register bits and the content of the Activity Register of the activated APEs can be updated with data on the Data and Activity Bus respectively during the write phase.

The four phases of execution are supported with APE activation functions and active APE procedures.

2.1.1 APE activation functions

During the execution of an APE activation function, all APEs simultaneously compare the contents of their registers with the states of the Data and Activity Busses. The matching APEs (match on both registers) are either directly activated (e.g. by updating their activity registers) or initiate inter-APE communications to indirectly activate other APEs. A match is recorded when the content of the APE's Data Register and the state of the Data Bus are identical and the content of the APE's Activity Register is a sub-set of the state of the Activity Bus.

2.1.2 Active APE procedures

Active APE procedures execute read or write operations in those APEs which match the state of the Activity Bus, and simultaneously update their Activity Registers.

2.2 ASP software

Application programs for the ASP are written entirely in a block-structured high-level language. The present software implementations use Modula-2 to express the ASP operations for performance evaluation of the architecture for certain applications; e.g. text processing, image processing, image generation, Prolog implementation, WSI applications, etc. The ASP programs are constructed from a set of built-in APE activation functions and active APE procedures. The structure of the language allows the program to include calls to external pre-compiled routines from a routine library.

2.3 Evaluating the ASP architecture for VLSI

The ASP architecture is a fine grain, regular structure with distributed logic due to the associative nature of the memory local to each processing element. By distributing the processing power the processing rate increases, allowing higher integration.

For the VLSI implementation of an architecture to be cost-effective, regularity is the main requirement. Certainly, the ASP architecture is regular; e.g. identical APEs. The regularity of the ASP structure extends also to the system level. An ASP based system will be using homogeneous ASP modules. The ASP string regularity in association with the lack of addressing requirements, due to the associative nature of the ASP processing, increases the reliability of an ASP based system, because simple cost-effective fault tolerance techniques can be used to sustain the system operation. Faulty processing elements are logically isolated, using simple bypass techniques, and replaced by auxiliary ones with only slight degradation in processing or inter-APE communication.

There is an additional feature of the ASP structure which must be emphasized. The pin-count of the architecture is independent of any future improvements in device density. The string structure of the ASP allows a constant pin interface for any number of processing elements integrated on an ASP module. The pin-count problem is a severe handicap for other architectures, where improvements in density allow more logic on chip but no more pins (because of architectural considerations) are available to deliver additional data.

The really big hardware issue in parallel processing may ultimately be one of packaging, that is, how to make a parallel architecture scalable (a design is scalable if it can be adjusted up or down in size or number without loss of functionality to scale effects) with respect to processing power the same way sequential architectures have become expandable with respect to memory capacity. More explicitly, one would like to plug more processors into a parallel machine to improve its performance in a computer-limited application just as one can today plug in additional memory cards in a sequential machine to enhance memory-limited performance. One of the main advantages of the ASP structure is that it is scalable without any modification of the system's hardware and software. In contrast with other scalable machines (e.g. The Connection Machine [6], The Massively Parallel Processor (MPP) [7], etc.), which have limited extendibility because extra bits for the address space have to be integrated in the original hardware and software designs, the ASP architecture is incrementally scalable, as the only interface between ASP modules is the LAP to RAP interface which in current ASP implementations (e.g. the SCAPE chip) is a single bit/pin interface.

2.4 Information processing with the ASP

The ASP is a very flexible and effective structure for general purpose information processing. All abstract data structures can be represented and manipulated using the Associative String Processor.

Sets map naturally to the string structure of the ASP, with an APE being allocated for each set element. The activity bits can be used as flags to identify set membership of a set. The set operations such as union, intersection, labelling and comparison are easily implemented using the associative nature of the ASP architecture, in simultaneously manipulating the activity bits of elements which are members of a particular sub-set.

Strings and linear arrays map naturally into the ASP format. The elements of these two data structures are stored in a sequence of neighboring APEs, with each element occupying a single APE. The ASP architecture is capable of shifting arbitrarily large segments of data between neighboring blocks of processing elements in 'unit' time. Therefore, insertion and deletion operations, very common to string applications, are accomplished very efficiently. Also each APE can operate as a finite state machine for pattern recognition applications, useful in areas such as artificial intelligence, speech recognition, string matching in text processing, execution of declarative languages etc. The time for the pattern recognition is proportional to the length of the search argument.

Applications involving arrays and matrices are the most common areas of today's supercomputer. The elements of an array map onto the ASP format,

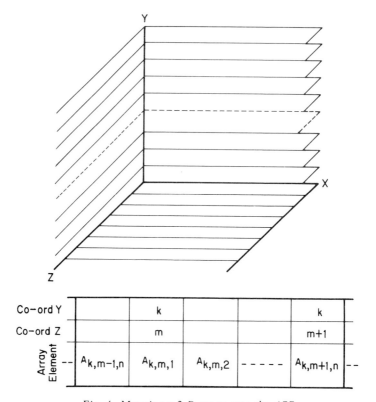

Fig. 4. Mapping a 3-D array onto the ASP.

by concatenating linear arrays with their index reference markers associated with each dimension as shown in Fig. 4. Array operations, low-level image processing is a typical application area, involve mainly arithmetic operations (e.g. multiplication, division etc.) and local summation of the products. Such operations benefit from the flexible high-speed APE inter-communication network, capable of transferring large blocks of data, and the high degree of integration which allows very large arrays of data to be accommodated within a relatively small number of ASP modules (integrated circuits).

The manipulation of non-linear data structures, e.g. trees, graphs etc., is also supported by the ASP architecture, despite the fact that such structures are not always well defined and not as regular as the linear structures discussed previously. On the ASP, the non-linear structures are stored as records of the type:

in-tags	value	out-tags

with the associated tags indicating the inputs and outputs of the particular

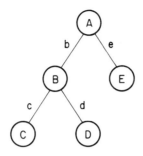

in-tags		b	c	d	e
out-tags values	A	B	C	D	E
	b	c	0	0	0
	e	d	0	0	0

Fig. 5. Mapping non-linear structures onto the ASP.

node. Each record is stored in a single APE. Fig. 5 shows the representation of a binary tree on the ASP architecture. The inter-record (inter-mode) communciation is performed using the inter-APE communication network. The network can support asynchronous and irregular communications, i.e. string activations, remote symbol activations, as well as regular communications. The manipulation of non-linear data structures involves global associative searches for the appropriate nodes and propagation of the search results to the appropriate node using the inter-APE communication network. The propagation of the search results can be simultaneous for multiple non-linear structures.

3 THE SCAPE CHIP

The SCAPE (Single Chip Array Processing Element) chip [8, 9, 10] is a practical VLSI implementation of the Associative String Processor, which has been optimised for numerical computation. The SCAPE chip is a versatile addition to the bit-serial SIMD Single Instruction control of Multiple Data streams (SIMD) class of parallel processing VLSI chip architectures. It integrates a string of 256 identical processing elements, each comprising of 37-bits of content-addressable memory (32-bit Data Register and 5-bit Activity Register), a 1-bit full adder and logic for communication with other processing elements. SCAPE chips can be linked together to configure a chain, increasing linearly the processing power of the system; the chip interconnection strategy is transparent. SCAPE chips can be linked together to form multiple channels for supporting computational configurations such as SIMSIMD and MIMSIMD.

All SCAPE chips in a SCAPE chain or SCAPE channel are controlled by the SCAPE chain controller, which comprises the standard bit-slice microprocessor components of typical high-speed microprogram controllers. The chain controller also buffers data transmitted between the SCAPE chain and the host environment.

The SCAPE chip floor-plan is shown in Fig. 6. It comprises four major functional blocks, configured in an array of "exactly butting" quadratures. The function of each block is described below.

Every one of the four AMA (Associative Memory Array) blocks comprises 64 AMA-rows (word-rows) of content addressable memory, each formatted as a 32-bit data field and a 5-bit activity field.

Every one of the two BCL (Bit Control Logic) blocks is composed of 37 similar bit-column controllers in support of bit-serial operations on programmable declared serial fields or bit-parallel operations on byte or 32-bit word fields. The BCL comprises a Serial Field Partition Register to support programmable partition of the AMA data field to up to three serial data fields; Pointer and Marker Registers, identified with each serial field, enable or inhibit associated bit-planes of the AMA for bit-serial processing. Additionally, the Data Interpretation Logic (DIL) allows bit-masking of AMA bit-columns during search and write operations (e.g. tertiary mode).

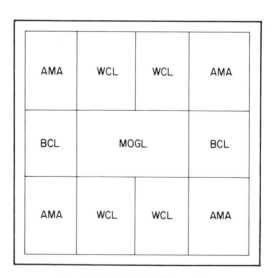

Fig. 6. SCAPE chip floor-plan.

Every one of the four WCL (Word Control Logic) modules includes 64 similar local processing elements. Closely integrated with the local AMA block, each module provides manipulation of the match vector, temporary storage, bit-arithmetic functions and inter-APE communication. Each WCL block incorporates: a match network for mapping multiple AMA match vectors into a single overall match vector; the match network determines which AMA registers have matched a content-search. An adder block supports bit-arithmetic functions; each local processing element has a 1-bit full-adder to support bit-serial addition and subtraction operations. A TR12 block incorporates two 64-bit Tag Registers TR1 and TR2 to staticise the "result vectors" of search operations; TR1 also provides a synchronous data channel for shifting of the 'result vector'. An alternate network distributes alternately into the TR1 and TR2 the matching elements for pairing and divide-and-conquer algorithms. An activation network provides a data dependent asynchronous channel for the support of activation mappings between staticized 'result vectors' and the processing elements selected for subsequent read or write operations.

The inter-APE communication network of SCAPE chip consists of the serial communication channels implied in the alternate, TR12 and activation networks; these channels are multiplexed onto the single-bit ports (viz. left link port and right link port) of the SCAPE chip interface.

The MOGL (Micro-Order Generation Logic), during SCAPE operations, issues dynamic micro-orders to the BCL and WCL functional blocks, derived from the static micro-orders and operation code of each micro-instruction and the current time slot issued by a timing generator. Input-output multiplexing (to minimize pin-count and package dimensions) and internal clock generation are also performed in the MOGL.

4 IMAGE REPRESENTATION ON SCAPE

The subject of image representation on string architectures is of prime importance, as it greatly affects the design of image processing algorithms. Methods used for image input and output are also affected by the choice of data structure. In many cases, the choice of a data structure for a set of problems can even influence the design of a machine architecture for efficiently solving those problems. For example, mesh-connected architectures map naturally into hardware the two-dimensional array data structure used most commonly to represent images on sequential machines. Similarly, the string nature of the ASP architecture affects the way used to represent images on it.

The majority of image processing algorithms designed for parallel processor arrays assume that the array operates in the pixel parallel mode: a processing element is assigned to each image pixel. Digital images typically contain 10^4 to 10^6 pixels. Having a physical array of the image size presents several problems, mainly by being very large in size and cost ineffective (despite the advantages offered by the semiconductor technology e.g. VLSI). Therefore, parallel image processing architectures have to cope with the situation where the array processor has many fewer processing elements than there are pixels in a typical image. Hence, consideration must be given as to how these 'oversized' images are mapped onto the array.

Array processors with many bits of memory per processing element alleviate the problem to some extent by using the concept of virtual processing elements. This is accomplished by actually storing more than one pixel per processing element and operating only on the pixel data when it is actually required. A SCAPE-based image processing system has a limited number of memory cells per processing element (32 data bits and 5 activity bits); in addition, there is no provision for individual processing elements to interface with external memory. Therefore, for gray-level image processing applications it is rather difficult to implement virtual processing elements on the SCAPE chain. If 8 bits are devoted for the pixel information of the input image, only a small number of memory cells (24 data bits and 5 activity bits) remain available to be used as work-space.

The obvious choice of performing image processing with a SCAPE system, when the image size is larger than the size of the SCAPE chain, is to repeat the load-process-unload sequence of operations on sub-images of the input image until the whole image is processed. Each sub-image is called image patch. The image patch is defined as a sub-set, $n \times m$ pixels, of the input image. A SCAPE image patch must contain, in the best case, as many image pixels as processing elements are available in the SCAPE chain.

The image patches are defined using the scan-line approach to image representation. In order to avoid the communication problems arising from the concatenation of entire image scan-lines in the SCAPE chain, the SCAPE image patches contain only part of each scan-line. In that way the severe communication (very long distance communications) obstacle is somewhat cut down. Therefore, an entire scan-line is contained in a number of adjacent image patches. Figure 7 shows a digital image divided into eight image patches. Each image patch is loaded into the SCAPE chain by concatenating patch scan-lines. Hence, if $p(m, n)$ is a pixel corresponding to mth line and nth column of the patch, then Fig. 8 depicts the way the patch containing this pixel is distributed in the SCAPE chain. The size of the image patch is selected on the base that will give an optimal ratio between computation and communication portions of the processing time for a given image. The aim is to maximize this ratio, therefore minimize the contribution of the communication operations. This can be achieved if the patch size, in the scan-line direction, is kept small; but that could lead to an increased number of load-process-unload sequence of operations, which might eventually increase the overall image processing time.

More than one image patch might be processed simultaneously on a SCAPE chain, depending on the relation between the operating patch size and the number of processing elements available in the SCAPE chain. The patches are being concatenated in the SCAPE chain; the first scan-line of the

Fig. 7. Dividing an image into patches.

following image patch follows the last scan-line of the previous image patch. The computational techniques applied to the SCAPE chain are identical for either case: single-patch or multi-patch processing, which shows how flexibly parallelism is exploited using the ASP architecture.

A disadvantage of the patch processing techniques is that a number of the available processing elements in the SCAPE chain make no useful contribution during image processing algorithms based on local techniques. This is a combination of the nature of the local techniques (which require all the pixels in a defined neighbouring area to be present during the computation) and the definition of an image patch where only part of image scan-lines exist in a patch. Therefore, if $p \times q$ is the size of the local operator, there will be $(p - 1) \times (q - 1)$ processing elements per image patch, which will perform no useful computational task. The image pixels assigned to these processing elements may be envisaged as occupying "guard strips" around the image

$P_{m-1,n-1}$		$P_{m-1,n}$		$P_{m-1,n+1}$
$P_{m,n-1}$		$P_{m,n}$		$P_{m,n+1}$
$P_{m+1,n-1}$		$P_{m+1,n}$		$P_{m+1,n+1}$

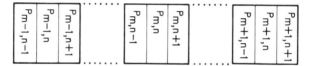

Fig. 8. Pixel distribution in SCAPE chain.

patch. The pixels included in these strips have to be repeated in the adjacent patches, where they will be processed, together with the neighbouring pixels necessary for the computations. Due to the overhead of redundant pixels in a patch, the choice of the patch shape is becoming a very important factor. The aim is to select such a patch shape, which will maximize the number of the actually processed pixels in it. This will minimize the number of image patches required to cover the entire image. More details on patch based image processing can be found in [11].

Earlier in this section it was mentioned that the main reason for not implementing virtual processing elements with the SCAPE chain is the combination of limited amount of memory available per processing element and the number of bits required to represent the gray-level information of each image pixel. Image segmentation and higher level image processing algorithms use binary pixel representation, where only a single bit is sufficient to represent the pixel information. In addition, the processing of binary images is dominated by logical operations which do not demand as much workspace as the arithmetic operations dominant at the low-level image processing. If binary representation is used, then virtual processing elements can be implemented in the SCAPE chain. In that case individual SCAPE processing elements contain information sampled from identical locations of different image patches. With that representation up to 32 pixels can reside in each SCAPE processing element. Although the processing time remains the same when virtual processing elements are used, because the processing will be sequential, the performance of the SCAPE chain is considerably enhanced because the I/O time, a significant percentage of the overall processing time, is reduced and in many occasions minimized; e.g. a 256×256 binary image needs to be loaded and unloaded once on a 16-chip SCAPE chain.

5 A SCAPE-BASED IMAGE PROCESSING SYSTEM

The configuration of a SCAPE-based Image Processing Module (IPM) is depicted in Fig. 9. The SCAPE Module in this configuration consists of a chain of SCAPE chips as shown in Fig. 10, with all the processing elements of the chain performing the same instruction simultaneously. The instructions are generated and broadcasted from the Control Module, which also performs all operations on scalar variables. The Patch Buffer Module, shown in Fig. 11, acts as the interface of image patch transfers between the Frame Store Module and the SCAPE Module. SCAPE devices are able to exchange 32-bit words in a single operational cycle (100 ns), which in effect overlaps the loading and unloading of image patches. Because the width of the I/O word is 32 bits (four 8-bit pixels) the effective I/O bandwidth is 8 bytes per 100 ns or 80 Mbytes/sec. Independent SCAPE channels can operate simultaneously to load/unload different portions of the SCAPE chain. This is based on the autonomy characterising the ASP modules comprising the SCAPE chain, which is a significant difference from the two dimensional architectures. It is

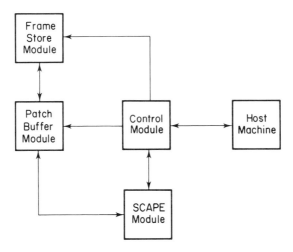

Fig. 9. SCAPE-based Image Processing Module (IPM).

A. Krikelis and R.M. Lea

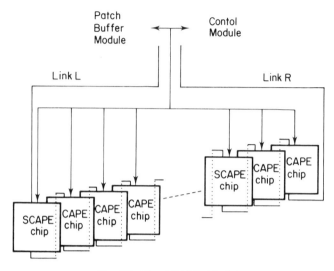

Fig. 10. The SCAPE Module.

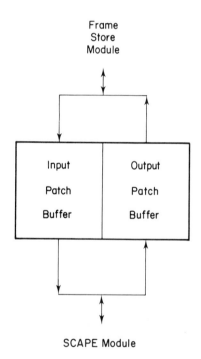

Fig. 11. The Patch Buffer Module.

necessary for the Patch Buffer Module of the SCAPE Image Processing Module to satisfy the demand for the high-speed I/O requirement by the SCAPE channels. That will require either very high-speed hardware or double buffering techniques which might increase the cost of the module.

The Frame Store Module provides storage for a sequence of image frames. The Host Machine is the interface between the application environment and the SCAPE-based Image Processing Module. It provides software and hardware for generating, testing and running application programs. In operation, the Host Machine requests the execution of an image processing task on a selected image stored in the Frame Store. The Control Module initiates the transfer of image patches from the selected image to the SCAPE Module through the Patch Buffer Module. When a patch is loaded onto the SCAPE Module the Control Module initiates the execution of the requested image processing task. When the process is completed the processed patch is unloaded and a new patch is loaded onto the SCAPE Module. The patch processing is repeated until the full image frame is processed.

5.1 The Control Module

The design of the Control Module is shown schematically in Fig. 12. The module consists of four sections. A more detailed design of the SCAPE Control Module is discussed in [12].

The SCAPE Chain Controller (SCC) broadcasts instructions to all processing elements in the SCAPE Module. The Scalar Buffer Unit (SBU) is used to support I/O operations for image processing constants and scalars used in the SCAPE Module which are not literal data within SCAPE instructions; in addition it stores scalar results leaving the SCAPE Module (e.g. histogram counts). The Principal Control Unit (PCU) performs all tasks in an image processing application environment not dealing directly with image data. It initiates all image manipulation tasks executed by the SCAPE Module and all data exchanges between Patch Buffer Module and the SCAPE Module. The Scalar Processor (SP), a fast sequential machine, is used for the computation of scalar attributes associated with the image processing tasks executed in the SCAPE Module (e.g. histogram manipulation). The SP manipulates data resident in the Scalar Buffer Unit.

5.1.1 The SCAPE Chain Controller

The SCC must not only generate instructions for the SCAPE Module, it must synchronize the SCAPE instructions and the scalar data and operations (when needed), must compute any conditions for program branching and other program control structures in addition to setting and sensing various command and feedback lines (e.g. Match Reply (MR), End Of serial Field (EOF), the chain links (LINKL and LINKR) etc.).

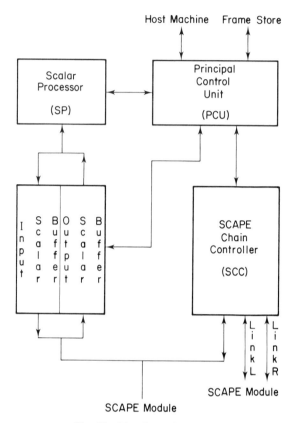

Fig. 12. The Control Module.

In general, programs in the SCC perform short routines which cause the SCAPE Module to perform such operations as image addition, multiplication, shifting etc. The SCAPE instructions for such operations are stored in memory local to the SCC. Image processing tasks are performed as a sequence of routine calls initiated from the PCU. The interface between the PCU and the SCC is a sequence of routine calls. As each routine is finished the next is begun.

5.1.2 The Principal Control Unit

For an image processing task, the PCU performs much like a sequential machine. Its task is to perform all non-image manipulation tasks and to generate image manipulating routine calls by broadcasting the address of the routine to the SCC and placing the appropriate parameters in the Scalar Buffer Unit. It also initiates the data transfer between the Patch Buffer Module and the SCAPE Module and provides the main interface to the Host Machine.

5.2 The SCAPE Module

The SCAPE Module, as shown in Fig. 10, consists of a simple chain of SCAPE chips. The module provides in-place processing of an image patch. The SCAPE chain can be organized to SCAPE channels, loaded simultaneously, for faster loading of the SCAPE chain overall. This is because the load time depends on the number of processing elements to be loaded. In order to maximise the processing period available to the SCAPE Module it is essential that image loading can be accomplished in the shortest period. The length of a channel can vary from a single SCAPE chip to the full length of the SCAPE chain in the SCAPE Module. Every SCAPE channel must have its own patch buffer sub-module, if simultaneous loading of the SCAPE channels is required. Each SCAPE channel can support a transfer rate of 80 MBytes/sec (32 bit words, one in each direction, can be transferred every 100 ns).

6 SCAPE PERFORMANCE

Table 1 is indicative of the performance of a single SCAPE chip. The system performance increases linearly with the number of SCAPE chips in it; for example Table 2 is indicative of the performance of a system with 16 cascaded SCAPE chips.

Table 1
Single SCAPE chip performance (MOPS)*

	8-bit operands	16-bit operands
Addition/Subtraction	250.000	125.000
Scalar-Vector Multiplication	37.500	6.500
Vector-Vector Multiplication	23.750	4.375

* 1 MOP is 10^6 operations per second.

Table 2
16-SCAPE chip system performance (GOPS)*

	8-bit operands	16-bit operands
Addition/Subtraction	4.00	6.00
Scalar-Vector Multiplication	0.60	0.10
Vector-Vector Multiplication	0.38	0.07

* 1 GOP is 10^9 operations per second.

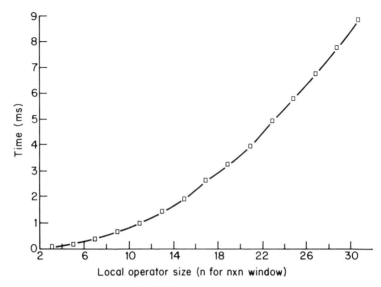

Fig. 13. SCAPE convolution performance.

Figure 13 depicts the performance (based on simulation) of a SCAPE-based image processing system for image convolution.

The following Tables show estimated performance (based on simulation results), for a number of computer vision tasks, of a SCAPE-based image processing system, consisting of only 16 SCAPE chips. The performance of SCAPE-based systems increase linearly with the number of SCAPE chips in the chain.

Table 3
Median filtering (ms)
Chain Length 16-SCAPE chips

	3×3	5×5	7×7	9×9	11×11
256×256	19.45	25.72	44.89	93.43	153.56
512×512	41.69	66.41	91.35	143.62	201.47

Table 4
Fourier transform (ms)
Chain Length 16-SCAPE chips

256×256	26.73
512×512	94.57

Table 5
Sobel filtering (ms)
Chain Length 16-SCAPE chips

256 × 256	3.67
512 × 512	14.69

Table 6
Image histogramming
Chain Length 16-SCAPE chips

256 × 256	6.31
512 × 512	25.24

REFERENCES

[1] Lea, R.M. (1986). VLSI and WSI associative string processors for cost-effective parallel processing, *The Computer Journal*, 29, 6, pp. 486–494, 1986.
[2] Lea, R.M. (1986). VLSI and WSI associative string processors for structured data processing, *IEE Proc.*, 133, Pt. E, 3, pp. 153–162, 1986.
[3] Kisylia, A.P. (1968). An associative processor for information retrieval, *Report R-390 (AD 675310)* Coordinated Science Lab., Illinois University, 1968.
[4] Lee, C.Y. (1968). Content-Addressable and Distributed Logic Memories. In *Applied Automata Theory*; J.T. Tou ed. Academic Press, New York, 1986, pp. 76–92.
[5] Hwang, K., and Briggs, F.A. (1984). Computer Architecture and Parallel Processing, McGraw Hill, 1984.
[6] Hillis, W.D. (1985). The Connection Machine, MIT Press, 1985.
[7] Batcher, K.E. (1980). Design of a Massively Parallel Processor, *IEEE Transactions on Computers*, C-29, pp. 48–56, September 1980.
[8] Lea, R.M. (1982). SCAPE: a Single-Chip Array Processing Element, Original specification, February 1982.
[9] Lea, R.M. (1986). SCAPE: a single-chip array processing element for signal and image processing. *IEE Proceedings*, 133, Pt. E, 3, pp. 145–151.
[10] Jalowiecki, I.P., and Lea, R.M. (1987). A 256-element associative parallel processor, *Proc. ISSCC*, February 1987.
[11] Krikelis, A. (1987). Computer Vision with Fine-grain Parallel One-dimensional Structured Computer Architectures. PhD Thesis, Brunel University.
[12] Lancaster, J. (1987). Functional Specification of SCAPE Chain Controller. Internal Report, Brunel University, Alvey Contract MMI Number 043, March 1987.

Chapter Seven

Meshes and Hypercubes for Computer Vision

Anthony P. Reeves

Department of Computer Science
University of Illinois at Urbana–Champaign
Urbana, Illinois, 61801

1 INTRODUCTION

The high computation rates required for computer vision applications has spurred interest in high performance computer architectures. The computation characteristics of the highly regular low level vision algorithms have led to the consideration of highly parallel computer architectures. While a large number of parallel computer architectures have been proposed, very few have been built and tested with real applications. The two main exceptions to this are mesh connected processor arrays and hypercube multicomputers. Both of these schemes have been commercially implemented by a number of vendors and have been investigated by a large number of researchers for real applications. The merits of these architectures for computer vision tasks are considered in this paper.

Highly parallel systems offer a mechanism for increasing processing speed beyond that possible by technological improvements alone. Unfortunately, efficient programs for these architectures cannot be developed in conventional programming languages and are more difficult to develop than conventional programs. This has been a major impediment to their acceptance by the general high speed processing community. This situation may be changed as better programming tools and environments are developed and second generation systems offer better performance improvements over conventional systems.

In the next section the basic mesh and hypercube architectures are described then in subsequent sections the important topics of computer vision algorithms, programming environments and performance measures are considered.

MULTICOMPUTER VISION
ISBN 0-12-444818-6

2 HIGHLY PARALLEL ARCHITECTURES

In highly parallel systems we are interested in utilizing the resources of hundreds or thousands of processors. Such systems can take full advantage of the high functional complexity made available with VLSI technology and also with full wafer technology as it becomes available.

The classical memory processor bottleneck of conventional and pipelined processors is avoided by using VLSI processors which are matched in speed to current high density memory technology and by providing each processor with its own fast memory. The new problem which this creates is the need to communicate information between the different processors.

We are interested here in highly parallel systems by which we mean architectures which are not fundamentally limited in the degree of parallelism. A key concept in designing algorithms for such systems is to make them independent of the number of processors used. In this way higher speed for the algorithm may be achieved by simply adding more processors. This is in contrast to serial processors and "vector" processors which offer a limited amount of parallelism for existing conventional programs but which are not able to take advantage of any additional hardware parallelism.

There are two main computation models of highly parallel architectures; these are frequently termed SIMD and MIMD. In a SIMD system a single instruction stream broadcasts instructions to a number of slave processing elements (PEs). In the MIMD case a number of independent processors work together on a single task. Mesh and hypercube refer to the topologies used for the interconnections between processors; however, for the systems considered here, a further distinction is that the mesh systems are SIMD and the hypercube systems are MIMD. A significant exception to this is the Connection Machine which is a SIMD machine with a hypercube interconnection scheme.

The near-neighbor mesh scheme connects each processor via four ports to its four adjacent neighbors in a two-dimensional grid as shown in Fig. 1. Other versions are possible in which processors are connected to 6 or 8 adjacent neighbors. For an n processor system, this scheme has a complexity of $O(n)$ and is very simple to implement since a two-dimensional mesh maps directly onto a two-dimensional surface. This scheme is very effective for a large number of algorithms which require near-neighbor operations but may be inefficient for some other data permutations. End-around connections, which can be selected by software to connect opposite edges of the mesh array together, are implemented with some two-dimensional mesh schemes.

The hypercube scheme is similar to the near-neighbor mesh except that the processors are located at the vertices of a hypercube with each processor being connected to its *log n* near neighbors. This scheme is much more powerful than the mesh scheme for algorithms which do not map simply to the mesh; it is also more difficult to implement and has complexity $O(n \log n)$. The first five hypercube networks are shown in Fig. 2. The number below each network indicates its dimension (D).

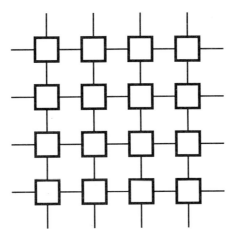

Fig. 1. Mesh Interconnection network.

An important feature of the hypercube scheme is that many different important topologies may be efficiently embedded within a subset of the hypercube connections. These topologies include mesh, tree, pyramid and the FFT butterfly. One advantage of this emulation is that algorithms based on these other topologies can be easily implemented on the hypercube. A second advantage is that much needed research into new algorithms for various topologies can be done without developing special hardware.

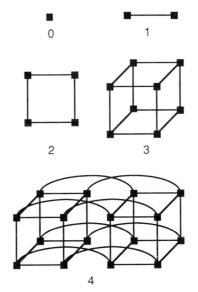

Fig. 2. Hypercube Interconnection network.

2.1 Mesh SIMD computers

The concept of SIMD systems is to use a large number of ALUs to simultaneously process a number of data elements. Usually, these systems consist of a set of Processing Elements (PEs) each of which contains an ALU and some local memory. There is a single "host" program control unit which broadcasts the same instruction to all PEs. The advantage of such systems is that very large numbers of PEs (many thousands) may be efficiently used for suitable applications. The main disadvantage is that users must very carefully map their problems onto the system. Conventional serial languages such as Fortran are out of the question. Usually an array based high level language is used.

A design strategy for high hardware efficiency is to use a very large number of simple PEs in combination with one complex, fast instruction unit which does not waste any PE cycles. For this type of architecture to be most effective there should be at least as many data elements to be processed as there are PEs and the algorithms should be well structured for the near neighbor interconnection structure. In practice, most systems of this type have bit-serial PE architectures; that is, the basic word size in each PE is only one bit wide. A number of such PEs can be fabricated on a single chip. The advantages of the bit-serial approach over more conventional multi-bit words include more effective use of hardware, more optimal use of storage and the possibility of adjusting the processing time (possibly dynamically) to fit the actual precision of the data; i.e. short data words are processed faster than longer data words. In a multi-bit organization, processing is restricted to multiples of the machine "word" size which must be larger than the data precision. A precursor for these advantages is the two conditions listed above (i.e. degree of parallelism and appropriate structure). When this is true, then the processor array is a very efficient computer architecture with much more of the hardware dedicated to processing the data than with more conventional organizations.

Processor arrays have been made commercially available to both the general scientific and the image processing communities. An early processor array for scientific applications was the Illiac IV which had an 8 × 8 array of 64-bit PEs, constructed with ECL technology. The ICL Distributed Array Processor (DAP) [1] consists of 4096 bit-serial PEs organized in a 64 × 64 mesh, several DAP processors have been built and a large number of scientific programs have been run on them. A smaller 32 × 32 DAP which is hosted by a MicroVax has recently been announced by AMT.

For the image processing community a number of bit-serial processor arrays have been developed based on special VLSI chips. One of the earliest of these is the CLIP4 processor. It consists of a 96 × 96 mesh of bit-serial PEs; there are 8 PEs with their local memory on a single chip. The CLIP chip has much less local memory than the DAP (32 bits compared to 4096 bits) due to the main intended application of processing short word integers rather than floating point numbers. At the time of the development of these systems memory was a very expensive item. The lack of sufficient memory has been a severe limitation on the range of problems for which these systems have been used. The CLIP processor has direct connections to its eight near neighbors rather than 4 neighbors for the general scientific systems; it involves a near neighbor processor which can directly compute functions on a subset of near neighbor values. It is also possible to configure the system for a 6 neighbor interconnection pattern. This is to optimize performance for a hexagonal class of binary image topological and shape processing operations which are common to some image processing algorithms. A number of more dense VLSI chips of this type have been recently developed which includes the NCR GAP Chip with 72 PEs [2] and the OKI Data chip with 64 PEs.

For the future, the development of much cheaper processor arrays that take advantage of VLSI technology may be anticipated. ITT is predicting the development of a single board 120 MFLOP processor array which can be attached to a conventional IBM PC/AT [3]. The processor array architecture is also highly suitable for wafer scale integration when it becomes available. An interesting wafer scale implementation for this type of architecture is described by Nudd et al. [4]. For this system, a technology has been developed to enable data connections to be made vertically through a wafer. Several wafer types have been developed each of which implements an array of simple functions such as memory, bit-serial addition, or mesh interconnections on the wafer. A processor array is constructed by vertically connecting together a stack of these wafers. The exact architecture of the PE and the size of the memory is determined by the types of wafers used to build the stack.

An interesting recent system is the Connection Machine which is manufactured by TMC [5]. The Connection Machine has 65,536 bit-serial PEs. The PEs are implemented with a special VLSI chip; each chip contains 16 PEs. This system has two interconnection networks, a two-dimensional mesh and a hypercube-like network. The hypercube network is supported by automatic routing hardware which enables arbitrary data permutations to be implemented with good efficiency. This significantly expands the nature of the problems and the types of algorithms which can be implemented. A large amount of the space on the processor chip is used by the hypercube routing implementation.

The Massively Parallel Processor consists of 16,384 bit-serial Processing Elements (PEs) connected in 128×128 mesh [6, 7]. That is, each PE is connected to its 4 adjacent neighbors in a planar matrix. The MPP offers a simple basic model for analysis since it involves just mesh interconnections and bit-serial PEs. The minimal architecture of the MPP is of particular interest to study, since any architecture modifications to improve performance would result in a more complex PE or a more dense interconnection strategy.

2.2 The MPP processing element

The MPP processing element is shown in Fig. 3. All data paths are one bit wide and there are 8 PEs on a single CMOS chip with the local memory on external memory chips. Except for the shift register, the design is essentially a minimal architecture of this type. The single bit full adder is used for arithmetic operations and the Boolean processor, which implements all 16 possible two input logical functions, is used for all other operations. The NN select unit is the interface to the interprocessor network and is used to select a value from one of the four adjacent PEs in the mesh.

The S register is used for I/O. A bitplane is slid into the S registers independent of the PE processing operation and it is then loaded into the local memory by cycle stealing one cycle. The G register is used in masked operations. When masking is enabled only PEs in which the G register is set perform any operations; the remainder are idle. The masked operation is a very common control feature in SIMD designs. Not shown in Fig. 3, is an OR bus output from the PE. All these outputs are connected (ORed) together so that the control

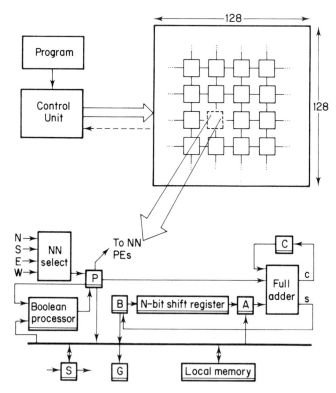

Fig. 3. The MPP processing element.

unit can determine if any bits are set in a bitplane in a single instruction. On the MPP, the local memory has 1,024 words (bits) and is implemented with bipolar chips which have a 35 ns access time.

The main novel feature of the MPP PE architecture is the reconfigurable shift register. It may be configured under program control to have a length from 2 to 30 bits. Improved performance is achieved by keeping operands circulating in the shift register which greatly reduces the number of local memory accesses and instructions. It speeds up integer multiplication by a factor of two and also has an important effect on floating-point performance.

2.3 Hypercube MIMD computers

There ae two main architecture models for MIMD systems: shared memory systems and distributed systems. In the shared memory architecture a number of independent processors have access to a single logical address space implemented by means of a number of memory modules and a processor-to-memory interconnection network. In the distributed approach each processor has its own local memory. Successful shared memory systems have been developed for small numbers of processors; however, these systems are difficult to extend to high degrees of parallelism since the memory latency and memory contention increase with the number of processors in the system.

With the distributed MIMD organization, a processor has simple fast access to its own memory but to access the memory of another processor it must communicate through an I/O channel to that processor. Typically this is done by a processor interrupt which involves a large amount of overhead for both processors. Consequently, the data processing operations and communication operations are usually separated and block data transfers are used as much as possible between processors to offset the overhead of performing a transfer. While the programming environment of a loosely coupled system is much less convenient than for a shared memory system, the potential advantage is that a very large number of processors may be used.

It is only in the last few years that commercial systems with a distributed MIMD organization for scientific applications have been developed. These systems are based on the Cosmic cube design [8] which has been used to demonstrate a number of scientific applications; all these systems involve a hypercube interconnection scheme. The first Cosmic cube consisted of 64 Intel 8086 microprocessors; such a system does not have a high processing performance but it did demonstrate that hypercube systems could be effectively programmed for scientific applications. Commercial hypercube systems have recently been introduced by Intel, Ametek, NCUBE, and FPS.

A typical node of a hypercube system is shown in Fig. 4. The heart of the node is a conventional microprocessor which performs all general control functions and some arithmetic computations. Each node has a number of I/O ports which connect it to other nodes. Typically, a node in a D-dimensional hypercube system has D + 1 ports; the extra port is for I/O to the outside world. With an

Bit-Serial I/O Ports

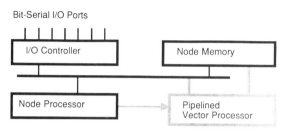

Fig. 4. *A Hypercube Node Processor.*

I/O port on every processor, the potential for very high I/O bandwidth exists. With the FPS T-series and optionally with the Intel system, a VLSI pipelined floating-point processor is used for vector arithmetic.

The hypercube MIMD system is characterized by a highly flexible hardware organization which is capable of supporting many different software strategies. However, current programming environments are in a very primitive state of development and do not permit the systems capabilities to be easily exploited. In order to control an ensemble of independent processors, an operating system is required. For a hypercube multicomputer, the operating system is to support only a single user (in some cases multiple users is also a possibility). A major feature of this system is the technique used for message passing since this dramatically impacts the performance of the system and the development of algorithms.

2.4 Hypercube operating systems

The basic programming tools provided with current hypercube systems are very similar. The usual programming environment is a conventional high level language such as Fortran or C with a library of message passing subroutines which allow data to be conveyed between different nodes. Programming environments for hypercube systems are currently a very active research area. There are a number of important issues in the method chosen for message passing and process management. Some of the main issues are as follows:

Process Management. Nodes are frequently based on conventional micropro-cessors; therefore they are capable of running a number of processes concurrently under an operating system. In fact, this is necessary if the I/O is done with DMA. However, it is not clear how to manage a number of processes in a single application environment. Interesting unconventional scheduling strategies are possible. For example, since task switching takes a significant amount of time, one strategy is to only swap tasks when the running task is blocked. A different novel strategy being explored at JPL, for real-time applications, is the time-warp concept. With this scheme all messages are time stamped and the process to be scheduled is selected by the waiting message with the oldest time stamp. Processing backtracking may be necessary when messages arrive out of sequence. Yet another school of thought is that multiple application processes are unnecessary and better performance is to be obtained with a single process scheme.

Message Addressing. A second issue is the way in which processes address messages to other processes. At the lowest level, a process may send a message to a node where any process on that node may receive it. At the next level a message address may specify a process within a node. The highest level is for a process to address a message to a specific process; the target process in this case could be moved to a different node. The successive levels described above involve increasing overhead costs; they also directly impact the types of algorithms which can be implemented.

Message Protocols. Perhaps one of the most controversial issues of hypercube design is the protocol used for message transfer. The central issue is how to most effectively utilize the bandwidth of the hypercube interconnection network; the most appropriate protocol depends on both the available hardware facilities and the properties of the messages such as length distribution, frequency, and coherence of the message paths. The message properties are highly application dependent. A first issue is should data transfers be DMA or processor polling; polling may require less overhead for synchronized processes and DMA may be more efficient for unsynchronized long messages. Second, how should a message be routed through a sequence of nodes. Possibilities include: (a) only near neighbor data transfers are permitted; (b) messages are transferred between adjacent nodes and then automatically routed towards their destination. This scheme requires a scheduling policy at each node to select between messages which want to use the same I/O port; (c) messages may create virtual circuits between source and destination nodes; all intermediate links are reserved until the complete message has been transferred.

Another issue is whether synchronous or asynchronous messages are supported. In the synchronous case a receiving process must acknowledge that it has received a message before a sending process is permitted to continue execution; in the asynchronous case the sending process continues execution without waiting for an acknowledgement. One problem, especially with asynchronous message passing, is that message buffers are required at each node for transferring messages and for pending messages. Since messages can be of a variable size it is very difficult to allocate the appropriate amount of each nodes memory for message buffers; most current systems have limited buffer pools and cannot recover if the messages exceed the allocated space. One approach to this problem is "packetizing" the messages into fixed length packets; this greatly simplifies the message buffer management. An extension of this concept is to combine packetizing with the virtual switch concept such that short messages use the strict virtual circuit while long messages can be interrupted to permit other traffic to flow. The more complex protocols have very attractive bandwidth properties at the cost of additional message processing overhead. Different applications (and algorithms) are suited to different communication protocols. It is quite possible that the optimal solution for some problems may involve the use of several protocols.

Hardware Support for Communication. Each of the communication protocols mentioned above could be made more efficient if a special hardware I/O processor was designed to implement them. Most current systems use simple DMA I/O ports since these are familiar from conventional processor systems. Greatly improved I/O hardware may be anticipated in future designs when the interprocess communication properties of hypercube systems are better understood.

2.5 Hypercube systems

The first generation hypercubes have been built with off-the-shelf components. A node consists of a conventional microprocessor with a standard VLSI communication chip used for each of the I/O ports. Typically a node occupies a single board.

A technologically innovative hypercube system has been developed by NCUBE [9]; the system environment it supports is representative of most other hypercube systems. Each processor node on the NCUBE system consists of a specially designed VLSI chip, which is claimed to have a computation performance similar to a VAX 11/780, and six memory chips which provide 128 Kbytes of memory. This minimal memory size will be expanded in the future with the availability of larger memory chips. The special 32-bit processor has 11 bit-serial bidirectional data channels with DMA support. The floating point performance is about 0.5 MFLOPS for scalar register operations. A single processor board contains 64 interconnected processors; i.e. a 6 cube. Most other hypercube systems have in the order of one processor on a board. An NCUBE system may contain 16 processor boards, for a total of 1024 processor nodes, in a single cabinet; i.e. a 10 cube.

Each node runs a simplified Unix-like operating system and will support C and Fortran programs with message passing primitives. The bandwidth between adjacent nodes is about 1 Mbyte/second with a start-up latency of 300 µs. A store-and-forward policy is used for transferring messages between nonadjacent nodes which means that message buffers are required at each node for in-transit messages.

While the integer performance of current hypercube systems is adequate for some applications, the floating point arithmetic is much too slow for most scientific applications. For these applications each node should be enhanced with a floating point accelerator.

The FPS T-series is also a technologically innovative design which is significantly different from most other hypercube systems [10]. The node for the FPS T-Series consists of a control processor and a vector pipeline for floating point arithmetic. The control processor is a Transputer which is a high-speed 32-bit microprocessor with 4 bit-serial data channels that are under direct program control. Multiplexers are used to give each node 16 channels. The processor and memory are contained on a single board and a cabinet holds 16 node processor boards. A very large system of this type could, in theory, consist of 4,096 nodes housed in 256 cabinets; however, current systems are used in experimental environments and consist of one or two cabinets. Each processor has a pipelined vector processor which has a peak processing rate in the order of 12 MFLOPS for 64-bit numbers. There is 1 Mbyte of memory on each node which could be made larger on future systems.

Hypercube systems are still in a very early stage of development. The current systems based on off-the-shelf components are good research vehicles on which to base future designs. Highly improved interprocessor communication speeds may be anticipated as recently developed architectures, which have been designed for hypercubes, are realized in VLSI components.

3 COMPUTER VISION OPERATIONS

The implementation of algorithms for computer vision applications is considered in this section. Three levels of computer vision algorithms are considered: low, intermediate and high. The boundaries between these levels are not very clearly defined; furthermore, a number of applications do not involve all three levels. For this paper the distinction between the levels will be characterized by the input and output data representations. A low level algorithm operates on an image matrix of pixels and generates an image result. An intermediate level algorithm operates on an image matrix and generates a list of features which is typically not in a matrix form. Finally, a high level algorithm receives as input either a feature list from an intermediate level or an image matrix and produces a scene description which typically will itemize each of the major objects in the scene and also record their size and location.

The remainder of this section is a general discussion of the relative merits of the mesh and hypercube architectures for the three vision algorithm levels. For a qualitative comparison we consider a hypercube computer to have in the order of 100 to 1,000 processors, which have an architecture as shown in Fig. 4, while the mesh computer has from 10^4 to 10^6 bit-serial PEs. Furthermore, if both system types are ideal for an algorithm then the mesh SIMD scheme should be considered the best since it intrinsically involves less hardware for an equivalent processing bandwidth.

3.1 Low level computer vision

Low level image processing is concerned with the initial processing of the raw data from the image sensor. Initial processing usually consists of radiometric correction followed by spatial invariant filter operations. These operations are characterized by highly regular near neighbor operations performed uniformly to all elements of the image array. Such ideal parallel algorithms are ideally matched to the capabilities of the mesh computers. The interprocessor communication requirements are low enough that efficient implementation of these algorithms on hypercube systems is usually possible.

Spatially varying image processing operations such as affine transforms and image warping can be effectively implemented on mesh computers but there is some loss in efficiency. Algorithms which have been implemented on the MPP include image rotation, image warping and stereo matching. It is difficult to comment on the performance of these algorithms on hypercube systems since very few such algorithms have been implemented. In many cases the hypercube implementation will be highly efficient; and in most cases some of the inefficiencies of the SIMD implementation will be overcome in the hypercube implementation.

The fast Fourier transform (FFT) can be effectively implemented on most current mesh systems which have in the order of 10,000 PEs. However, if the number of PEs was much larger then the difficulty of implementing the FFT butterfly on a mesh topology would make the FFT implementation very inefficient. The hypercube topology is ideal for implementing FFT butterflies; a requirement for efficient FFT implementation on such systems is that the interprocessor bandwidth must be similar to the processing bandwidth.

Pyramid building is a low level vision operation of increasing interest. On mesh systems horizontal pyramid operations are efficiently implemented by near neighbor filter operations [11]. Vertical pyramid operations are made not very efficient due to the mismatch of the permutation with the mesh topology. Hypercube systems should be very efficient for most pyramid algorithms [12]. Lower level vertical pyramid operations are performed without any interprocessor communication and for the highest levels the pyramid topology can be directly embedded into the hypercube.

3.2 Intermediate level computer vision

Intermediate level algorithms transform a pixel based image representation to some other data form. Typical intermediate level algorithms include segmentation, line following and region growing.

Most intermediate level algorithms require different sequences of operations to be applied to subsets of the image data. While it is still possible to implement many such operations on an SIMD system there is usually a severe loss in efficiency. A good example of this is region growing. For a very large number of small regions the mesh computer is very effective. However, as the number of regions diminishes the efficiency of the mesh system is reduced as the whole image matrix must still be processed.

A second example is edge following. The parallelism of the problem depends upon the number of lines being followed. Once again the mesh architecture may be very effective if the number of edges to be followed is very large; but it is not effective when only a few edges are involved.

The MIMD organization of the hypercube system is highly suitable for these applications. Furthermore, the lower parallelism of the system makes it more effective when a small number of features compared to the number of pixels in the image are being processed. Finally, it is possible on an MIMD system to concurrently examine an image for different types of features while only one feature type may be considered at a time on a SIMD system.

3.3 High level computer vision

High level computer vision in this paper refers to the generation of scene descriptions from the scene features generated at the intermediate or low levels. The main operations performed at this level are pattern recognition and sub-graph matching. There are two main computation methods for high level vision: classical statistical pattern recognition and symbolic graph matching.

In statistical pattern recognition, identification is made by the location of a parameterized feature or shape in an n-dimensional hyperspace. Depending upon the application, a scene analysis may involve the identification of a large number (1,000) of features or a relatively small number (10–100) of objects. In parametric recognition, where the hyperspace is partitioned by a small number of parameters, the SIMD architecture may be effective if the number of features to be identified is large since the features may be distributed in the array and the parameters applied, one at a time, from the host. However, the SIMD scheme will not be good if only a small number of objects are to be identified, since the parallelism of the input data and matching algorithm is much lower than the parallelism of the system. A hypercube system will be better than a mesh system when the number of objects is small, due to its lower degree of parallelism.

For non-parametric pattern matching, such as nearest neighbor determination, the mesh architecture can be very efficient. The database is distributed in the processor array and objects are processed one at a time in the host processor.

The hypercube computer is also very effective for this task. The matching problem is made more difficult if the database is too large to be completely stored in each node. Features must be sent to enough processors to completely cover the database; however, the interprocessor communication in this case is not very large. Furthermore, when the number of features is large, the MIMD system can make use of fast serial search techniques in each processor which is not possible with a SIMD organization.

For symbolic matching techniques little use has been made of highly parallel systems to date. Much work in this area is programmed in either conventional Lisp or Prolog which only have a limited intrinsic parallelism that is difficult to exploit. Some symbolic matching operations could be implemented by highly parallel processors. Mesh computers can be used as associative processors for some of these applications. In general, the hypercube is more flexible than the mesh scheme and can run a number of Lisp or Prolog tasks concurrently (at least one in each processor). It would only be less effective than a mesh computer for some string matching applications which can take advantage of the bit-serial architecture.

While many high level symbolic problems exhibit little direct parallelism, this situation could change with future algorithm development. The most powerful high level vision system, the human brain, is obviously using highly parallel techniques in order to make decisions as fast as it does.

4 PROGRAMMING ENVIRONMENTS

Highly parallel computer systems cannot be effectively programmed with conventional serial languages such as Fortran. For SIMD systems only a limited set of programming strategies are possible; a typical language is outlined in the following section. In contrast, for hypercube systems a wide range of programming strategies are possible and only a few have been tentatively explored.

4.1 SIMD languages

High level programming languages for mesh connected SIMD computers are well developed; they usually have operations similar to matrix algebra primitives since entire arrays are manipulated with each machine instruction. The features of a typical high level language for processor arrays, called Parallel Pascal, are outlined below.

Parallel Pascal [13] is designed for the convenient and effective programming of parallel computers and is an upward compatible extended version of the standard Pascal programming language. It is the first high level programming language to be implemented on the MPP. Parallel Pascal was designed with the MPP as the initial target architecture; however, it is also suitable for a large range of other parallel processors.

Parallel Pascal includes parallel expressions and a mechanism for processor array allocation. In addition, there are three fundamental classes of operations on array data which are frequently implemented as primitives on array computers but which are not available in conventional programming languages, these are: data reduction, data permutation and data broadcast. These operations have been included as primitives in Parallel Pascal. Mechanisms for the selection of subarrays and for selective operations on a subset of elements are also important language features.

Parallel expressions. In Parallel Pascal all conventional expressions are extended to array data types. In a parallel expression all operations must have conformable array arguments. A scalar is considered to be conformable to any type compatible array and is conceptually converted to a conformable array with all elements having the scalar value.

Parallel data declaration. In many highly parallel computers including the MPP there are at least two different primary memory systems; one in the host and one in the processor array. Parallel Pascal provides the reserved word *parallel* to allow programmers to specify the memory in which an array should reside.

Reduction functions. Array reduction operations are achieved with a set of standard functions in Parallel Pascal. The numeric reduction functions *maximum, minimum, sum* and *product* and the Boolean reduction functions any and all are implemented.

Permutation functions. One of the most important features of a parallel programming language is the facility to specify parallel array data permutations. In Parallel Pascal three such operations are available as primitive standard functions: *shift, rotate* and *transpose*. The shift and rotate primitives are found in many parallel hardware architectures and also, in many algorithms. The shift function shifts data by the amount specified for each dimension and shifts zeros (null elements) in at the edges of the array. Elements shifted out of the array are discarded. The rotate function is similar to the shift function except that data shifted out of the array is inserted at the opposite edge so that no data is lost. While transpose is not a simple function to implement with many parallel architectures, a significant number of matrix algorithms involve this function; therefore, it has been made available as a primitive function in Parallel Pascal.

Distribution functions. The distribution of scalars to arrays is done implicitly in parallel expressions. To distribute an array to a larger number of dimensions the *expand* standard function is available. This function increases the rank of an array by one by repeating the contents of the array along a new dimension. The first parameter of expand specifies the array to be expanded, the second parameter specifies the number of the new dimension and the last parameter specifies the range of the new dimension. This function is used to maintain a higher degree of parallelism in a parallel statement which may result in a clearer expression of the operation and a more direct implementation. In a conventional serial environment such a function would simply waste space.

Sub-array selection. Selection of a portion of an array by selecting either a single index value or all index values for each dimension is frequently used in many parallel algorithms; e.g. to select the ith row of a matrix which is a vector. In Parallel Pascal all index values can be specified by eliding the index value for that dimension.

Conditional execution. An important feature of any parallel programming language is the ability to have an operation operate on a subset of the elements of an array. In Parallel Pascal a *where-do-otherwise* programming construct is available which is similar to the conventional *if-then-else* statement except that the control expression results in a Boolean array rather than a Boolean scalar. All parallel statements enclosed by the where statement must have results which are the same size as the controlling array. Only result elements which correspond to true elements in the controlling array will be modified. Unlike the if statement, both clauses of the where statement are always executed.

4.2 MIMD languages

The usual programming environment on current hypercube systems consisting of a conventional language plus message passing subroutines is at much too low a level for a user programmer. Typically the user writes a single program which runs on every processor. A unique processor identifier is used to determine where to send messages. While the environment has a superficially familiar appearance, the organization of programs is much more complex due to the message passing between processes. In effect, the user is now expected to program many functions which are conventionally done by the operating system.

For a large number of structured scientific applications a SIMD style of operation is used. In this scheme each node runs a single user process and is responsible for processing a contiguous block of a data array. A library of subroutines supports the distributed array data structures in a similar way to a SIMD language. For example, subroutine procedures may be available to perform total array transpose, matrix multiply or FFT operations. The message passing is hidden from the user who only has to specify the dimensions of the array to be processed and call the appropriate function. This environment is similar to that of the early array processors; while it is reasonably simple to use existing library functions it is very difficult for the user to specify new functions.

An alternative to the library approach is to implement a SIMD language such as Parallel Pascal. This provides the user with a convenient method of developing new functions while still hiding the message passing details. A major advantage of this approach is that the user programs the whole problem at a high level rather than attempting to do the subtask decomposition and develop a program which works on one block of the problem. Parallel Pascal has been ported to the FPS T-series [14].

For applications which do not fit the SIMD constraints a special purpose operating system is possible. With this approach, the user programs a problem by means of a sequence of task oriented system primitives; different sets of primitives may be implemented for different applications. The user only specifies the computation process and the format of the input and output data. The system performs all subtask decomposition, allocation and scheduling to best fit the available resources. While this is the most difficult approach to implement, it offers the greatest promise for the future.

With an appropriate high level software environment, the system, rather than the programmer, is able to determine which processes and which data elements will be allocated to which nodes. This flexibility has two important consequences. First, the system can implement fault tolerance strategies. If a node fails then the system can allocate its processes to other nodes. Second, dynamic load balancing techniques are possible; if some nodes have completed the work allocated to them then they may be reassigned to take some of the load of any remaining busy nodes.

In summary, a critical component of a hypercube computer is the software system. Current programming environments are very difficult to use; however, for specific tasks, effective systems have been demonstrated. More research in the software area is necessary for hypercube systems to come close to realizing their full potential.

5 PERFORMANCE MODELING AND EVALUATION

Simple conventional performance measures, such as processor bandwidth, are not, by themselves, suitable for characterizing the performance of parallel processors since they do not consider the effects of task distribution, interprocessor communication and processor synchronization. For mesh systems, conventional measures can be supplemented with a table of permutation costs [15]. From these figures it is possible for programmers to estimate the effectiveness of an algorithm during its development.

Hypercube systems may require more parameters for characterization; for example interprocessor communication latency and task switching time are important measurable performance parameters. When a SIMD programming paradigm is used then permutation cost tables may be developed in a similar manner to SIMD systems. For more autonomous programs, performance is very difficult to predict since it often depends upon a combination of the data set contents and the tasking strategy used in addition to the large number of relevant parameters.

6 CONCLUSION

Two important highly parallel computer architectures have been considered in this paper which are at radically different levels of development. Mesh systems have been in use for a number of years now. Their behavior is predictable and a significant number of algorithms have been developed for them. While more work is needed, the basic strengths and limitations of these systems are becoming well understood. The mesh computer is highly efficient for low level computer vision applications and also for some types of high level vision algorithms. For regular near-neighbor algorithms it is ideal.

The hypercube systems are at a much earlier stage of development; furthermore, they are much more flexible and a large amount of research still needs to be done to determine the best programming strategies and operating environments for such systems. They can emulate a mesh computer but will not be as effective for algorithms which are ideal for a mesh system. A major strength appears to be in intermediate level and a large range of high level computer vision algorithms. These systems show much promise for a wide range of applications; however, improvements in hardware design and operating environments will be needed before these systems can successfully compete with more conventional alternatives.

While current MIMD research has centered on systems with hypercube interconnections; research to date has neither vindicated nor indicted the hypercube topology. The interconnection topology is not the main issue at this time; effective algorithms and operating environments are more important.

For a complex computer vision system it is possible that a combination of architectures will offer the best solution in many cases. A mesh computer would be used for low level vision while a hypercube computer could be used for higher level scene analysis.

REFERENCES

[1] S.F. Readdaway. (1979). *Infotech State of the Art Report on Supercomputers.*

[2] NCR Corporation. (1984). *Geometric Arithmetic Parallel Processor*, NCR, Dayton, Ohio.

[3] S.G. Morton, E. Abreau, and F. Tse. (1985). ITT CAP-Toward a Personal Supercomputer, *IEEE Micro*, pp. 37–49 (December 1985).

[4] G.R. Nudd, R.D. Etchells, and J. Grinberg. (1985). Three-Dimensional VLSI Architecture for Image Understanding, *Journal of Parallel on Distributed Computing* **2**, pp. 1–29.

[5] K.A. Frenkel. (1986). Evaluating two Massively Parallel Machines, *Communications of the ACM* **29**(8), pp. 752–758 (August 1986).

[6] K.E. Batcher. (1981). Design of a Massively Parallel Processor, *IEEE Transactions on Computers* **C-29**(9), pp. 836–840 (September 1981).

[7] A.P. Reeves. (1986). The Massively Parallel Processor: A Highly Parallel Scientific Computer, *Data Analysis in Astronomy II*, ed. V. Di Gesu, pp. 239–252. Plenum Press.

[8] C.L. Seitz. (1985). The Cosmic Cube, *Communications of the ACM* **28**(1) (1985).

[9] J.P. Hayes, T.N. Mudge, Q.F. Stout, S. Colley, and J. Palmer. (1986). Architecture of a Hypercube Supercomputer, *Proceedings of the 1986 International Conference on Parallel Processing*, pp. 653–660 (August 1986).

[10] J.L. Gustafson, S. Hawkinson, and K. Scott. (1986). The Architecture of a Homogeneous Vector Supercomputer, *Proceedings of the 1986 International Conference on Parallel Processing*, pp. 649–652 (August 1986).

[11] A.P. Reeves. (1986). Pyramid Algorithms on Processor Arrays, *Pyramidal Systems for Computer Visison*, ed. V. Cantoni and S. Levialdi, pp. 195–213. Academic Press.

[12] Q.F. Stout. (1986). Hypercubes and Pyramids, *Pyramidal Systems for Computer Vision*, ed. V. Cantoni and S. Levialdi, pp. 75–89. Academic Press.

[13] A.P. Reeves. (1984). Parallel Pascal: An Extended Pascal for Parallel Computers, *Journal of Parallel and Distributed Computing* **1**, pp. 64–80 (1984).

[14] A.P. Reeves and D. Bergmark. (1987). Parallel Pascal and the FPS Hypercube Supercomputer, *Proceedings of the 1987 International Conference on Parallel Processing*, (August 1987).

[15] A.P. Reeves and C.H. Moura. (1986). Data Manipulations on the Massively Parallel Processor, *Proceedings of the Nineteenth Hawaii International Confer-, ence on System Sciences*, pp. 222–229 (January 1986).

Chapter Eight

Image Processing Experiments on a Commercial MIMD System

L. Carrioli‡, S. Cuniolo† and M. Ferretti†

† Dipartimento Informatica e Sistemistica, Pavia, Italy
‡ I.A.N. C.N.R. Pavia, Italy

1 INTRODUCTION

This paper describes some experiments carried out to evaluate the performance of the multiprocessor machine "Sequent Balance 8000" in image processing. Goal of these tests is to verify if a general purpose commercial MIMD machine can support image processing tasks, which, at the early processing level, require the elaboration of a great amount of data. Although much work has been done to develop dedicated machines (a good review of such architectures can be found in [1–3]) by means of which true "real time" can be reached in the low-level image processing, it is worth noting that other kinds of machines can be successfully used in many cases. The main advantage in using commercially available machines is the completeness of these systems both from hardware and software point of view. In fact they do not require any front-end computer for man-machine interface and for mass storage manipulation, any controller, any ad-hoc input device and any particular programming language. Moreover the flexibility of a MIMD machine permits both low-level and high-level image processing. From the user point of view the availability of a well known operating system (with all its programming facilities) and of parallelization tools inserted in the language structure allows a quick design and an easy implementation of the algorithms.

After the description of the machine (that is a common bus multiprocessor machine) some experimental results are illustrated. They have been collected on a set of three well known image processing tasks ("thresholding", mathematical morphology "closing" and "distance transform"); in measuring performance, we have used a set of parameters which try to capture all sources of overhead introduced by system activity and parallelizing strategy. The results show that, for this kind of algorithm, good performances are achievable; in some cases the gain due to parallelization almost equals the theoretical one.

2 SYSTEM OVERVIEW

The Balance series of multiprocessor systems is an integrated hardware and software environment to support high performance, general purpose applications. It consists of three elements:

(a) a shared memory, common bus, parallel architecture, built around industry standard microprocessors;

(b) Dynix operating system, which is an extension of Unix 4.2 Bds, to support Balance parallel architecture;

(c) standard interfaces, such as Multibus and Ethernet.

According to Flynn's taxonomy [4], the system fits into the MIMD class; each of the up to 30 identical processors executes a private task on private or shared data streams. Topologically, the architecture is best described as a tightly coupled multiprocessor system, owing to the central role played by the common bus; moreover, no hierarchy is superimposed on the set of processors, which have equal priority in accessing shared resources, most notably the common memory subsystem. Similar designs can be found in the "family" concept of the EMMA multiprocessor [5], in the "processor cluster" of the Multicluster system [6], in PICAP II [7] and in other multiprocessors.

A problem common to this kind of architectures is the possible bottleneck arising from contention in bus accesses; therefore, all these systems are based on special purpose, high bandwidth busses and extensively exploit cache mechanisms in memory management. This is the case in Balance systems as well, which moreover are equipped with a dedicated, single-bit serial bus, connecting special purpose ASIC circuits called SLIC (Serial Link and Interrupt Controllers), located on each board of the system and devoted to the management of interrupts and to synchronization of accesses to critical sections of kernel data structures.

A unique feature of Balance systems is the provision of hardware locks to support access to shared memory sections by different processors: these locks, called Atomic Lock Memories (ALM in the following) are placed in the Multibus adapter board and can be used to implement software synchronization protocols of different types (spin-locks, semaphores, monitors, etc.).

In the following, a deeper description of the system components is given; more details can be found in the pertaining system documentation [8].

2.1 The system bus

The system bus links the system's CPUs, the memory and I/O subsystems. It is operated synchronously at a clock rate of 10 MHz and accommodates a 64 bits data paths multiplexed in time with 32 bits addresses, yielding a maximum channel bandwidth of 80 Mbytes per second. Current devices use only 32 bits data paths and 28 bits addresses, resulting in a sustained transfer rate of up to 26.7 Mbytes per second.

The system bus supports read and write operations from and to memory in packets of 1, 2, 3, 4 and 8 bytes; furthermore bus operation can be pipelined. Bus arbitration is handled by a clock/arbitration board: control of the bus is granted partly according to fixed priorities (boards are ranked on the base of their location in the backplane and are split into two classes, high priority and low priority ones), partly through a round robin policy (for boards of the same priority class, such as those containing the CPUs).

2.2 The memory subsystem

A Balance system can contain up to four "memory modules", each consisting of a controller board (which contains 2 Mbytes of RAM) and of an optional expansion board (up to 6 Mbytes). Each module responds to read requests in three bus cycles (300 ns) and to a 4 or 8 bytes write request in two cycles; memory interleaving on alternate 8 bytes addresses can be exploited, provided that the subsystem contains at least two 8 Mbytes boards.

2.3 The SLIC bus

To aid in the management of interrupts and of low level control signals among the various boards, the system is equipped with a 1-bit data path in the backplane; it interconnects special purpose chips, called SLIC, located on every board. The functions carried out by the SLICs are configuration management at system power-up, interrupt handling and mutual exclusion mechanism to synchronize accesses to the operating system kernel data structures. This last feature is based on low level hardware locks, called "gates", which can be acquired and released by issuing special commands to the SLICs. The management of these locks is invisible to user tasks; in particular, ALM are completely disjoint from "gates".

2.4 The processors pool

The CPUs in the system are packaged on dual-processor boards, all of them functionally equivalent. Each board hosts two National Semiconductors Series 32000 CPUs, which operate independently of each other and of all others; each CPU comes with supporting circuitry, namely a memory management unit, a floating point coprocessor, 8K of local RAM and 8K of cache memory, plus a SLIC circuit. While the role of the SLIC is to unload the CPU from the management of interrupts and arbitration in accessing kernel data structures, the cache memory aids in effective usage of the bus by keeping most recently used blocks of system memory; the local RAM instead only helps in making the implementation of the operating system as efficient as possible, since it is devoted to storage of certain frequently used kernel code and read-only data structures. The operation of both local RAM and cache memory is totally transparent to user tasks, but the effects of the cache invalidation policy do appear at the application level when frequently updates to shared blocks of memory occur, as shall be seen later.

3 OPERATING SYSTEM SUPPORT OF PARALLEL PROGRAMMING

The Dynix operating system is an enhanced version of Unix 4.2 bds, modified to support multiprocessing; furthermore it offers compatibility with Unix System V. It is not the purpose of this paper to fully describe the implementation of Unix in such an environment; it suffices to say that the distribution of system workload among the CPUs is completely transparent to user tasks and that kernel processes running on different CPUs synchronize themselves by using the SLIC bus.

From the point of view of the application developer, Dynix comes with the standard facilities of both Unix 4.2 (signals and Inter-processor Communication) and of Unix System V (message queues, counting and blocking semaphores); so, a parallel application might exploit these mechanisms in conjunction with the availability of more CPUs. Applications relying strongly on "message passing" techniques can be easily adapted to the multiprocessor environment, without extensive code modifications. Other types of applications make little use of "message passing" and require extensive concurrent access to large data structures; to them, an efficient mechanism to shared memory is a crucial factor.

Actually, controlled access to shared memory is the straightforward way to exploit Balance system multiprocessing capabilities explicitly. The Dynix operating system offers a simple method to generate common sections of system memory and a set of synchronization routines relying on ALMs.

As in standard Unix environment, the "mmap" system call can be used to map any file or region of the system's physical address space into a process' virtual address space. But, unlike standard systems, such regions can be shared among different processes in either of two ways: cooperating, but otherwise different processes (such as two processes which have been created through the "exec" call by distinct "fathers") can map in their private address space the same portion of a file; alternatively, processes, which have been spawn through the "fork" system call by a single process, inherit and share such a region which has been acquired by the common "father".

Whichever means is used to create such shared region, mutual exclusive access to it can be obtained with a proper use of the ALMs. Atomic Lock Memories are locations in the physical address space mapped in the Multibus adapter board of the system; such locations are actually hardware locks which implement the test-and-set protocol as an indivisible, uninterruptible operation. Thus ALMs can be used to realize software synchronization mechanism, such as simple spin-locks, or more advanced ones, such as semaphores or monitors. There exists 16K ALMs in each Multibus adapter board. Since ALMs reside at specified addresses in these boards, which in turn occupy specific ranges of the physical address space of the system, it is necessary that processes map such memory location in their common section of the virtual address space; this can be done either by the "father" before forking, or by the processes themselves, once "exec-ed".

The software environment offered by Dynix to manage shared memory and ALMs is organized in a "parallel library" which can be used by high level language compilers, such as those for the C Language and for Fortran. The routines in the library allow:

(a) acquiring, allocating and releasing shared memory and ALM locks;
(b) initializing, locking and unlocking of "software locks"; these are actually spin-locks and are the only type of locks available in the library, while semaphores and other synchronization mechanisms must be realized explicitly using ALM as building blocks;
(c) initializing and using "barriers"; "barriers" are synchronization points which allow more processes to "rendez-vous" at a pre-established position before proceeding in the execution;
(d) determining the number of processors available for use.

Since "software locks" rely on ALMs, which are physically accessible only through the system bus, their implementation is based on the concept of "shadow lock"; variables declared as "software lock", once accessed for the first time, are copied in the cache of a processor and the test-and-set routine spins on this shadow copy, until the processor which first acquired the lock releases it. This causes the block of cache containing the lock to be written back into memory and the corresponding blocks in other caches to be invalidated. The next read performed onto the lock will bring into the caches the up-to-date version; this implementation minimizes bus usage, which might otherwise become extremely heavy.

Beyond the parallel library support, Dynix offers also a "microtasking" facility which can be used to handle semi-automatic execution of loops; it is of little interest for applications in which the explicit management of shared data structure is the major concern.

4 ALGORITHMS AND PARALLELIZATION

The performance of Balance 8000 is analyzed by using a set of algorithms for low-level image processing. The main feature of low-level tasks is to deal with a great amount of data because the transformations are of the kind "image to image". For this reason the machine is tested on tasks which need a large number of transfer operations between shared memory and local memory. This allows to measure the efficiency of the invalidation mechanism of the private page of memory of each processor (cache controller) and of the devices which manage the communication on the common bus. Moreover the performance measured by means of algorithms of common use in the field of computer vision is especially interesting in this case because the Balance system is a commercial machine with a user-friendly operating system which guarantees to the programmer the transparency of the operations above mentioned.

Three algorithms belonging to three different classes have been implemented: "threshold", "closing" and "distance transform". From a functional point of view, the first one performs a point transformation on the image (the pixel value depends only on the corresponding input pixel value), the second one a local elaboration and the third a global one. This classic partition of low-level tasks imposes no mandatory strategy to the process of translating the "problem statement" into an actual "parallel algorithm"; many alternatives exist that depend both on the characterization of the algorithm and on the architecture at hand [9]. There are two main kinds of algorithm parallelization on a MIMD machine: **function partitioning** (heterogeneous multi-tasking) and **data partitioning** (homogeneous multitasking). The first one involves the creation of processes performing different operations on a set of private or shared data: with this approach, sometimes a few steps to be done in temporal sequence on the whole data must be identified in the program. Each step is assigned to a single process which puts its results in a buffer that furnishes the input data to the process used for the execution of the next step. On the other hand, homogeneous multitasking is based on identical processes and on data partitioning among them. This partition depends on the type of algorithm. Since it is not always possible to split the data into not overlapping segments, when more than one process tries to update the same shared segment at the same time, conflicts arise that can be solved by exclusive access to the data or by means of private editions of the shared memory.

The kind of parallelism chosen for the implementation of three above mentioned algorithms is **data partitioning**. In fact, the operations required are highly uniform across the whole image and data dependencies are kept to a minimum. When a large amount of data has to be processed, as in this case, on machines in which the processors contend the access to the communication bus, most of the parallel implementation overhead comes from the limited bandwidth of the bus channel; indeed, homogeneous multitasking minimizes explicit inter-process communication, which is a specific requirement of heterogeneous multitasking.

In our case data partitioning is exploited for all algorithms because also the distance-transform computation is achieved by a sequence of parallel and homogeneous operations. In particular, it is performed by means of "erosions" and "sums", local operations whose duration does not depend too much on the input data.

Moreover, data partitioning allows to structure the algorithms in a way that naturally adapts to the number of processors available; the resulting software can be easily ported on systems of different sizes in terms of CPUs.

There are two main strategies to assign the data to the processes: **static** and **dynamic allocation**. Static allocation divides the image in a number of segments that equals the number of processors (they are often overlapping). On the other hand, dynamic allocation divides the image in more segments: each process deals in sequence with more than one segment, choosing among the unprocessed ones, every time it becomes free. This technique requires the use of an index of the segments to be processed, that must be shared by all the processes; it is updated when a process gets a segment to work on.

Dynamic allocation is more convenient than the static one when the elaboration time strongly depends on the input data; on the other hand it generates overhead because of contention for the shared index, which must be guarded through a "software lock". Since the algorithms of our benchmark have a computation time "lightly" dependent on the context in which they work, static allocation is more efficient than the dynamic one.

The parallelization procedure is based on the replication of a "father" process in some "children" processes by means of the system call "fork" (see Fig. 1). All children have to access the image to read their segment and must return to the father the results of their elaboration; so, a shared area of memory is defined, containing the input and the output images. Although this

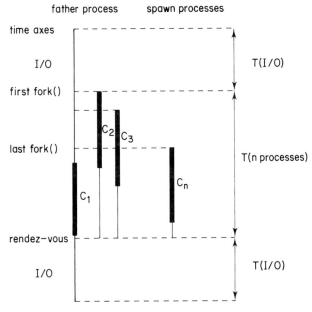

Fig. 1. Parallel process execution profile.

area is shared among all the processes, collisions are reduced because each process writes on the assigned segment. However, there are situations in which synchronization is unavoidable; this happens when a task is split into more steps, during which each process produces partial results in shared memory. To maintain data consistency, all processes have to finish the n-th elaboration step, before proceeding to the next one. Process synchronization is achieved with the library function "p_wait_barrier", that creates a meeting point for more processes. When a process meets a "p_wait_barrier" call, it lets the system know that it is present at the barrier. When all processes are present, parallel execution starts again. The wait mechanism on the barrier is realized with shared variables updated and tested by each process.

5 MEASURING APPLICATIONS PERFORMANCE

Any performance evaluation of multiprocessor systems requires a precise statement of the architecture at hand and, most important, of the tools to be used to collect measures.

In the domain of image processing, a possible approach is to analyze the suitability of the various architectures in performing representative tasks [10]; such an analysis requires the evaluation of the number of elementary operations needed to execute the task and leads to closed-form formulas which quantify the execution time. The advantage of this approach is the possibility to estimate the performances both of real machines and of proposed new ones; also, it offers a theoretical framework to assess the "match" between an algorithm and a specific architecture.

However, when dealing with a general purpose multiprocessor which is being used for image processing, such a detailed analytic procedure is extremely difficult and actually misplaced. A more direct measurement of the true execution time of the selected algorithm is the straightforward means to assess the performance of the system; in the present case, we are in the nice position to be able to compare execution time on the same system when used as a single processor or as multiprocessor.

Still, there remains the problem of choosing a reasonably complete set of parameters characterizing the system; a possible set of measures has been proposed by Siegel [11] for the class of SIMD machines. Although the architecture of Balance systems does not fit into such a class, the kind of algorithms we have realized (homogeneous multitasking) is very near to SIMD operation.

In his definitions, Siegel characterizes the complexity of task through the number M of pixels to be processed and the architecture through the number n of processors available. The parameters defined are:

Execution time $T_n(M)$
It measures the time to perform the algorithm for a task of size M on an n-

CPUs system; it can be expressed as

$$T_n(M) = c_n(M) + o_n(M)$$

where $c_n(M)$ is the time spent performing computations which are actually part of the task, while $o_n(M)$ is the "overhead", or time spent performing operations required to "manage" the parallelism. In our situations, the overhead is mainly due to process creation through the "fork" systems call, to conflicts in bus accesses and to time spent by processes at synchronization points.

Speed $V_n(M)$

Speed $V_n(M) = \dfrac{M}{T_n(M)}$ is the number of pixels processed per unit time.

Speed-up $S_n(M)$

The speed-up is defined as:

$$S_n(M) = \frac{T_1(M)}{T_n(M)}$$

and is obviously proportional to speed; ideal speed-up is N which means $o_n(M)$ is zero.

Efficiency $E_n(M)$

It is defined as

$$E_n(M) = \frac{S_n(M)}{m}$$

and gives an idea of how the achieved speed-up compares to the ideal one. Efficiency is always less than 1 in multiprocessor systems, unless the overhead is zero.

Overhead ratio $O_n(M)$

It is measured as

$$O_n(M) = \frac{o_n(M)}{T_n(M)}$$

and, if the speed-up is ideal, $O_n(M) = 1 - E_n(M)$.

Utilization $U_n(M)$

It is the fraction of time during which the processors are executing computations of the algorithm. It can be measured as the average of the computation time $c_n(M)$ over execution time $T_n(M)$:

$$U_n(M) = \frac{\sum_{i=0}^{i=n-1} (c_n(M))_i}{n * T_n(M)}$$

Redundancy $R_n(M)$

It is the total computing time of all processors compared with the execution time in the mono-processor case, expressed as:

$$R_n(M) = \frac{\sum_{i=0}^{i=n-1} (c_n(M))_i}{T_1(M)}$$

This is another way of estimating overhead, but it only keeps track of time spent in resources contention.

These definitions have been translated in our environment by using a model of the execution profile of the algorithm, illustrated in Fig. 1.

A parallel algorithm is logically split into two phases, a serial and a parallel one. In the former, a single process exists (the "father") which performs standard initializations, I/O operations required to load into memory the image and to store it back to disk; in the latter, there exist n processes, among which the "father", all of them in execution on different CPUs.

We define $T_n(M)$ as the time elapsed between the creation of the first child process and the moment when all processes have reached the final rendez-vous point (a barrier). Accordingly, $c_n(M)$ is measured since the moment when a process starts execution pertaining to the task until it ends and queues at the barrier; for the father process, this time interval starts immediately after the creation of the last child.

The most difficult measure is clearly $o_n(M)$; we have chosen to estimate it by adding the time required to the father process to generate all of the children and the time wasted during the final synchronization. This explicitly captures two components of the overhead, while it misses the effects of contention in bus access. However, redundancy gives an indication of this source of overhead. Furthermore, when an algorithm consists of more parallel phases, as is the case in "closing" and "distance transform", separated by various synchronization points, the execution profile model has been applied to each phase.

To measure time, the system call "ftime" has been used; on the Balance 8000 system, we have measured an average execution time of this routine as 0.5 ms and an interval discrimination of 10 ms.

6 RESULTS AND COMMENTS

The experiments have been carried through on a system configured with 6 Mbytes of memory, four processor boards, that is with 8 CPUs, each a NS32032 operating at 10 Mhz; the three algorithms have been run on a set of images with dimensions ranging from 64 x 64 pixels up to 512 x 512; also, each algorithm has been run many times, to even out possible minor fluctuations in execution time.

Figures 2 through 4 show speed-up and overhead ratio for each algorithm and for each image. It can be easily noted that the achieved speed-up is well

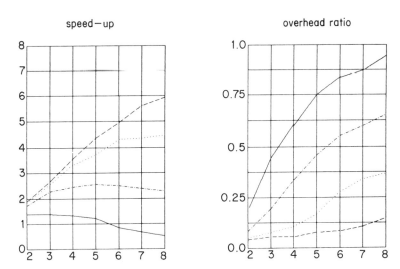

Fig. 2. Threshold; speed-up and overhead ratio against the number of processors.

above the over-pessimistic logarithmic assumption of Minsky's conjecture [12] and compare fairly well with the theoretical maximum speed-up in most cases.

A few facts are worth noting. Image size plays a major role in affecting speed-up, especially in thresholding and closing. It is certainly unrealistic to use images smaller than 512 x 512 pixels in actual image processing tasks, but it has proved extremely useful in highlighting overhead contributions arising from system activity. In fact, an image of 64 x 64 pixels, which contains 4 Kbytes, is composed of exactly four pages of system memory. The thresholding algorithm, which is a point transformation, has been coded with a single buffer to host input and output image sectors: therefore, as soon as the number of processors is larger than 2, the cache invalidation policy completely cancels out the benefits of multiprocessing, since image sectors allocated to processors extend beyond page size. With even more processors, the parallel algorithm performs worse than the serial one. For larger images, this effect becomes negligible and the flattening in speed-up is due much more to bus contention and to the overhead caused by the time necessary to generate children processes.

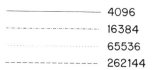

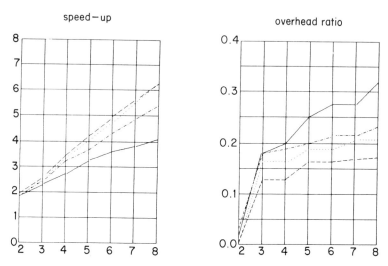

Fig. 3. Closing; speed-up and overhead ratio against the number of processors.

When the algorithm is more complex, such as for closing and medial axis transform, which consist of more parallel phases, the achieved speed-up is higher and the overhead ratio much slower, even for very small images. This is largely due to the fact that these algorithms use distinct buffers for input and output image sectors at each stage. Reducing process synchronization to a minimum is a very convenient strategy; if the algorithms can be formulated as a succession of local operations, data partitioning allows for minimum synchronization overhead and leads to speed-up factors which compare fairly well with the theoretical limit.

In this situation, bus architectures, such as Balance systems, originally designed for general purpose applications, provide a viable solution also in parallel image processing if the bandwidth of the bus channel is sufficiently wide.

7 CONCLUSION

Benchmarks design has always been a very difficult activity; a critical analysis of the recent DARPA benchmark can be found in [13]. With reference to the

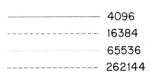

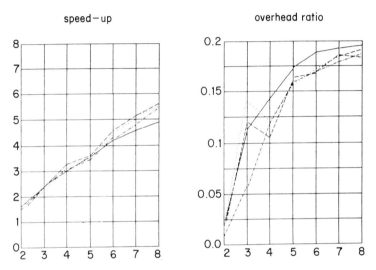

Fig. 4. Distance transform; speed-up and overhead ratio against the number of processors.

set of algorithms chosen for that benchmark, we do not claim that the experiments performed on the Balance system are in any way complete or exhaustive; for one thing, they address only that sector of image processing which involves only image to image transformations. However they show the importance of evaluating true system performance against a precisely defined set of measures.

A very important issue which has been raised is that of programming effort: no benchmark keeps into account the impact of converting algorithms to run on a multiprocessor system. So far, explicit parallelism is a strict requirement on general purpose multiprocessor systems; in our case it has proved extremely easy to realize thanks to the software environment and to the data partitioning strategy adopted. The serial version of the algorithm is the body of the parallel version as well: the use of fork and of synchronization barriers adds a minimum of coding and makes the structure of the parallel algorithm linear and self explanatory.

ACKNOWLEDGMENTS

We wish to thank ELEDRA SYSTEMS S.p.A. for giving us the possibility of performing these experiments on their Balance 8000 system.

TRADEMARKS

Balance and Dynix are registered trademarks of Sequent Computer Systems, Inc.
UNIX and UNIX System V are registered trademarks of AT&T
ETHERNET is a trademark of Xerox Corporation
MULTIBUS is a trademark of Intel Corporation

REFERENCES

[1] Duff, M.J.B. (ed.) (1983). *Computing Structures for Image Processing*, Academic Press, London.
[2] Kittler, J. and Duff, M.J.B. (eds.) (1985). *Image Processing System Architectures*, Research Studies Press Ltd., Letchworth, Hertfordshire, Great Britain.
[3] Duff, M.J.B. (ed.) (1986). *Intermediate Level Image Processing*, Academic Press, London.
[4] Flynn, M.J. (1972). Some Computer Organization and Their Effectiveness, *IEEE Trans. on Comp.*, C-21, n. 9, pp. 948–960.
[5] Appiani, E., Barbagelata, G., Cavagnaro, F., Conterno, B. and Manara, R. (1985). EMMA-2, an Industry-Developed Hierarchical Multiprocessor for Very High Performance Signal Processing Applications, *Proc. SCS-85, St. Petersburg, Florida*, pp. 310–319.
[6] Reeves, A.P. and Jeon, C.H. (1986). Computer Vision Task Distribution on a Multicluster MIMD System, in [3], pp. 193–208.
[7] Kruse, B., Gudmundoss, B. and Antonsson, D. (1980). FIP: the PICAP II Filter Processor, *Proc. 5th Intern. Conf. on Pattern Recognition, Miami*, pp. 484–488.
[8] Sequent Computer Systems, "Balance Technical Manual", MAN-0110-00, Nov. 1986.
[9] Jamieson, L.H. (1986). The Mapping of Parallel Algorithms to Reconfigurable Parallel Architectures, in [3], pp. 53–63.
[10] Cantoni, V., Guerra, C. and Levialdi, S. (1983). Towards an evaluation of an Image Processing System, in [1]. pp. 43–56.
[11] Siegel, L.J., Siegel, H.J. and Swain, P.H. (1982). Parallel Algorithm Performance Measures, in *Multicomputers and Image Processing: Algorithms and Programs*, L. Uhr ed., Academic Press, pp. 241–252.
[12] Minsky, M. and Papert, S. (1971). On Some Associative, Parallel and Analog Computations, in *Associative Information Techniques*, E.J. Jacks ed., N.J., 1971.
[13] Rosenfeld, A. (1987). A Report on the DARPA Image Understanding Architectures Workshop, *Proc. Image Understanding Workshop, Los Angeles, CA.*, 23–25 Feb. 1987, pp. 298–302.

Chapter Nine

One Dimensional SIMD Architectures— The AIS-5000

Stephen S. Wilson

Applied Intelligent Systems Inc.
110 Parkland Plaza
Ann Arbor, MI. 48103

1 INTRODUCTION

The most well-known form of interconnection between SIMD (Single Instruction Multiple Data) fine grain parallel processors is that of a two-dimensional N × N square mesh, such as the MPP [1] with an array of 128 × 128, the DAP [2] with a 64 × 64 array, and the CLIP4 [3] with a 96 × 96 array. It is obvious that the mesh connected architectures are superb at low level vision processing and enhancement using neighborhood computations. The programming model for mesh connected systems is fairly straightforward due to the regularity and isotropy of the architecture. Through programming, these mesh systems can operate on sub-images, and are able to piece together computations for any reasonable image size. An advantage of this type of architecture is that as technology progresses, the mesh can grow in size so that the processing throughput increases with the number of processors.

However, this interconnection scheme is not as effective for many high-level vision algorithms and for many types of applications which involve global or long distance communication paths. A significant part of the cost of these systems is in:

(1) the overhead in electronics to support the handling of neighborhood connections at the edges of subimages;

(2) hardware to support "corner-turning" data so that the byte serial format of I/O data can be converted to the bit-parallel format that the mesh requires;

(3) extremely complex controllers which are needed so that an instruction stream to the parallel array can be updated at a rate generally around 10 MHz;

MULTICOMPUTER VISION
ISBN 0-12-444818-6

Other disadvantages are that

(4) the instruction set must be kept simple due to the limited pinout in LSI chips, and

(5) the number of processors can not be simply arbitrarily expanded by adding boards since the complexity of the inter-processor wiring increases by 2N.

2 THE ONE-DIMENSIONAL ARRAY

The AIS-5000 is a SIMD architecture which is a N × 1 dimensional array, where the size can span from 128 × 1 to 1024 × 1. In this system the array is as wide as the image, i.e. there is one processing element for every column in the image, and there is enough memory directly coupled to each processing element (PE) to hold the entire column of the image along with a large amount of storage space for intermediate results of computations. A single image operation is processed by loading an instruction into the PEs, and then reading rows of data from the associated memory to the PEs, performing the transformation, and then writing the resulting transformed rows back into memory. Rows are read and written sequentially until the entire image is processed.

Advantages of this architecture are:

(1) there is little need for hardware to support neighboring connections of subimages since there are no subimages in the horizontal dimension;

(2) corner turning I/O data is much simpler;

(3) PE instructions can be generated at a much slower rate, since the instruction, once loaded, is valid for the entire vertical span of the image. Only a regular pattern of memory addresses of the SIMD array need to be updated at a high speed;

(4) complex PE instructions can be loaded in serially and therefore use fewer pins since instruction loading speed its not critical;

(5) circuit board and backplane layout is simple and the number of PEs can be expanded by adding more boards, without expanding the complexity of the backplane.

Disadvantages of the one-dimensional array concept are:

(1) The image width is fixed by the number of processors. Although images or regions of interest narrower than the number of processors can be accommodated, some processors would remain idle thus lowering the efficiency of the system.

(2) The processor concept does not easily lend itself to expansion by

adding more PEs. It is true that more rows of PEs can be added, but by definition, the system would no longer be one dimensional. (The CLIP7 [4], for example, is an exceptional mesh connected system in that it has an array size of 512 × 4, and is configured to process 512 × 512 images.)

(3) Compared with a mesh architecture, the one-dimensional array may be confusing in that the architecture is essentially anisotropic where the horizontal direction can be considered as "massively parallel", and the vertical direction is a "general purpose ALU" dimension.

Further analysis of the one-dimensional SIMD architecture is given by Fisher [5, 6], where a number of different implementations are discussed. He suggests that one way around the second disadvantage listed above is to run several arrays in a parallel pipeline. A more formal analysis comparing the performance of the one-dimensional linear array, pyramid, and hypercube architectures is given by Fountain [7]. His conclusion is that the linear array is obviously in a lower cost category than the other two architectures and it is also lower in some aspects of performance. The anisotropic nature of the architecture can be hidden by a software layer for low level processing, and used to great advantage in higher level processing.

3 THE AIS–5000

The Applied Intelligent Systems Inc. AIS-5000 parallel processor can be used in conjunction with a graphic workstation, or as a standalone unit. A development environment, which runs on the workstation, provides a means of programming applications that execute on the parallel processors. A configuration that is used for program development also includes mass storage devices and a communication mechanism (e.g. Ethernet). The workstation contains a Motorola 68020, a high resolution black and white monitor, a large amount of memory, a keyboard, and pointing device. The workstation is used for software development, while the AIS-5000 performs the computationally intensive tasks. There is no emulation of the parallel processor done on the workstation and, when doing image analysis, there is no need to transfer images across the network since the AIS-5000 has its own 68000 host, real-time monitors, memory, and storage.

In many applications, the parallel processor is intended to be unplugged from the workstation for installation in a factory or office. Software that has been developed using the program development tools of the workstation can be directly used in the detached parallel processors which then operate as dedicated devices. It is currently the only massively parallel computer built to operate as a standalone unit in these environments.

Users have a range of tools that can be used to develop software for the parallel array. The C Programming language is one of the primary means of developing algorithms. It provides full access to the capabilities of the parallel architecture through a library of functions which a C programmer can call directly. There are functions that can be called from C that can be used to program the parallel array using its most fundamental operations (i.e. those that are directly supported by the individual processing element hardware) as well as functions that perform high-level operations on the parallel array.

3.1 The system

The AIS-5000 system consists of three major components:

(a) a general purpose 68000 host processor and peripherals;

(b) special purpose high speed input/output hardware for the parallel processor;

(c) a SIMD array parallel processor and controller.

Figure 1 shows the system and identifies the host, I/O, and parallel processor components. The 68000 host part of the system also includes memory and peripherals and is conventional in its design and the way it is programmed. The I/O sections transfer data in and out of the memory associated with the PEs (i.e. the parallel memory), and contain the corner-turning logic. The data destined for the parallel memory can come from a number of sources including cameras and standard 68000 addressable RAM. The data coming out of parallel memory can go to a number of destinations including video monitors and 68000 RAM. Details of the modules in the AIS-5000 system are given in reference [8]. The parallel processor part of the AIS-5000 consists of

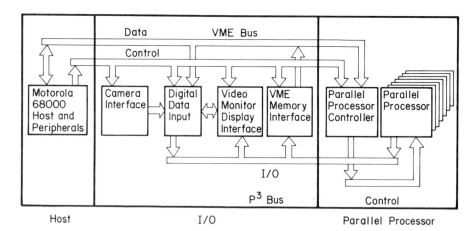

Fig. 1. The AIS-5000 system.

the SIMD processing elements, their associated memory, and the controller which directs their operation. These units will be described in the next sections.

3.2 The parallel array

The linear array can contain up to 1024 programmable, bit-serial PEs, each of which tightly coupled to its own local single bit memory and connections to two neighboring PEs as shown in Fig. 2. The memory consists of commercially available byte-wide chips which are in the $32 \text{ K} \times 8$ format. Each memory chip therefore services 8 PEs where each PE is accessing one bit of the 8 provided by the chip. There are 8 PEs per chip, 128 processors per circuit card and up to 8 cards in the system. The data in adjacent memory columns can be accessed by a PE through its connections to its two neighboring PEs. The PEs on the end of the array only communicate to one neighboring PE on their left or right. The other neighbor connection is always a zero.

The processing elements and I/O channels for the AIS-5000 are built on a custom integrated circuit. Each circuit with 8 PEs and 3 I/O channels is shown in Fig. 3. The processing elements on the custom gate array chip can perform three distinct types of functions: Boolean, Neighborhood, and Arithmetic. These functions are performed on single bits read from the memory and the results of the functions are written back to memory. The

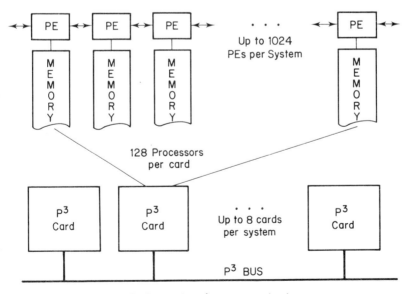

Fig. 2. Processing element organization.

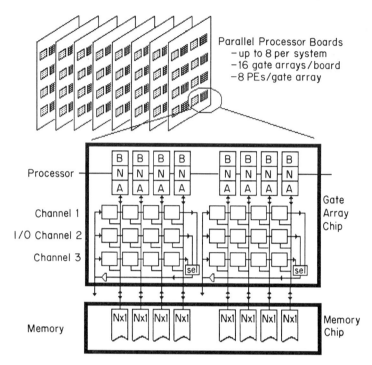

Fig. 3. The parallel array.

boolean and arithmetic functions are typical of those found in more conventional computer architectures. The neighborhood functions are unique to certain parallel architectures which provide direct connections between processing elements. All three types of functions are programmable so that the host processor (and ultimately the programmer) can specify the particular boolean, neighborhood or arithmetic function the processing elements are to perform. In addition, the pattern and addresses of memory reads and writes can be programmed.

The custom chip contains not only the PEs but also an I/O section that facilitates getting data in and out of the parallel memory. This I/O section operates independently of and asynchronously with the processing elements. The I/O section and the PE section of the chip share the line to memory. The I/O section consists of three separate channels, each of which operates at 7.15 MHz. When parallel memory is to be accessed, the data in the I/O channel is read from or written into the memory chip connected to the PE chip in a one cycle non-maskable interrupt. In this manner, the data passing through the I/O channels to or from memory does not disturb the processing elements on the PE chip. There are two physical I/O lines per chip which are connected to a special purpose bus on the backplane of the system. Management of the channels is under program control.

Since the I/O channels on the gate array chip are independent, they can contain different data going in different directions. This allows data to be read from parallel memory at the same time data is being written to parallel memory. For example, camera input can be loaded into parallel memory at the same time as video output is being read from a different place in parallel memory. This allows a great deal of overlap in I/O and processing functions with very little overhead. Maximum utilization of the I/O channels results in about 5% of the memory duty cycle being used for I/O leaving 95% of the available memory duty cycle for the processing elements. Typical I/O results in memory duty cycles dedicated to I/O functions that are less than 1%.

3.3 The processing element

In the following discussions the boolean, neighborhood and arithmetic operations will be covered in more detail. The C language function calls are used in examples that demonstrate the programming of the PEs. All data paths and registers in the following diagrams are one bit wide.

Boolean Operations. There are three types of boolean operations characterized by the number, either 2, 3 or 4, of input variables. For all boolean operations, the source inputs are bits read from parallel memory. The sources are transformed according to a truth table supplied by the programmer. The boole4 function causes the processing element to read four bits from memory, transform them according to a truth table into a one bit result and write the result back to memory, as shown in Fig. 4. The truth table defines, for each possible combination of the 4 source bits, whether a 1 or a 0 should be written

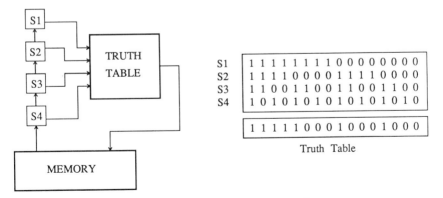

Fig. 4. PE in boolean operation mode.

back to the memory. Both the source addresses, the logical function and the destination address are specified in the C language call to the function for example,

Boole4(OxF888,srcl,src2,src3,src4,destination);

The truth table is given as a 16 bit hex value. In this example, OxF888 (Ox is the notation for a hexadecimal number) would result in a truth table of 1111 1000 1000 1000 which is the logical function (src1 AND src2) OR (src3 AND src4). The source and destination parameters are parallel memory addresses. This function will therefore perform the specified transformation on all four full bitplanes of parallel memory and put the result into a fifth bitplane. Boole3 and boole2 functions act identically to boole4 except that they use only 3 and 2 source bit planes respectively. For convenience popular boolean functions such as

AND4(srcl,src2,src3,src4,destination); and
XOR(src1,src2,destination);

which are for example a four input AND and an exclusive OR, are also in the library.

Neighborhood Operations. The direct access of the PE to its east and west neighbors allows many different types of neighborhood functions to be programmed. A neighborhood function acts much like a boolean function in that a truth table transformation is performed upon a set of bits (in this case four bits) to produce a one bit result. The differences between the neighborhood and boolean functions are that, in the neighborhood function, the East and West bits used as operands come from neighboring processing elements, and a logical function can be performed on the output of the truth table. This can be seen in the connections shown in Fig. 5. In a neighborhood

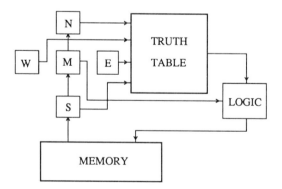

Fig. 5. PE in neighborhood operation mode.

transformation operation, the controller causes a shift up of consecutive rows of bits of the image read from the memory, and the result is written back into the memory. Each shift of a new row of bits to the South register, S, will cause the previously stored rows in the S, M and N to shift up, thus creating a new set of neighborhood data in only one read operation. The row in the top North register, N, will be discarded as the M row takes its place. As an example, the function

erode_nbr(Oxf888,source,destination);

causes an erosion of a neighborhood according to the specified truth table. In erosions, the output logic is an AND function, so the above example will transform a neighborhood according to the rule ((N AND S) OR (E AND W)) AND M. Other common neighborhood functions are included in the library such as a dilate east and west which is written as

d_ew(source,destination);

For a system with 1024 processing elements, the effective performance is 3.5 billion neighborhood operations per second. More complex 3 × 3 or M × M neighborhood transformations can be built up from sequences of the 4 nearest neighbor transformations and are also in a library.

Arithmetic Operations. When performing bit-serial arithmetic, the PE configuration used is shown in Fig. 6. It is conventional for a bit serial processor in that a sum and carry are generated simultaneously. This function is similar in operation to boolean operations in that two bits are read and shifted into registers, the operation is performed, and the result is written back to memory. The source and destination addresses are specified in the call to the function, for example,

add(sourcel,source2,destination);

where source and destination parameters are parallel memory addresses of consecutive bitplanes, called byteplanes, which are interpreted as numbers.

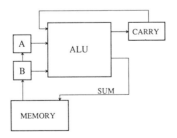

Fig. 6. PE in arithmetic mode.

The add function will perform additions on two byteplanes and put the result into a third byteplane. For a 1024 processor system, over 250 million byte wide arithmetic operations per second can be performed. Arithmetic operations of any precision are supported.

3.4 Parallel memory organization

The physical memory can be logically viewed as a three-dimensional array of bits where the location of any bit can be given by specifying its row, column, and bitplane within the 3D memory block. The hardware and firmware of the AIS-5000 supports this view and alleviates the programmer from having to cope with details of memory addressing. Bits in parallel memory are logically referenced by their row, column, and bitplane index which respectively specifies the memory location along the height, width, and depth. The width of the memory block is always equal to the number of PEs in the system. The height and depth of the memory block are parameters which can be dynamically set to any desired value that is within the bounds of the physical memory present. A block of memory of a specific width and height but only one bit deep is referred to as a bitplane.

4 THE CENTIPEDE

A new custom PE chip called the "centipede" is under development. It will be used in one-dimensional array systems with an architecture very similar to the AIS-5000, where there is one PE per image column. The boolean, neighborhood and arithmetic processing section of the centipede will be the same as the AIS-5000 with a few extra modes. The major enhancements are in data communication and manipulation. Major additions to the PEs are:

(1) a sixteen bit accumulator,
(2) capability of an 8 × 8 transpose on subarrays,
(3) indirect addressing of the parallel memory,
(4) a byte wide arithmetic mode, and
(5) a "sum-or" capability.

The centipede architecture is arranged in groups of eight consecutive PEs. A number of operations will use these logical groups for byte wide computations. Other operations such as boolean, neighborhood, and bit serial arithmetic will use each PE individually as in the AIS-5000. Figure 7 shows a rough block diagram of the Centipede PE architecture where the top block refers to 8 ALUs, each very similar to the AIS-5000 PE without the data I/O channel. The next two blocks are each identical groups of 8 × 8 registers called the high and low accumulators. The fourth block is used only

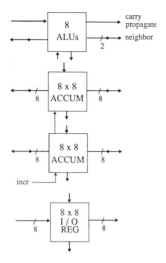

Fig. 7. Diagram of Centipede PE architecture.

for data I/O. A custom CMOS chip of about 10,000 gates and 120 pins would contain 16 PEs, and operate at 20 MHz.

For data input from an external source such as a digitized camera raster stream, the data is shifted to the right a byte at a time until the entire row of I/O registers for all PEs are full. Then the register data is shifted down into the parallel memory in eight cycles. A full row of data to be output can then be shifted from the parallel memory into the I/O shift registers in 8 cycles, and then shifted to the right. No further corner turning hardware is needed. This method of data I/O was also recognized by Fisher [5].

4.1 Accumulators

The accumulators have several functions. As indicated by the arrows in Fig. 7, the accumulators can shift 16 bit words east or west at each clock cycle, resulting in a very high bandwidth of horizontal data communication. The accumulators can also shift down. This mode is used during reading and writing the parallel memory. The accumulators also act as 16 bit counters with count enable inputs coming from parallel memory. Accumulators and counters are not new in the SIMD literature [1, 9], however the combined functions in the one accumulator allow new functions to be performed which would otherwise be rather difficult. The accumulators also connect to the ALUs so that the parallel memory and accumulators can serve as inputs to the ALU with the resulting output going back to either the memory or accumulators. Fewer parallel memory read or write cycles are required when the accumulators are used in arithmetic operations.

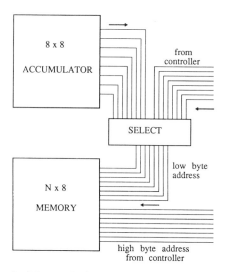

Fig. 8. Detail of Centipede direct and indirect addressing selection.

4.2 Indirect addressing

It has been mentioned [5, 9] that a very useful addition to the PE in a SIMD array would be the capability for each PE to control the address of its local memory, rather than only using the mode where a controller broadcasts the same address to every parallel memory. This is called indirect addressing. It is also acknowledged that the major difficulty with indirect addressing is that the memories would have to be integrated on the chip since there would be a large number of wires leading from the indirect address register to each memory. With multiple PEs per chip, using VLSI technology, limitations in the required number of pin-outs would occur before gate count limitations are encountered.

In the Centipede, indirect addressing is done in the byte-parallel mode of the PEs. Figure 8 shows that the low byte accumulator on the right of the 8×8 block is used as the register for indirect addressing where a selector can choose either the indirect or direct mode of addressing. The 8 bit output of the selector serves as the low byte of address for a byte wide memory chip coupled with the group of 8 PEs. The high byte of the address is always direct.

4.3 Transpose

Another important function of the 8×8 block of accumulators is to transpose data. Small 8×8 subimages can be transposed, but the more important function is to transpose bytes from a "vertical format", as in Fig.

(a)

A0	B0	C0	D0	E0	F0	G0	H0
A1	B1	C1	D1	E1	F1	G1	H1
A2	B2	C2	D2	E2	F2	G2	H2
A3	B3	C3	D3	E3	F3	G3	H3
A4	B4	C4	D4	E4	F4	G4	H4
A5	B5	C5	D5	E5	F5	G5	H5
A6	B6	C6	D6	E6	F6	G6	H6
A7	B7	C7	D7	E7	F7	G7	H7

(b)

A0	A1	A2	A3	A4	A5	A6	A7
B0	B1	B2	B3	B4	B5	B6	B7
C0	C1	C2	C3	C4	C4	C6	C7
D0	D1	D2	D3	D4	D5	D6	D7
E0	E1	E2	E3	E4	E5	E6	E7
F0	F1	F2	F3	F4	F5	F6	F7
G0	G1	G2	G3	G4	G5	G6	G7
H0	H1	H2	H3	H4	H5	H6	H7

Fig. 9. Data formats in parallel memory storage. (a) Vertical format. (b) Horizontal format.

9(a), to a "horizontal format" as in Fig. 9(b). Eight bytes, A to H, are shown where least to most significant bits are numbered from 0 to 7. Bytes in the vertical format can be used in bit serial arithmetic similar to the AIS-5000, where in the horizontal format, bytes can undergo arithmetic operations in parallel, where the PEs can send the carry out signal to PEs on the right, as shown by the carry propagate line in Fig. 7. (In another mode the carry propagate also acts as a "sum-or".)

The horizontal format is necessary when indirect addressing is used. Since the parallel memories are addressed as bytes, the data must be used as bytes.

The parallel memory input pathways from the various blocks are shown in Fig. 10(a), where most paths are conventional for SIMD machines in that lines from various parts of each single PE are connected to a single memory wire. Unconventional paths are the eight lines from the right side of the 8 × 8 low accumulator to the data lines of the memory. These lines are called the "transpose out" lines because data stored in the accumulators in the vertical format will be transferred to memory in the horizontal format after 8 memory read clock cycles, while the low byte accumulators are simultaneously shifting to the right.

Parallel memory output pathways are shown in Fig. 10(b) where most paths are also conventional in that each individual memory output wire connects to each single PE. A set of connections called "transpose in" couple to the input of the left side of the 8 × 8 low accumulator group wherein data is also transposed between vertical and horizontal formats.

5 APPLICATIONS

Because of the unusual nature of the Centipede SIMD architecture, a few examples are needed to illustrate the usage of the accumulators, transposing, and indirect addressing for both low level and high level applications.

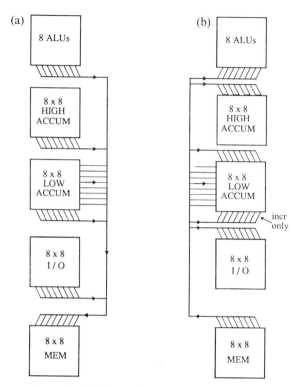

Fig. 10. Data pathways in the Centipede PE. (a) Memory input. (b) Memory output.

5.1 Convolutions

Eight bit data can be multiplied by constants by shifting and adding, while summing numbers directly into the accumulator. The entire accumulator contents can be then shifted east or west to pick up data from neighboring elements of the convolution kernel. Other SIMD processor designs [10] have separate accumulator and data communication paths so that the accumulator results remain stationary, and the data moves. Usage of an accumulator is three times more efficient than reading and writing intermediate results into the parallel memory. A 3×3 convolution of arbitrary weights can be done in about 5.7 msec for a 512×512 image.

5.2 Look-up-table

A look-up-table transform of an 8 bit number to another 8 bit number would take advantage of the indirect addressing mode. The table is first stored in the

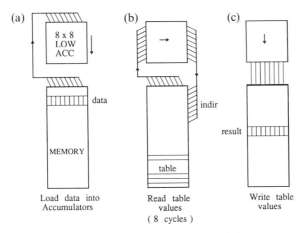

Fig. 11. Data flow for look-up-table operation. (a) Load data into accumulators in the vertical format. (b) Read table values and transpose to vertical format in accumulators. (c) Write results into memory in vertical format.

parallel memory in the horizontal format where, in general, a different table could be stored in the parallel memory corresponding to each group of eight PEs. 256 consecutive memory locations are required. Since the most significant parallel memory address is always direct, the beginning of the table must be registered with an address which is a multiple of 256, for example 0, as shown in Fig. 11(b). A row of data stored in the vertical format, as shown in Fig. 11(a) is read into the low accumulator block in the vertical format. The data byte in the right accumulator serves as an indirect address to the parallel memory, as shown in Fig. 11(b), where the direct, high address byte points to the beginning of the table. The value of the horizontal byte is read out of the memory into the "transpose-in" of the left accumulator, where a shift-right command will cause the right data byte to be lost thereby exposing the next data value as the next indirect address. The cycle shown in Fig. 11(b) clocks a total of eight times until all the original data values are displaced and replaced with the look-up-table values. These new values are then shifted back to parallel memory in the vertical format, as shown in Fig. 11(c). A total of 24 clock cycles are required for each row. With a 20 MHz clock, a 512×512 image could be transformed in 0.62 msec.

5.3 Feature extraction

Suppose low level processing has resulted in a number of feature bytes scattered through the image as in Fig. 12(a), where the MSB of each feature is a 1, and acts as a tag bit. The other seven bits encode the particular feature

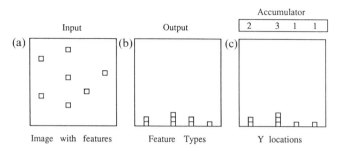

Fig. 12. Feature extraction. (a) Input image. (b) Output format for features. (c) Output format for Y locations.

type. It is desirable to stack the features at the bottom of a byte plane, as shown in Fig. 12(b), so that they can be located in order N time rather than order N^2 time. The Y locations must also be stored in another byte plane, shown in Fig. 12(c). The X location is implicit in the particular column the feature is located.

Feature extraction can be provided in 4 cycles. The accumulators all start out filled with zeros. First, in Fig. 13(a), assuming that features are transformed to the horizontal format, the data byte, which might be a candidate for a feature, is transferred to the ALU. Second, the data is read back to the parallel memory indirectly (Fig. 13(b)). Since the accumulators are zero, the data is read to the base location of the most significant direct address byte, e.g. zero. Next, the Y axis is read into parallel memory from the controllers least significant address byte which is pointing at the row under consideration. It is also stored indirectly, but at a different base address as shown in Fig. 13(c). Finally, as shown in Fig. 13(d), the accumulator is incremented if the tag bit is 1. The four cycles are repeated for each image row. If the feature tag bit is zero for some column, then the accumulator will not be incremented, and the data in the next row will overwrite the previously stored data. As soon as a tag bit is 1, the accumulator will increment and point to the next consecutive location, and the next data byte will not overwrite a valid feature. When all rows are processed, the accumulator will contain the number of features in the column. Since the indirect addressing only has a span of 256 rows, the feature extraction process would be broken into subimages which are 256 pixels high. Feature extraction requires 0.41 msec for images 256 rows high.

5.4 Other functions

A number of other low to high level functions work well with the centipede architecture. For example, histograms can take great advantage of the

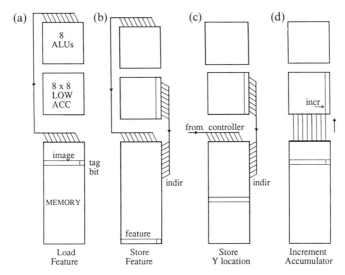

Fig. 13. Data flow for feature extraction operation. (a) Store feature in ALU in horizontal format. (b) Store feature indirectly into memory in horizontal format. (c) Store Y location indirectly in horizontal format. (d) Increment right-hand accumulator if tag bit is one.

indirect addressing mode. Areas and perimeter measurements can take advantage of the accumulator increment mode by performing a column add in 0.026 msec. An FFT can be computed in the vertical direction with no data movement. The image can then be transposed, in about 1.7 msec per bit-plane for a 512 × 512 image, then the horizontal FFT can be computed with no further data movement [11]. Neural processing can be done with each PE acting as one or more neural cells. Connection weights can be stored as matrices, and the process can run taking full advantage of the parallelism.

Hough transforms [12] are very efficient on the Centipede. It is first computed between plus and minus 45°, and then, for the remaining angles the image is rotated by 90°, and computed between plus and minus 45° again. To compute the Hough transform at a particular angle, the accumulator would be incremented by the data in the image, one row at a time. However, the accumulator must be shifted horizontally between rows at a slew rate according to the slope of the angle. The complete transform for 1° increments requires about 24 msec.

6 CONCLUSION

The one-dimensional linear array can have no more processing elements than the width of an image and, in one sense might be considered as an interim architecture which will become less valid in the future when advances in LSI technology allow low cost massively parallel mesh connected architectures to become available. However, this point of view is not accurate for several reasons. The linear array can more readily accommodate complex instructions, for example a truth table can enhance neighborhood and logic operations an order of magnitude over the simpler binary operations available in mesh connected systems. For this reason the AIS-5000 is able to perform the Abingdon Cross benchmark [14] in 20 msec—better than most mesh connected systems even though only 512 PEs are used. Only a few systems, such as the Cytocomputer [15], have truth tables available in hardware. The instantaneous vertical communication of data in the linear array architecture allows a large degree of parallelism in mid to higher level image processing such as the FFT, Hough transformations, feature extraction, and neural processing.

An arbitrarily high performance can be derived from the linear array simply by a pipeline of several of them in a M(SIMD) architecture. Thus, the one-dimensional linear array has a secure future as a low cost, high performance architecture. Systems beyond the centipede could take advantage of VLSI to include larger truth tables, pyramid structures, and bit-serial floating point arithmetic.

REFERENCES

[1] Batcher, K.E. (1980). Design of the Massively Parallel Processor. *IEEE Trans. Comput.*, C-29, pp. 836–840.
[2] Reddaway, S.F. (1973). DAP—A distributed processor array. First Annual Symposium on Computer Architecture, Florida, pp. 61–65.
[3] Duff, M.J.B. (1976). CLIP4: A large scale integrated circuit array parallel processor. *Proc. 3rd IJCPR*, Coronodo, CA, pp. 728–733.
[4] Fountain, T.J. (1985). Plans for the CLIP7 chip. In *Integrated Technology for Parallel Image Processing* (S. Levialdi ed.), Academic Press, London.
[5] Fisher, A.L. and Highman, P.T. (1985). Real time image processing on scan line array processors. *IEEE Workshop on Computer Architecture for Pattern Analysis and Image Database Management*, Miami, FL, pp. 484–489.
[6] Fisher, A.L. (1986). Scan line array processors for image computation. *13th Annual Symposium on Computer Architecture*, Tokyo, Japan, pp. 338–345.
[7] Fountain, T.J. (1986). Array architectures for iconic and symbolic image processing. *Proc. 8th Int. Conf. on Pattern Recognition*, Paris, France, pp. 24–33.
[8] Wilson, S.S. (1985). The Pixie-5000: A systolic array processor. *IEEE Workshop on Computer Architecture for Pattern Analysis and Image Database Management*, Miami, FL, pp. 477–483.
[9] Danielson, P-E., and Ericsson, T.S. (1983). LIPP—Proposals for the design of an image processor. In *Computing Structures For Image Processing* (M.J.B. Duff ed.) Academic Press, London.
[10] Fountain, T.J. (1983). A survey of bit-serial array processor circuits. In *Computing Structures For Image Processing*, (M.J.B. Duff ed.), Academic Press, London.

[11] Jamieson, L.H., Mueller, P.T. and Siegel, H.J. (1986). FFT algorithms for SIMD parallel processing systems. *Journal of Parallel and Distributed Processing*, Vol. 3, No. 1, pp. 48–71.

[12] Hough, P.V.C. (1962). "Method and means for recognizing complex patterns." U.S. Patent 3,069,654.

[13] Schmitt, L.A. and Wilson, S.S. The AIS-5000 Parallel Processor. Accepted for publication in *IEEE Patt. An. Mach. Int.*

[14] Preston Jr., K. (1986). Benchmark results—The Abingdon Cross. In *Evaluation of Multicomputers for Image Processing*. (L. Uhr and K. Preston Jr., eds.) Academic Press, Cambridge.

[15] Lougheed, R.M. and McCubbrey, D.L. (1980). The Cytocomputer: a practical pipelined image processor. *Proc. 7th Annual Symposium on Computer Architecture*, La Baule, France, IEEE. pp. 271–278.

Chapter Ten

Processor Arrays Compared to Pipelines for Cellular Image Operations

Robert P.W. Duin and Pieter P. Jonker

*Pattern Recognition Group, Department of Applied Physics,
Delft University of Technology, The Netherlands*

ABSTRACT

Processor arrays and pipelines are compared as parallel architectures for image processing. This is done on the basis of almost identical processing elements. In this way architectural differences can be studied most clearly. Quantitative and qualitative analyses show that pipelines tend to be smaller and slower, but may be extended with hardware options hard to realize for a processor array. Pipelines have a larger flexibility in addressing and particularly in image size. The position of linear processor arrays is in this context somewhere between pipelines and two-dimensional processor arrays.

1 INTRODUCTION

An image processing task can be split up into a series of operations that may influence all bits of all pixels of a number of images. If one is interested in designing hardware architectures that speed up or simplify the computational task then a number of parallel architectures may be considered like image parallel, pixel parallel, bit parallel and instruction parallel. Two or more of these types of parallelism may be combined. Some of them can be extended with certain types of hardwiring that make them very well suited for processing data of the image format. This especially holds for the pixel parallel and the instruction parallel architectures. They are discussed and compared in this chapter on the basis of some general features.

In Fig. 1 the fundamental difference between these two architectures is illustrated. Figure 1a shows the image processing task: a stream of pixels (an image) has to be processed by a series of instructions. In the pixel parallel approach, Fig. 1b, this is done by a *processor array* (PA) of identical *processor*

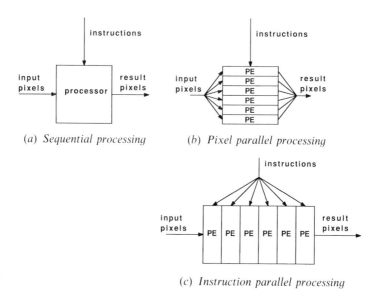

(a) Sequential processing   (b) Pixel parallel processing

(c) Instruction parallel processing

Fig. 1. The principles of pixel parallel and instruction parallel image processing.

elements (PEs), running the same program (SIMD architecture) by the following steps:

(1) load the input pixels in the PEs of the PA.
(2) load and execute a stream of instructions constituting the operation to be performed.

In the instruction parallel approach the steps are made in a different order as here a stream of pixels is passing a series of PEs (a *pipeline* (PL)), each performing the next instruction (Fig. 1c):

(1) load all instructions into all PEs.
(2) process a stream of pixels.

For both architectures it is assumed for the moment that all pixels are processed by the same set of instructions.

We will now compare these two types of architecture on the basis of an analysis of speed, hardware complexity and flexibility. In order to make this comparison as fair as possible almost identical PEs will be assumed for both, the PA and the PL: 1-bit cellular processors, operating in a $3 * 3$ environment either on 1-bit images or on a grey value image in a bit serial fashion. In Section 2 the features of this hypothetical PE are considered. In Sections 3 and 4 the possibilities are discussed of realising this PE in a processor array, respectively a pipeline configuration. As the resulting PA and PL are thereby made as similar as possible in image processing capabilities, their essential differences come out most strongly. This is illustrated in Section 5 by a quantitative example. In Section 6 the results are summarized and discussed in a more qualitative way, together with other features of PAs and PLs.

2 THE PROCESSING ELEMENT FOR CELLULAR OPERATIONS

We will consider here cellular operations on 2-D images represented on a square grid. It will be assumed that the pixels are to be treated in an 8-connected way. These choices are not essential, but they give a framework for the discussions. In Fig. 2 the eight neighbouring pixels are shown, that together with the central pixel are used for computing a new central pixel value. These computations have to be carried out over all pixels in an image. In principle any function of the following form is possible:

$$x'_0 = f(x_0, x_1, x_2, x_3, x_4, x_5, x_6, x_7, x_8)$$

in which x_0 is the central pixel, x'_0 is its new value and x_1–x_8 are the eight neighbour values. In order to be able to combine results from different images of from several operations on the same image, also functions like:

$$x'_0 = f(x_0, y_0)$$

have to be supported, in which y_0 is the pixel in another image that corresponds to x_0.

A pixel value x may have any (non-negative) value. For computational feasibility its accuracy has to be restricted to, say, B bits. In order to keep the pixel interconnection scheme simple and the accuracy flexible, we will consider only single bit, or bit-serial connections. The possibility of using more bits for pixel input and output is by this assumption not affected. The

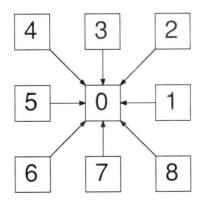

Fig. 2. A 3 * 3 cell of neighbouring pixels in an image.

processor that computes the results needs to have access to some memory for storing and retrieving pixels of other bitplanes that are results of previous operations or belong to other images. The following inputs and outputs can now be distinguished for the PE (see Fig. 3):

8 one-bit inputs from the neighbouring pixels;
1 one-bit input from some image memory containing the central pixel;
1 one-bit input from some image memory containing the value of the corresponding central pixel of another image;
1 carry input bit for the case that results of different bitplanes have to be combined;
1 one-bit output for storing the result value into the memory;
1 one-bit output for showing a pixel value (not necessarily identical to the result value) to the neighbours;
1 carry output bit.

Carry input and output are distinguished from the memory in order to gain flexibility. The output pixel value to be shown to the neighbours may be identical to the computed result, but also to the original input value, or even to some other value. This *general PE* has an 11-bit input and a 3-bit output. It is assumed to be *fully programmable* which implies that its instruction set is such that for all 11-bit input values any 3-bit output value can be specified. We will call such an instruction a *basic operation*. If the PE is not fully programmable a basic operation takes a number of instructions instead of just one for producing the same result. Each instruction may take one or more processing cycles, depending on the hardware. If the PE is *generally programmable* all basic operations can be performed in a finite number of instructions. Below some examples of operations will be discussed for this PE, together with an estimate of the number of basic operations needed for computing one result pixel. This illustrates the possibilities and limitations of cellular image processing.

Cellular logic operations. The computation of the hit-or-miss transform with a

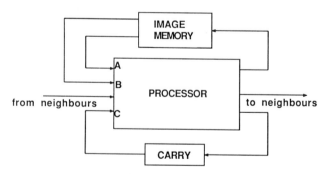

Fig. 3. A general processing element for cellular image operations.

3 * 3 structuring element takes for the one bit case just one basic operation as all necessary information can be shown on the inputs simultaneously.

*3 * 3 Convolution.* Let us assume that pixel values and weights have a B-bit accuracy. Then it takes B steps to show the neighbourhood pixel values to the PE. In each of these steps the 9 input bits have to be combined with the corresponding B bits of the weights. Thereby $B^2\log(9)$ basic operations are needed at least as the output bits are produced serially.

Dyadic operations. For the combination of two images by addition, subtraction, logical operations, etcetera., the neighbourhood connections are not needed. By using just the two inputs from the memory and the carry bit, in B steps B-bit results are computed. For some operations, results can not be computed bit serial, like for multiplication. In this case at least B^2 basic operations are needed.

Table-look-up. All monadic grey value pixel operations (e.g. adding a constant, taking the logarithm, shifting the pixel value two bits down) can be realized by table-look-up. However, this is not a simple task at all with the proposed PE. It takes at least as many processing steps as there are entries in the table, multiplied by the number of bits by which the table values are represented. In case of B bits/pixel on input and output this takes at least 2^BB basic operations.

The general PE as defined here is focused to cellular operations in a 3 * 3 environment. Operations in larger neighbourhoods have to be built up by series of basic operations. For global operations like a Fourier transform of a complete image this PE is not suited. Also image rotation is not easily implemented. Object dependent operations can be realised by using one of the input bits for labelling the area's in the image that have to be processed.

In order to set conditions on the image boundary special features have to be added, dependent on the hardware architecture. A number of limitations for the general PE may be removed by adding other hardware features. One is the inclusion of registers for accumulating input bits before processing by which the instruction can depend on previous input bits. Result bits may be accumulated in these registers as well, offering the possibility of direct recursion. Such a register will increase the power of the PE considerably. Another feature is the availability of the address of the pixel to be processed, which would allow for certain address dependent operations, especially if it can be used for addressing the PE local memory (data dependent addressing). These features are at this point excluded from the general PE in order to avoid unnecessary complications in the comparison of the two architectures.

3 PROCESSOR ARRAYS

In this Section processor arrays will be described with PEs similar to the ones defined in the previous section. In Fig. 4 an 8-connected interconnection

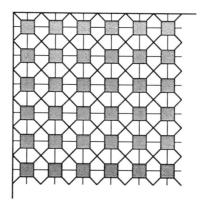

Fig. 4. An 8-connected processor array network.

scheme is shown between the processor elements. On each node a processor element is available, together with a local memory containing the pixel values. All processing elements are identical and run the same program. An external controller feeds all PEs simultaneously with the program instructions. At the edges of the processor array special hardware is available that takes care of setting the boundary conditions.

The hardware as described above may be simplified in one or more of the following ways:

4-connected processors instead of 8-connected processors;
serial interprocessor connection instead of parallel interprocessor connection (communication with one processor at a time);
carry bit output equal to neighbour output;
neighbour output equal to result;
computation of the two or three output bits in a serial way instead of a parallel way;
restrictions on the ways the input bits may be logically combined to output values (not fully programmable).

All these simplifications are used in the various processor arrays that have been constructed or proposed, e.g. see Preston and Duff [1] and Fountain [4, 5]. Only the last of these simplifications is in all cases really necessary: an 11-bit input can take on 2048 different states, which requires for full programmability a $2048 * 3$ (the number of output bits) bit wide program path to all processors in order to be able to set a new instruction in each programming step. This is completely out of the question. The processors have thereby to be restricted in their possibilities considerably. The PEs become thereby less powerful than the general PE described in Section 2. If this is done carefully most of the desired possibilities for image processing algorithms can be kept, but a considerable part of the basic operations can only be realized in a number of processing steps. This non-full-programmability is an important disadvantage of processor arrays.

The present state of technology forces the processors to be very simple if one wants to integrate thousands of them in a single machine. For that reason most nowadays PAs lack the possibility of data dependent (instead of programmatic) memory addressing and address dependent instructions as discussed in Section 2. This would simplify, for instance, the table-look-up operations considerably. Features that are available in most processor arrays are the execution of object dependent operations and the availability of programmatic feedback. For the execution of an instruction for the object pixels only it is necessary that certain processors, say those with a '1' in some register perform the THEN clause of an IF statement, while the other pixels perform the ELSE clause. Programmatic feedback implies that the result of one instruction, e.g. a pixel count, influences, again by a conditional statement in the PA controller, the execution of following instructions.

In an image processing machine where all pixels in an image are treated simultaneously it is not possible to program recursive operations. Results are just available in the following pass of an algorithm and not in the present one. For one and two pass recursive algorithms this may imply that a sequential processor is finished after two passes through the image, while the processor array may need several hundreds of steps. This is the case, for example, if some image boundary value has to be propagated over large parts of the image. On account of the large number of PEs a processor array is for this operation still much faster than a sequential processor. However, in relation to the amount of hardware a processor array is for these operations relatively inefficient.

The size of a processor array may be smaller than the size of the actual images to be processed. This may be caused by the fact that images tend to grow larger and larger. It can also be done more intentionally for economic reasons. There are several ways in which a PA can scan a larger image, in software as well as in hardware. Two essentially different ways of mapping an image of M pixels on a smaller array of m PEs are the so called window mapping and the crinkle mapping, also called pyramidal mapping, see Fountain et al. [3] and Pass [7].

In the crinkling method the pixels in subimages of $\lceil M/m \rceil$ pixels are mapped entirely on one single PE. Each PE takes care of computing results for all pixels in its subimage. As neighbouring pixels are stored in the same PE (with an exception for the subimage boundaries), the PE-PE interaction is minimized. Pass [7] calls this an advantage, however, we will emphasize strongly here the disadvantage that the special PA configuration is hardly used in this case. To be more specific, it is in this configuration impossible to reach all neighbour pixels simultaneously. As the corresponding pixel values are usually within the same memory of one PE they have to be treated sequentially, possibly resulting in decrease in processing speed by a factor 8.

The processing in the crinkling mapping method is done in a way that resembles the image parallel type of architectures. It speeds up processing not more than proportional to the number of PEs. However, two advantages can be noticed. First, certain types of large neighbourhood operations may be faster, even with a smaller number of PEs, compared to the case of window mapping, as here the number of pixel shifts is smaller. Secondly, it does not have the complicated window boundary problem (see below).

In the case of scanning an image using window mapping the image is divided into windows of the size of the processor array. Corresponding pixels in windows are piled up into the PE memory. In this technique the principle of neighbouring PEs processing neighbouring pixels is preserved for pixels inside a window. The processing of the window boundary is a rather complicated problem. Values of pixels neighbouring the actual position of the PA in the image have to be made available to the edge pixels in the PA. This may be done by special edge hardware, or by a software shift of these values to the right position in the array followed by a special edge processing pass. The overhead caused by this is expressed by a factorial overhead A_1. This means that if the image has M pixels and the PA has m processors ($m < M$), the processing time is $\lceil M/m \rceil * A_1$ times the time needed for processing an image with $m = M$. The value of A_1 depends upon the available shift and addressing features. Processor arrays that are designed for using hardware scanning may have an almost neglectable overhead. For other ones this overhead can be much larger. A complete software solution may show overheads of larger than 100 as shown by Buurman [14].

As explained, the PE of a processor array is often not fully programmable. This means that for most basic operations more than one instruction is needed. Processing each instruction takes a number of cycles for loading data from memory, loading the desired instruction and for storing the final result. Let A_2 be the average number of cycles that is needed for a basic operation. The total processing time needed by a PA with m processors for processing N basic operations on an image of M pixels of B bits is now given by:

$$t_{PA} = A_1 * A_2 * \lceil M/m \rceil * B * N * t_c \qquad (1)$$

in which t_c is the time needed for processing one cycle.

At the moment the use of linear processor arrays is investigated on several places, see Fountain [4, 5]. They consist of a one-dimensional array of m PEs that scans a larger image. Some of them scan in one direction, others scan in two directions. For the first class one of the image sizes is determined by the array size. The second class is more flexible and may scan images of any size. In Fig. 5 the configuration of such a linear array is shown. One advantage of a linear processor array over a two-dimensional processor array is that it can be made to be more flexible: variable image size, and a smaller scanning overhead A_1. A second advantage is that it is possible to use more powerful PEs as fewer have to be integrated in the system. Operations will thereby need less instructions: smaller A_2. In order to perform basic operations in just one instruction 9 pixels should be made available simultaneously from the PE memories, see Fig. 5. This requires some kind of quadro-ported memory access as the memory should also be accessible from the data bus. This is a

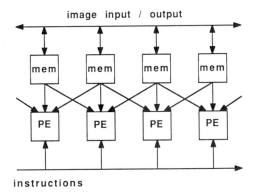

image input / output

instructions

Fig. 5. A linear processor array configuration.

heavy hardware demand. The disadvantage is of course that because of the fewer PEs the amount of parallelism is reduced.

4 PIPELINES

In this Section we will restrict ourselves to the use of pipelines for image processing. For a more general discussion on the basic arguments for using pipelines we refer to Kung [17].

In a pipeline a number of instructions are performed in parallel by a series of processors on a sequence of pixels, see Fig. 6. Generally these processors are different, have different hardware and run different instructions. After each processing step the addresses are updated and the pixels in the pipe are shifted one position. The instructions may be dyadic (on two streams of input pixels), monadic (on one stream of pixels) or windowed. In the last case a shift register inside the processor has to keep a complete neighbourhood available for processing, see Fig. 7.

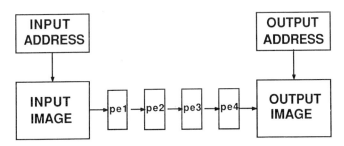

Fig. 6. A pipeline configuration.

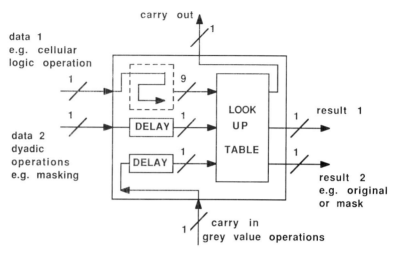

Fig. 7. A processing element for a pipeline.

In order to make pipelines more powerful they are often combined with the bit-parallel concept. Their hardware may be 8 or 16 bits wide. If the pixels have B bits and the pipeline is b bits wide and if $B > b$ then processing of all B bitplanes may take at least $\lceil B/b \rceil$ passes through the image. This is only possible if the hardware is specially prepared for this, using an image wide memory for carry bits. Usually $B \leqslant b$.

In most pipelines the PEs have different hardware. In that case the architecture of each PE is focused to a particular set of image operations. In order to keep such a pipelined processor as flexible as possible the interconnection scheme has to be made reconfigurable. By this the order of the processors can be changed or some of them can be left out for a certain operation.

It is also wise to have at least one very generally programmable processor unit in the pipeline. This may slow down the process when it is used, but it keeps the range of operations as wide as possible.

In contrast to the processor array it is in a pipelined processor possible to create recursiveness for neighbourhood operations, but this is not simple. For realization the result of the operation should replace the original pixel in the shift register before the next neighbourhood is processed. This will slow down the process as processing steps within the recursive operation can not overlap.

A feature that is very standard in the sequential general purpose processors, and that is hard to realize in PAs is the mixture of data and addresses. In a PL architecture this is possible, but not always available. It is needed for the computation of histograms, for table-look-up, for edge following (e.g. by data dependent addressing of the input image), etc.

In this study we assume the PEs to be identical, for reasons of comparison and because we are interested in investigating the principle of pipelining. The general PE discussed in Section 2 can very well be used in a pipeline. A point to note is that these PEs have no local data memory in a pipeline configuration. This implies that intermediate results and image planes with object masks have to be passed through the PEs in a separate pixel stream. Such a stream may be passed unchanged: output equals input. The PEs may or may not be loaded with different instructions. If they are equal this corresponds to n iterations of the instruction over the image if there are n PEs in the pipe.

Adapted to the PL architecture a PE may look as shown in Fig. 7. The internal shift register takes care of creating a $3 * 3$ neighbourhood. By using table-look-up with $2^{11} = 2,048$ entries with a 3-bit outcome it can be made fully programmable. Thereby the operational overhead as defined in the case of processor arrays does not exist here: $A_2 = 1$. When desired a recursive pipe like described above may be used instead of the non-recursive one (in that case also the non-recursive option should stay available). Realised on the lowest level of instructions recursiveness does not slow down the computational speed. If a number of PEs take care of a number of iterations of the same transformation their tables are identical. For different transformations, tables are different. Before the pipe is started the tables of the PEs have to be loaded, resulting in an additional overhead A_3. This overhead is proportional to the number of PEs to be loaded. Frequently used tables may be stored in ROM if the overhead of this loading process can not be neglected. If two tables are used loading may be done concurrent to processing, resulting in $A_3 = 0$.

In Fig. 8 an 8-bit wide pipeline configuration is given with 4 PEs in each bit stream. Carry bit connections enable grey level processing. For synchronisation higher bitplanes have to be delayed. The bit significance has to be reversed in case of operations that need downward passing of carry bits.

The total time that is needed for processing an operation of N instructions over an image of M pixels of B bits by a b-bit wide pipeline of n processors

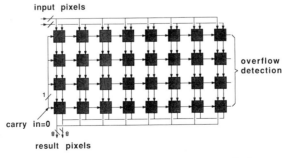

Fig. 8. A pipeline with 8 parallel series of PEs.

can now be written as:

$$t_{PL} = \lceil N/n \rceil * M * \lceil B/b \rceil * t_c + A_3 * n * t_c \qquad (2)$$

t_c is the time needed for a single processing step. Usually the last term can be neglected.

There are several pipelined processors produced commercially that (can) use a series of identical cellular PEs similar to the one defined here (see also Preston and Duff [1]), e.g. the Cytocomputer (Sternberg [15]), the SNAP board of Datacubes' MaxVideo System and the Leitz TAS system. These processors are non-recursive. An example of a recursive pipelined cellular processor is described in the next section.

5 A CASE STUDY

In this Section the concepts of the PA and of the PL are compared on the basis of cellular image processing. We will use for that purpose the CLIP4 processor array, see Duff [2], and a cellular pipelined architecture under design by the authors in cooperation with others, based on the DIP pipelined image processor, see Gerritsen [10].

The CLIP4 is a processor array with 8-connected one-bit processors. The values shown by the neighbours are combined (by masking and or-ing) together with the carry-bit and the B-register (typically the pixel value of another bit-plane or of another image) to one input of the processor. The A-input is the value of the pixel under consideration. There are two outputs, one is the result value to be stored in the memory, the other is the value shown to the neighbours and simultaneously the carry bit in case of grey value operations. See Fig. 9, in which some connections needed for operating the processor in the 'binary column arithmetic mode' are not shown.

The binary processor (2 bits in, 2 bits out) is fully programmable, for which 8 input control bits are needed. Together with the 8 bits necessary for masking the neighbour connections and two bits for enabling B and C this yields 18 control bits to be set for each processing step. Within the PA concept they are identical for all processors.

A CLIP4 processing step consists of loading the registers A and B, loading the instruction, processing and storage of the result. This corresponds to what we have called an instruction in this paper. Such an instruction needs about 25 CLIP4 processing cycles. The cycle time of the most recent version of the CLIP4 chip is 400 ns.

In comparing the CLIP4 PE with the general PE as given in Fig. 3 it can be concluded that the CLIP4 PE, including the neighbour relations is not fully programmable, as that would require much more control bits. However, the selection that has been made here is such that most cellular logic operations like erosion, dilation, contour detection, etc., need just one processing step. An important exception is the skeletonisation, which needs many more steps as several checks have to be made in relation to the connectivity, e.g. the

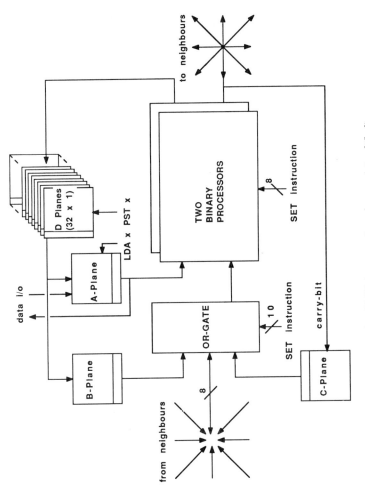

Fig. 9. The CLIPA processing element (simplified).

algorithm by Arcelli et al. [6] needs 16 steps for each iteration. Using the carry bit, dyadic grey value operations are possible. However, grey value table-look-up is difficult as in any PA.

A special feature of the CLIP4 is the "free propagation". In this mode the whole array acts as a combinatorial circuit. After it is stabilized the machine takes again its synchronized mode. By this feature some algorithms that would need otherwise a number of iterations over the whole array can now be processed by a single free propagation. This mode replaces some recursive operations in other architectures. However, it only operates in one bitplane at a time.

The CLIP4 system as it is designed by University College, London, has a $96 * 96$ processor array, with 32 bits of memory for each processor, see Duff [2], or Duff and Preston [1]. A scanning version, the CLIP4S has a $512 * 4$ array that performs a one-dimensional hardware scan over a $512 * 512$ image, see Fountain et al. [3]. The overhead for hardware scanning using the CLIP4 is estimated by Buurman [14] at a factor 4. A commercial version of the CLIP4 system is manufactured by Stonefield Electronics Ltd. This system uses the same CLIP4 chips, but adds an external 2048 bit of memory to each processor. A software scanning system is available. The overhead of this system, as measured by Buurman [14] varies from $A_1 = 3$ for complicated operations to $A_1 = 250$ for 1-bit operations in a $3 * 3$ neighbourhood that can be performed in a single instruction.

For the CLIP4 estimates for the constants in (1) can now be substituted. The hardware scanning overhead A_1 is about 4 (Buurman [14]). The number of cycles A_2 needed for a simple basic operation is about 25. However, for some operations, like the skeleton many more instructions per iteration are needed as indicated above. It depends completely on the algorithm and on the application how far this influences the total system performance. For the moment we will neglect the effect of the free propagation as well as the fact that some operations like the skeleton need more than one instruction per operation. We intend to make estimates of A_2 based on a large set of operations in the future.

The time needed for processing N basic operations over M pixels of B bits using a processor array of m CLIP4 chips is now given by:

$$t_{PA} = 100 * \lceil M/m \rceil * B * N * t_c \tag{3}$$

Note that this is a hypothetical result, as neither the CLIP4 nor the CLIP4S can scan images of an arbitrary size.

A VLSI design for a pipelined version of the general PE is under development, see Jonker and Duin [12] and Kraaijveld et al. [13]. It is based on earlier developments by Gerritsen and Aardema [8] and Boekamp et al. [11]. The chip, called Cellular Logic Processor (CLP) will consist of one PE, suitable for pipelining. It includes a recursive pipe as well as a non-recursive one. The tables are realized in a Writable Logic Array, a downloadable PLA.

Table look-up can be expressed as a completely specified logic function

$x'_0 = f(X_n)$ if $x'_0 \in \{0, 1\}$ and X_n is the boolean input vector with length n and $x_i \in \{0, 1\}$. This function may be reduced using some logic minimisation algorithm yielding a reduced logic function $x'_0 = g(X_n)$ with $x_i \in \{0, 1, 2\}$ in which 2 is the don't care value. In this way a table with 2^n entries is reduced to a set of m product terms or m structuring elements $(m \ll 2^n)$.

In this way significantly less terms have to be loaded than by using RAM tables. Table loading can be done concurrent to processing, so $A_3 = 0$. All basic operations can be realised in one instruction. This also holds for the recursive operations. Gerritsen [10] has shown that using these operations one skeleton step (a conditional erosion over an entire image) can be done in one basic operation. In the recursive pipeline under discussion this takes just one instruction, using 26 product terms of the WLA instead of one non-recursive and three recursive tables with length 512 (2^{11}). A number of CLP-chips may be placed in parallel, for grey value operations, or in series for computing more instructions in one run, see Fig. 8. The cycle time for the chip will be about 100 ns. This equals the time needed for processing one instruction over one pixel. The processing time of the discussed pipelined architecture is given by:

$$t_{PL} = \lceil N/n \rceil * M * \lceil B/b \rceil * t_c \qquad (4)$$

This is, like (3), a hypothetical result as the chip discussed above does not exist yet.

In the following it is assumed that the technology dependent processing cycle time t_c is equal for both systems. The results (3) and (4) are compared in Table 1 for three image sizes. The average number of processing cycles per basic operation are given. (This is equal to the processing time divided by the cycle time t_c and the number of processing steps N). Three different processor array sizes are given as well as three pipelines of the above discussed chips configurations: just one chip, ten serial chips and eight parallel lines of ten

Table 1

The average number of processing cycles needed for one basic operation over a whole image for three PA and three PL configurations and for three image sizes

image size (M)	$32 * 32$	$128 * 128$	$512 * 512$
bits/pixel (B)	1	8	8
PA (CLIP4)			
$32 * 32$	25	13,000	200,000
$128 * 128$	25	200	13,000
$512 * 512$	25	200	200
PL(CLP)			
$1 * 1$	1,000	130,000	2,000,000
$1 * 10$	100	13,000	200,000
$8 * 20$	50	800	13,000

serial chips. Note that PAs that are larger than the image do not have to scan, so $A_1 = 1$ in (1).

From the table we see that a non-scanning PA is always superior. However, if scanning is necessary, 10 pipelined PEs are as powerful as a $32 * 32$ PA and 160 pipelined PEs are as powerful as a $128 * 128$ PA. It, of course, completely depends upon the application whether these numbers can actually be reached. The relative power of the two types of PEs can also be derived more generally by dividing (3) by (4) and neglecting the $\lceil . \rceil$ operation:

$$t_{PA}/t_{PL} = n * b * 100/m \qquad (5)$$

which says that one PL element may be as powerful as 100 PA elements. It is interesting to compare this with the complexity of the chips. The CLIP4 chip has 8 PEs on board and is realized with 3000 transistors. The CLP chip has just one (pipelined) PE and needs about 30,000 transistors (which includes the writable logic array). The factor 100 is thereby paid by a much higher chip density.

It is realised by the authors that the value of the given example is limited. It mainly illustrates the difference in computational power of the two architectures. How far the given numbers can actually be reached depend on the application, the software support and hardware environment of the configuration.

6 DISCUSSION AND CONCLUSIONS

The above comparison is based on small neighbourhood operations. If one is interested in image processing algorithms that consist of more global types of operation, the presented discussions are of limited use. The discussed pipeline can only treat larger neighbourhoods in an iterative way. Processor arrays with a one to one pixel-processor relation are less suitable for addressing distant pixels then PAs with the crinkling type of pixel mapping. Duff [16] has presented some interesting thoughts on the evaluation of architectures for image processing based on the number of PEs, their internal complexity and the complexity of the interconnection scheme. This should be brought in relation to the different goals of the various levels of image processing, of which only the lowest level is considered in this paper.

A pipeline can be characterized as a set of processors that operates on a stream of pixels using instructions that have been loaded before. A processor array can be characterized as a set of processors that operates on a set of pixels that have been loaded before using a stream of instructions, see Fig. 1. The processor array thereby needs an additional load and store of the image. The pipeline needs an additional loading and storage of instructions. As there are less instructions than pixels, the overhead of loading and storing them before is smaller. As the instructions need wider bit paths than pixels, it is better to have a stream of pixels than of a stream of instructions. Both arguments plead for the pipeline and against the processor array. This has been illustrated in this chapter.

Besides, images are usually scanned, transported, stored and displayed in a pixel-sequential way. This is in line with the nature of the pipeline concept and conflicts with the processor array concept. The sequential to parallel conversion of pixel data takes thereby additional provisions.

It has been explained how a pipeline can be constructed with PEs that are similar to the PEs of a PA. An important difference between the resulting PL and PA is the impossibility for a PA to construct fully programmable PEs in which simultaneously the input from all neighbouring pixels are used as that requires the input of a $2048*3$ bit instruction in each processing cycle. Another difference is that image data is fed from outside to the PL, while in a PA the image data is mapped in one way or another on the PEs. A PL can thereby treat easily images of arbitrary size. For the PA two mapping methods are discussed. In contrast to the crinkle mapping, the window mapping has the advantage that neighbouring pixels are mapped on neighbouring processors, preserving the possibility of parallel access. However, scanning a window over an image generates a large overhead. These two differences prove that in an example where two implementations are considered a PE in the PL configuration effectively processes two orders of magnitude more pixels per second than in the PA configuration. It needs further research to evaluate this conclusion for other PA and PL designs and to determine the algorithmic dependency of the figures.

An additional advantage of the PL is that it can easily be extended with other processing hardware for operations that are hard to realize otherwise (like pixel table-look-up for our PE).

In considering linear processor arrays, some of the above arguments against processing arrays in general have to be reconsidered. First, as the number of PEs in a linear array is small, a much more powerful design can be used. This may result, in our terminology, into PEs that have an instruction set that is much closer to the set of basic operations. This can only be reached completely if the instruction set is table controlled like in the discussed pipeline version of the PE. Second, as noticed before, it is for small, linear arrays much more feasible to include shift and addressing options that minimise the amount of scanning overhead. The PA-PEs may thereby become almost as powerful as the PL-PEs. See Basille et al. [18] for a further discussion on the applicability of linear arrays.

What remains are two differences, an algorithmic one and an architectural one. In a pipeline the pixel loop encloses the more inner instruction loop. In a processor array first the pixels are treated for one instruction and then all pixels are treated for the next instruction (for the linear PA this holds only logically). This may make a difference if one wants to use the final results of some pixels before addressing other pixels (possibility of result dependent addressing in a pipeline) or if one wants to use the result on the whole image in deciding what the next instruction should be (feedback possibility in controlling a PA). The hardware difference is the way the neighbour interaction is realised: by a shift register for each PE (PL) or by a quadro-ported pixel memory (PA).

Gerritsen [9] has stated that the PA is the most promising basis for future developments in architectures for image processing. Our conclusion from the comparison of PLs and PAs for cellular operations is that if the PA is smaller than the image size, a PL might be constructed that yields the same performance. As the PL has additional advantages (easier I/O and inclusion of other special purpose processing hardware) it may be preferred for certain applications. However, if one demands the fastest solution that is possible the answer is still for many image processing applications: build a PA of the desired size.

7 ACKNOWLEDGEMENT

This research was supported by the Netherlands Organisation for the Advancement of Pure Research (Z.W.O.).

REFERENCES

[1] K. Preston Jr. and M.J.B. Duff. (1984). *Modern Cellular Automata*. Plenum Press, New York.
[2] M.J.B. Duff. (1982). CLIP4, in: K.S. Fu, and T. Ichikawa (eds.), *Special Computer Architectures for Pattern Processing*, CRC Press, Inc., Boca Raton, Florida, USA, pp. 65–86.
[3] T.J. Fountain, H. Postranecky, and G.K. Shaw. (1987). The CLIP4S System, *Pattern Recognition Letters*, vol. 5, no. 1, January 1987, pp. 41–47.
[4] T.J. Fountain. (1985). A review of SIMD Architectures, in: J. Kittler and M.J.B. Duff (eds.), *Image Processing System Architectures*, Research Study Press, Letchworth, England, pp. 3–22.
[5] T.J. Fountain. (1986). Array Architectures for Iconical and Symbolic Processing, *Proc. of the 8th Int. Conf. on Pattern Recognition*, Paris, France, October 1986, pp. 24–33.
[6] C. Arcelli, L. Cordella, and S. Levialdi. (1975). Parallel thinning of binary pictures, *Electronic Letters* 11, 1975, pp. 148–149.
[7] S. Pass. (1985). The GRID Parallel Computer System, in: J. Kittler and M.J.B. Duff (eds.), *Image Processing System Architectures*, Research Study Press, Letchworth, England, pp. 23–35.
[8] F.A. Gerritsen and L.G. Aardema. (1981). Design and Use of DIP-1: A Fast, Flexible and Dynamically Microprogrammable Pipelined Image Processor, *Pattern Recognition*, vol. 14, 1981, pp. 319–330.
[9] F.A. Gerritsen. (1983). A Comparison of the CLIP4, DAP and MPP Processor-Array Implementations, in: M.J.B. Duff (ed.), *Computing Structures for Image Processing*, Academic Press, London, pp. 15–30.
[10] F.A. Gerritsen. (1981). Design and Implementation of the Delft Image Processor DIP-1, Ph.D. Thesis, Dept. of Applied Physics, Delft Univ. of Technology.
[11] R. Boekamp, F.C.A. Groen, F.A. Gerritsen, and R.J. van Munster. (1986). Design

and Implementation of a Cellular-Logic VME Processor Board, in: M.J.B. Duff, H.J. Siegel and F.J. Corbett (eds.), *Architectures and Algorithms for Digital Image Processing*, Proc. SPIE 596, pp. 41–45.

[12] P.P. Jonker and R.P.W. Duin. (1985). Considerations on a VLSI Architecture for Cellular Logic Operations, *Proc. IEEE Comp. Soc. Workshop on Comp. Architecture for Pattern Analysis and Image Database Management*, Miami Beach, Florida, USA, Nov. 1985, pp. 453–462.

[13] M.A. Kraaijveld, P.P. Jonker, R. Nouta, and R.P.W. Duin. (1986). The VLSI Realisation of a Binary-Image Processor, in I.T. Young, J. Biemond, R.P.W. Duin, J.J. Gerbrands (eds.), *Signal Processing III, Theories and Applications*, North Holland, Amsterdam, pp. 1231–1234.

[14] J. Buurman. (1987). Scanning Algorithms for the CLIP4 Processor Array, Thesis, Faculty of Applied Physics, Delft Univ. of Technology.

[15] S.R. Sternberg. (1978). Cytocomputer real-time pattern recognition, *Proc. 8th Auto. Imagery Pattern Recog. Symp.*, pp. 205–214.

[16] M.J.B. Duff. (1986). Complexity, in: M.J.B. Duff (ed.), *Intermediate level Image Processing*, Academic Press, London, pp. 307–314.

[17] H.T. Kung. (1982). Why Systolic Architectures, *Computer*, 15, 1982, pp. 37–46.

[18] J.-L. Basille, P. Dalle, and S. Castan. (1986). Iconic and symbolic use of a line processor in multilevel structures, in: M.J.B. Duff (ed.), *Intermediate level Image Processing*, Academic Press, London, 1986, pp. 231–241.

Chapter Eleven

Designing Memories for Cellular Processors

A. Mérigot

Institut d'Electronique Fondamentale, Université Paris Sud,
91405 Orsay Cedex, France

1 INTRODUCTION

Memory design has become one of the more crucial points in the organization of a conventional computer. A way to bypass memory size limitation, is the design of a unified multi media memory to offer a large virtual memory with a limited hardware and performance cost. To bypass limitations in the memory access time, RISC computers [1] aim at a performance improvement by means of a common microcode and program memory, and of a carefully designed hierarchy of memories (registers, cache, main memory, mass memory).

Cellular arrays, in the opposite way, generally rely on the same memory model: a single port, externally controlled, monolithic memory, coupled with special purpose registers. In this paper, we present solutions to improve the model. The first part describes the present models, and points out their limits. The second part presents the organization of a cellular processor with an hybrid memory, and algorithms than can take advantage of this feature. The third part proposes a way to implement an efficient indirect access to this memory.

2 APPROACHES IN THE DESIGN OF A CELLULAR PROCESSOR'S MEMORY

Cellular arrays are externally controlled processors, and accordingly, their memory is primarily used to store data. In most cases, the memory can only be addressed by the external control system. Two main techniques are used for the actual realization of the memory: using external standard memory chips, or integrating the memory on the chip. We shall discuss advantages and drawbacks of these choices.

MULTICOMPUTER VISION
ISBN 0-12-444818-6

2.1 Externally realized memory

This is the most frequently used method to realize a cellular array memory. Actually, it is the case in MPP [2], CLIP [3], DAP [4], Connection Machine [5]. The main advantages are the large capacity available from standard memory chips, and their low cost. This capacity ranges at the present time from 64 kbits to 256 kbits for static, byte organized memories. Accordingly, it is possible to get thousands of bits for up to 8 processing elements with a single memory chip.

On the other hand, this method presents several drawbacks:

(a) The access time of the memory will limit the performances of the machine.

(b) The access path between one processing element and the memory is limited to a unique bit, and thus one can only implement a one-address machine. This is a serious limitation in the execution of several basic operations, and it leads the designers of these machines to add special purpose hardware to bypass it. For instance, to perform a multiple operation with the classical bit serial algorithm, one must accumulate a properly shifted operand in an intermediate result. To accelerate the execution of this frequent operation, a variable length shift register is often used to directly recycle the intermediate results, whatever is the length of the operands [6].

(c) This technique is cost effective in terms of silicon area—if we except the special purpose operators—but it implies a large number of extra I/Os. Indeed, as the processors must directly access the memory, one needs one pin per processing element, and one memory chip for every 8 processing elements. Present integration scale would allow several hundreds of memoryless bit serial processing elements to be integrated in a single chip, but packaging technologies wouldn't. More, a largely integrated chip is useless at the board level: if we compare two methods to put a large number of chips, say N, on a board, one with a VLSI N PEs chip, and the other with LSI 8 PEs chips, the total number of chips is $N/8 + 1$ for the former solution, and $2N/8$ for the latter one. Accordingly, the best solution is to use 8 PEs chip, as a VLSI one would be much more complex to realize and presumably more expensive, and just would just divide by two the total number of chips on the board. Thereby, cellular machines with external memory chips don't scale well with integration improvements.

2.2 Using in-chip memory

In some cellular arrays, the memory is directly integrated in-chip. This is the case in the GAPP [7], PAPIA [8], and SPHINX [9]. The main drawback of this technique, is the important silicon area occupied by this memory that will tend to limit the integration scale on the chip. For instance, in SPHINX, the 128 bits memory represents roughly 50 percent of the processing element silicon area. Accordingly, either the memory will be limited to a small size, say 128 or 256 bits, or, for larger memory sizes, the number of integrated processing elements will be in inverse ratio to this size.

One advantage of this technique is the fast data access time, and consequently, the reduced instruction cycle. But more fundamentally, it is possible to tailor in-chip memories to specific needs. Examples of such customizations include providing a dual access to this memory, as is the case in SPHINX. With such a dual port memory, it is possible to perform a 2-arguments Read-Modify-Write within an instruction cycle time [10]. That can lead to a significant speedup in many basic operations, whilst providing an efficient instruction set for automatic optimized code generation. Indeed, the memory can be accessed in a way that directly simulates a special purpose piece of hardware, like a variable length shift register, a stack, etc. In SPHINX, to reduce the instruction length of this 3-address machine, and to make the control system simpler, this memory is accessed by means of a set of global pointers that are automatically incremented or decremented at the end of the instruction [10]. Another interesting customization is to allow a local addressing of the memory (see below). Many hardware tricks based on the physical characteristics of the memory are possible to fasten some basic operations: byte level memory to memory copy, byte level immediate write.

2.3 The ideal memory

None of the above solutions are fully satisfactory. We try to define the requirements of an ideal memory for a massively parallel machine.

(1) *Large memory space.* Though a limited 128 bits memory is sufficient for many basic Image processing operations, some situations require a much larger space. For example, large images folded over the array. A 1024 × 1024 image folded on a 128 × 128 array would completely saturate a 128 bits memory—even with 8 bits pixels; multiple images processing; image sequences; pixels coded with a large number of bits (32 bits floating points or more, multiband images, complex numbers); and peak memory requirements. This can happen when performing higher level vision tasks. For instance, the result of a segmentation algorithm can be to assign regions to individual pixels, and it should be possible to directly manipulate these root descriptors in the cellular machine, by means of message passing techniques. An example of a segmentation algorithm using message passing between root region descriptors can be founded in [11]. In that case, these root processors should store a large set of descriptors relative to that region (area,

shape, texture, etc.). Combined, these constraints lead to a memory of several kbits per processing element.

(2) *Flexible access.* A dual port memory seems to have interesting capabilities, especially for an optimized automatic code generation.

(3) *Indirect access.* Indirectly accessing the memory is useful either to implement lists of items, or to be able to use look up tables to compute a tabulated function. Many situations require a list processing when performing higher level vision tasks. An example can be found in [12], where an algorithm to perform a hierarchical manipulation of contours by means of a variable length list of end points manipulation is presented. More generally, lists are useful, in a high level process, to manipulate variable length descriptors such as chain codes, polygons, adjacent regions, and so on. This capability can also be necessary in a message passing strategy on a MIMD network to buffer transiting messages. Look up tables are a way to implement either complex mathematical functions or transitions functions in a cellular automation. We can notice that the constraints attached to these types of operations are quite different: look up tables requires large tables that can be global to all the processors, and lists manipulate local data of a generally much smaller size.

(4) *Fast access.*

(5) *Low cost realization.*

These different constraints are conflicting. Points (2), (3), and (4) would plead for an in chip memory realization, and points (1) and (5) for the use of standard memory chips.

A solution to conciliate different requirements would be to use in chip and off chip memories at the same time. The external memory would be used as an overflow storage for the internal memory, in the same way as a *virtual memory* for a minicomputer.

This dual memory should be as transparent as possible at the programming level, and the memory management should be done at run time by an intelligent controller that would perform the conversion between the logical addresses generated by a compiler and the real addresses. This conversion can be realized by a software routine, but, according to the control structure, can be accelerated by means of a standard microprocessor memory management unit.

As the external memory is just used to store data in case of a main memory overflow, its access does not need to be very fast. This should be taken into account to minimize IO cost.

Two ways to realize a virtual memory and algorithms to manipulate data will be presented below.

3 DIRECT ADDRESSING VIRTUAL MEMORY

We present in this Section a way to realize a virtual memory without indirect addressing capabilities on the external memory by the association of a processing elements chip, and of a standard memory chip.

3.1 Organization of the memory access

As the external memory is primarily intended for a low frequency virtual memory task, we tried to optimize its realization cost rather than its access time. Its cost depends on the number of extra IOs needed to access it, and on the number of memory chips attached to every processing element chip. A direct access solution (one IO pin per processing element, one memory chip for every 8 PE) was discarded because of its cost for largely integrated chips. Thus, we assume that the access to the memory is restricted to a single byte, and that we only use one memory chip. This way, the number of extra IO pins is limited, but we need a special purpose shift register to serially drive the data to their associated processing elements (Fig. 1). The access time for a N PEs chip is N/8. Most cellular arrays include a serial IO path to input or output images by means of monodimensional shift register. The pins associated to this path can be used to access the memory, provided there is a mechanism to avoid collisions when we concurrently try to use the memory and the IO path. This can be done in hardware by a duplication of the shift register, or by a software routine to temporarily shift the register content to the external memory when it is required.

To allow efficient list implementation, we assume that there is a local pointer that can address a location stored in the local memory. This pointer can be automatically incremented or decremented to allow an automatic access to bit serial variables. List operations frequently require a comparison between a local and a global value, for instance to perform an out of range test when traversing a list, and a fast initialization to a global value [14]. For

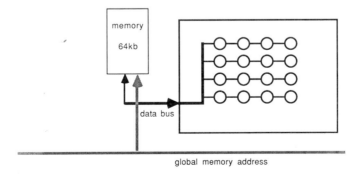

Fig. 1. Direct access virtual memory organization.

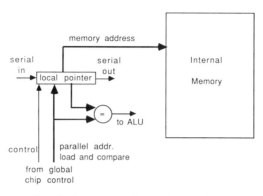

Fig. 2. Processing element local pointer.

that reason, we assume that it is possible to perform either of these functions in one cycle, the global value being part of the instruction. These functions can both be realized with a limited hardware cost.

A schematic of the local memory and of the associated pointer is presented in Fig. 2.

3.2 List manipulation

We present in this Section algorithms to manipulate lists of items with the previous operators. We use the following notations:

l is the maximum length of the lists.
s is the size of the allocated memory space to hold the list.
k is the time to access a bit stored in the external memory.
n is the number of bits of an item, and m the number of bits required to code its address.

We have chosen a representative set of list manipulation routines: extracting the first item of a list, list traversal, extracting an item inside a list.

Several representations can be used to store lists: a variable length monodimensional array with the head of the list at location 0 (connected array) or at any location (folded array), or a random set of items including an explicit pointer to the next element (pointer representation). We will only present here outlines of the algorithms, and results concerning the execution time for internally stored lists as well as externally stored ones.

We will assume an architecture close to the SPHINX one [9], but we will always ignore the constant processing time which is highly dependant on the actual instruction set. We will assume that it is possible to perform a global logical OR of a special purpose register of the different PEs of the array, and use it to test a premature completion of the list processing operation in order to avoid useless operations. Anyway, we will give minimum and maximum execution times. We will focus on the access time and model the element processing with a n bits copy to a specific memory location. A complete coding of the algorithms can be found in [14].

3.2.1 Extracting the first item of a list

When the list is stored internally, whatever its representation, then the execution time is small, thanks to the local pointer, and depends on the exact size of the different variables. The algorithms are straightforward.

For an externally stored list, with the connected array representation, we can immediately access the data, but we must scan the memory up to the end of the list to repack the array. For the folded array and pointer representations, this repacking is not necessary, but in the worst case the complete zone must be traversed.

	connected array	folded array	pointer
internal	n	$n + m$	$n + m$
external	$2knl$	kn (min)	kn (min)
		kns (max)	kns (max)

3.2.2 B-list traversal

A connected array internal list traversal is just a scan of the array. The number of steps, l, can be *a priori* determined, but we must use the local size to test the end of the list and stop further processing. With a folded array, one needs, besides, to check the frontiers of the allocated zone, and to reinitialize local pointers of the concerned PEs. Using the pointer representation is trivial.

With an external list, the connected array representation is straightforward to code. With a folded array, one needs a dual scan if the list is effectively folded. The pointer representation isn't really efficient as it may require a complete scan of the allocated zone to access every element.

	connected array	folded array	pointer
internal	$l(n + m)$	$l(n + m)$	$2ln$
external	kln	kln (min)	$2kln$ (min)
		$kn(s + l - 1)$ (max)	$knls$ (max)

3.2.3 Extracting an item inside a list

The main problem of this operation is to keep the list representation coherent after the item extraction.

When the list is in main memory, with a connected array representation, we systematically scan the memory, and enable the move operation when we reach the extract location. With a folded array, the technique is similar, but the scanning is performed by means of the local pointer, and with a unique pointer, we need to copy the data to move into a temporary location. Pointer representation allows a direct reconnection of the list after the extraction.

For an externally stored list, the connected array representation technique is unchanged. The folded array representation can be realized with a unique systematic memory sweep, even if the list is effectively folded. One needs to determine the list type first time, and to validate several active zones if necessary. The pointer representation isn't really efficient without indirect addressing capabilities, as it may imply two complete scans of the allocated area.

	connected array	folded array	pointer
internal	ln	$n(2l + m)$	$4m$
external	$2kln$	$2kln$ (min)	$2kln$ (min)
		$2kns$ (max)	$4kns$(max)

3.2.4 Conclusion

Using an external memory leads to algorithms that generally require a small number of scans of the allocated zone. The optimal representation is of the array type, but depends on the relative number of occurrences of the different operations. If the allocated zone is not much larger than the list length, the overhead for most operations is roughly equivalent to the access time of the external memory. The main problem is that coding of external operations tends to be tricky, and can't be efficiently deducted from generic internal list manipulation routines. Moreover, the former execution times assume that the compiler is smart enough to execute local operations during the idle periods of the transfer operations. Lastly, efficiently implementing look up tables is almost impossible.

4 INDIRECT ADDRESSING VIRTUAL MEMORY

Because of the previous model drawbacks, we tried to extend the indirect addressing capability to the external memory, with limited hardware and performances costs.

4.1 Organization of the access

A solution is presented in Fig. 3. To keep the IO pins and memory chip count small, we associate to every processor chip a unique memory chip. To perform indirect addressing on the memory, every chip must be able to generate an address for its companion memory chip. As we want to have indirect addressing capability, only one processing element can access the memory at any one time. Thus, as this chip is common to the different processing elements, the access must be serialized.

Special hardware is required to manage the sharing of the memory chip. We call it the External Memory Controller (EMC). It must take into account the exact memory access moment of the different PEs, and protect the data in the memory. For that reason, a specific memory zone (a page) will be allocated to every processing element. The PE will generate an address relative to that zone, and the EMC will have to make the conversion by using this relative address, and the identity of the accessing processor. The EMC will maintain a set of tables describing the memory. Several pages can be allocated to every chip, provided the instruction set can specify the actual number of the current one. The number of pages allocated to every PE can even be dynamically assigned, but it requires more complex processing capabilities for the EMC. Last, some pages can be common to all the PEs. This is useful to implement look up tables without memory waste, and with a reduced loading time.

As the access is serialized among the different processing elements, it is more efficient to perform a byte level memory access. Thus a common 8 bits tristate bus must be present in the chip. This fixes the external address length to a byte, and the size of a memory page to 256 bytes. The serialization and the mutual exclusion will be ensured by a fixed priority daisy chain-like mechanism. This daisy chain will select only one processor among the chip, and deselect it once the access has been performed. It will then select the next processor among a set of active processors. If the memory needs to be

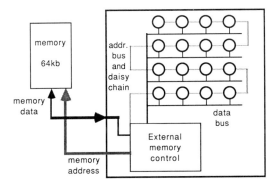

Fig. 3. Indirect virtual addressing organization.

accessed by a subset of the processors, it should be possible to check the global logical OR of an activity flag. This way, the external control system can stop the transfer operation as soon as it is over.

The time to access a byte for a N PEs chip will be at most equal to N. It is exactly the same as in the previous scheme, where it requires $N/8$ accesses to transfer a bit. But, if a small number of PEs need to access the memory, as can happen frequently for list processing operations, the access time is at most equal to the maximum of the cardinal of the active processors set in every chip. An outline of the memory organization is presented in Fig. 3.

4.2 Operation description

The external memory controller will perform the following sequence of operations:

While some processors are still active
    activate the daisy chain
    read the identity of the selected processor on the address bus
        and the logical address of the required data on the data
        bus
    compute the physical address in memory with the previous
        data
    if writing
        read the data sent by the processor on the data bus
        write it to the memory
    else
        read the data in the memory
        send it to the data bus for the selected processor
    endif
end while

To plainly use the external memory as an overflow storage (virtual memory swapping operation), one only needs a direct addressing capability. If the previous mechanism is too slow, the address should be directly generated by the EMC in a systematic way.

The architecture of the transfer part of the processing element is presented in Fig. 4. The internal step of the sequential scan of the processing elements should be as fast as possible, and thus should not include any kind of bit serial processing. Eight bit buffers are included in the processing element to temporarily store transferred data. As the write operation requires the concurrent emission of a memory address and of data, we need 2 buffers, the data and address buffers. The bit serial operations (more particularly transfers between the internal memory of the PE and these buffers) are performed in parallel on all the processing elements before and after the byte level transfer.

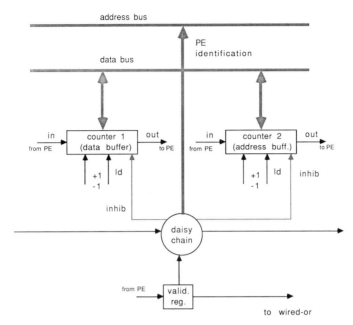

Fig. 4. Processing element buffers and control system.

The sequence of operations executed by the PE is the following:

Before the access, copy in parallel data to the buffer(s)
When the PE is selected
    if writing
        send the content of the address buffer to the data bus
            while the PE address is presented on the address bus
        send the content of the data buffer to the data bus
    else
        send the content of the address buffer on the data bus
            while the PE address is presented on the address bus
        write the content of the data bus in the data buffer
    endif
    reset the selected flag
end when
After all the accesses,
    when reading copy in parallel the content of the data buffer to
        the internal memory

This mechanism is relatively complex, and should be carefully designed not to be too time consuming. It is possible to realize the previous sequence in a 2 or 3 stages pipeline, according to the timing constraints. In that case the memory access time should be roughly equivalent to the instruction cycle.

With this model, it is generally more efficient to process lists coded with a pointer to the next item. Algorithms to manipulate such lists are straightforward to code with standard techniques. To improve indirect addressing, i.e. transforming a data to an address, data and address buffers should be banalized to immediately perform the indirect access to the next item without data movement. To get the successive element of a complex structure, one needs to increment the address. To avoid useless bit serial transfers, the buffers should be realized with counting/decounting capabilities.

This architecture provides a way to efficiently manipulate plain variables, tables and lists. Its main drawback is its relative complexity in terms of development, and silicon area.

5 CONCLUSION

High level operations in vision require more complex features for cellular processing elements. These features include larger sizes, faster access time, more sophisticated addressing modes, at a small cost. We have presented in this paper memory organizations that take into account these constraints. They rely on a hybrid structure using both internal memories and external standard chips to provide "virtual memory" functionality. This structure can be designed to effectively support non standard indirect accesses useful for higher level vision tasks. The next hardware version of the SPHINX pyramid machine will include a direct access virtual memory as it is described above. Scaling these structures with integration technology progress is possible if one concurrently takes into account the following points: the internal memory size (to limit the external memory access frequency); the number of processing elements on a chip (that tends to increase the external memory access time); and the number and the capacity of the external memory chips (to counter balance the previous effect). Real scale experiments for vision tasks should drive to the correct scale.

REFERENCES

[1] M.G.H. Katevenis. (1983). Reduced Instruction Set Computer Architectures for VLSI. October 1983. Ph.D. Thesis, U.C. Berkeley.
[2] K.E. Batcher. (1980). Design of a Massively Parallel Processor. *IEEE Trans. on Computers*, Vol. C29-9, Sept. 1980, pp. 836–840.
[3] M.L.B. Duff. (1976). CLIP4, a large scale integrated circuit array processor. *Proc. 3rd Int. Conf. on Pattern Recognition*, 1976, pp. 728–733.
[4] Flanders et al. (1978). Efficient high speed computing with the Distributed Array Processor, in *High speed computer and algorithm organization*, Kuck et al. (eds.), Academic Press.
[5] W.D. Hillis. (1985). The connection Machine. The MIT Press, Cambridge, Mass. (1982).

[6] K.E. Batcher. (1982). Bit serial processing systems. *IEEE Trans. on Computers*, Vol. C31-5, May, 1982, pp. 377–384.

[7] The GAPP reference manual. NCR Corp.

[8] V. Cantoni, M. Ferretti, S. Levialdi and F. Maloberti. (1985). A pyramid project using integrated technology in S. Levialdi (ed.) *Integrated technology for parallel image processing*, Academic Press.

[9] A. Mérigot, P. Garda, F. Devos and B. Zavidovique. (1985). SPHINX, a pyramidal approach to image processing. *Proc. 3rd Int. Workshop on Computer Architecture for Pattern Analysis and Image Database Management*, pp. 107–111.

[10] A. Mérigot, P. Clermont, J. Mehat, F. Devos and B. Zavidovique. (1986). A pyramidal system for image processing, in V. Cantoni, S. Levialdi (eds.) *Pyramidal systems for image processing, and computer vision*. Springer Verlag.

[11] T. Reeves. (1987). Communication Workshop on Multicomputers for High Level Vision, Roma, June 1987.

[12] P. Clermont. A. Belaid and A. Mérigot. (1987). A Pyramidal algorithm to orientate curves. *IAPR Conference*, Cefalu, Italy, Sept. 1987.

[13] Ph. Clermont and A. Mérigot. (1987). Real time synchronization in a multi-SIMD massively parallel machine. *Communication Workshop on Computer Architecture for Pattern Analysis and Machine Intelligence*, Seattle, Wash., Oct. 1987.

[14] A. Mérigot. (1987). Using indirect memory access on a cellular processor. *Internal Report, IEF*, Un. Paris Sud, Orsay, July 1987.

Chapter Twelve

The ISI Grapher: a Portable Tool for Displaying Graphs Pictorially

Gabriel Robins

Intelligent Systems Division
Information Sciences Institute
4676 Admiralty Way
Marina Del Rey, CU, 90292-6696, USA
gabriel@vaxa.isi.edu

ABSTRACT

The advent of inexpensive personal workstations with high-resolution displays has helped to drastically increase the productivity of end-users. However, the same technology has also served to highlight the deficiencies inherent in current pieces of software and existing user-interfaces. A small set of concepts (e.g. windows, menus, icons, etc) has established itself as a good model for user-interfacer design. We propose an important addition to this collection, namely the concept of a "grapher"; that is, the ability to interactively display and manipulate arbitrary directed graphs. We illustrate the usefulness of this idea, develop a practical linear-time algorithm for laying out graphs, and describe our implementation of a prototype, the ISI Grapher.

1 INTRODUCTION

The advent of inexpensive personal workstations with high-resolution displays, fast processors, and large memories, has helped to drastically increase the productivity of end-users. However, the same technology has also served to highlight the deficiencies inherent in current pieces of software and existing user-interfaces. In particular, it has been recognized now that

This research was supported in part by the Defense Advanced Research Projects Agency under contract number MDA903 81 C 0335. Views and conclusions contained in this report are the author's and should not be interpreted as representing the official opinion or policy of DARPA, the U.S. government, or any person or agency connected with them.

having a good user interface is often the single most important determinant of the usefulness and success of many kinds of systems. Considerable emphasis has been placed on the uniformity, universality, and consistency of user interface design [1].

A small and integrated set of concepts (e.g. desktops, windows, menus, icons, dialog boxes, forms, mouse clicks, etc.) has established itself as a good model for user interface design. We propose an important addition to this collection, namely the concept of a **grapher**, that is, the ability to interactively display and manipulate arbitrary directed graphs. We illustrate the usefulness of this idea, develop a practical linear-time algorithm for laying out graphs, and describe our implementation of a prototype, the ISI Grapher.

2 THE USEFULNESS OF A GRAPHER

Consider the following model of an interactive environment: several editor windows are active, each containing one or more objects which may reside over several files or machines. For the sake of concreteness, let us say that the objects being edited are procedures or semantic nets. It is very likely that due to the sheer complexity and number of these objects, the user soon loses track of which objects he has modified or of the relationships between these objects.

To alleviate this problem, we may introduce an additional **grapher window**, containing a picture of the relations between the objects that are being edited/inspected in other windows. In the following example, nodes represent functions and procedures, while edges represent static lexical scoping. Now the user has available a global view of the current state of his editing session. This grapher window is highly interactive; for example, clicking with the mouse on a graph node would cause the definition of the corresponding object to appear in an editor window whereupon the user may modify that definition. Pictorially, the scenario we envision may appear as follows:

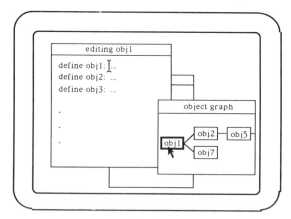

Fig. 1.

Other interpretations of the graphs are possible and are equally useful. For example, in an AI knowledge representation environment, nodes may represent concepts and edges may represent logical subsumption; in a grammar system, nodes may represent symbols (terminals or nonterminals) and edges may represent productions; in a file system, nodes may represent files and edges may represent directory containment; in a distributed environment, nodes may represent machines and edges may represent communication links, and so on.

3 PICTORIAL DISPLAY VS. SYNTACTICAL DISPLAY

If "a picture is worth a thousand words," then it can well be argued that "a graph is worth a hundred well-formed formulas." For example, consider the following directed graph, given by its edge set: G = {(D, H), (E, I), (C, G), (B, E), (F, J), (C, F), (K, B), (B, D), (K, C), (G, A)}. To visualize the structure of the graph G from this representation is not trivial. Suppose that we were told that G is in fact a tree; is it then obvious whether G is a binary tree? The answer is still not apparent at first glance. Even if we are told that in fact G is a binary tree, how easy would it be for us to determine what the root of G is? And even if we are further told that G is a binary tree with root K, how quickly could we determine whether G is a balanced tree?

The answers to all these queries follow immediately if instead of specifying G formally using set-theoretic notation, we had simply been given a pictorial diagram of G, as follows:

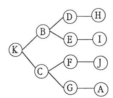

Fig. 2. The pictorial representation of G.

This discussion alludes to the following conclusion: since humans are good at pattern-recognition, it is often preferable to display the pattern pictorially rather than its equivalent formal syntactic representation. We may wonder why it is the case that certain properties are difficult for us to infer from formal descriptions, yet are trivially apparent from appropriate diagrams; this is partially due to the fact that *transitive closures* are difficult to compute mentally (is this related to the fact that the transitive closure predicate *can not* be specified in first order logic?). A compounding problem is that humans find it difficult to keep track of a large number of identifiers, even if they are mnemonic. However, the answers to such questions are best left for cognitive scientists to muse about.

The heart of any grapher would be an algorithm for laying out directed graphs. However, finding optimal layouts for graphs is quite a difficult problem; even in the special case of laying out binary trees optimally on the lattice plane, the problem turns out to be NP-hard, as is its approximation to within 4 percent! [2]. By *optimal* layout we mean a layout that minimizes some parameters, such as the total width of the resulting diagram, or the number of edge crossings. Other researchers have proposed various algorithms to layout and display graphs [3, 4], some of which are similar to the one adopted by the ISI Grapher.

Interestingly enough, laying out binary trees on the continuous real plane reduces to linear programming. This is a small consolation, however, as solutions to continuous problems do not directly map (via rounding) into solutions to the corresponding discrete versions, but the two can instead be arbitrarily far apart [5]. This is rather discouraging, as we would like to be able to layout large graphs (of several thousands of nodes) interactively, and in "real-time." Moreover, the notion of "optimality" with respect to a layout is quite subjective; in the above discussion, a reasonable set of "esthetic" heuristics with respect to binary trees had to be fixed. We then need to ask ourselves how important optimality is to us in the resulting layout; from this point on we use the assumption that users in most interactive applications would be willing to sacrifice some "beauty" in exchange for a considerable speedup.

4 DEFINITION OF THE PROBLEM

In order to make the problem more tractable and well-defined, we further relax it: we assume that nodes are to be represented by rectangles, and that edges are to be represented by straight line segments. Next, we constrain all the children of a node to appear in the layout to the right of all of their ancestors. Furthermore, we sidestep the problem of having to draw cycles, via a structure-preserving mapping of directed graphs to labelled acyclic directed graphs; this idea will be discussed later in a greater detail.

The problem then, is given an arbitrary graph (or relation), map the nodes (or identifiers) into the lattice plane (that is, assign coordinates to them), and display the result, in such a way as to exhibit the original structure of the graph as much as possible, also making it convenient for a user to inspect, browse through, and manipulate the resulting representation.

The ISI Grapher is an implementation of a solution to this problem: it is a set of functions which converts a given arbitrary directed graph into an equivalent pictorial representation, and then graphically displays the resulting diagram. Nodes and edges in the abstract graph now become boxes and lines on the workstation screen, and the user may then interact with the Grapher in various ways via the mouse and the keyboard. The ISI Grapher is both powerful and extendible, allowing an application-builder to easily and comfortably build other tools on top of it.

5 SALIENT FEATURES OF THE ISI GRAPHER

Other graphers and browsers exist, so the salient features of this system are now enumerated:

Portability. The ISI Grapher is implemented strictly in Common-Lisp, except for a tiny bottom-layer having to do with low-level graphics. This makes the ISI Grapher very portable. The ISI Grapher already runs on several versions of TI, as well as Symbolics workstations/environments, with only about a dozen lines of code of difference between the two implementations!

Speed. The ISI Grapher has a graphing speed of over 2,500 nodes/edges per minute (of real time, on a Symbolics 3600 workstation with garbage-collection turned off), almost an order of magnitude improvement over other systems. Moreover, the asymptotic time behavior of the ISI Grapher increases only linearly with the size of the graph being drawn. This was achieved through careful design of the data structures and the layout algorithm.

Nice layout. The layout algorithm employed by the ISI Grapher, in addition to being time efficient, compares favorably with the results of layout algorithms employed by other graphers. Figures 3 and 4 illustrate typical ISI Grapher displays.

Versatility. The ISI Grapher interfaces to other system tools, such as the editor and the inspector. This makes for a more uniform environment for the user/application-builder.

Extensibility. The design of the ISI Grapher allows other applications to be built on top of it quickly and elegantly. Several such tools will be described later. This is a very important property, because graph structures are a recurring theme throughout computer science (in data structures, knowledge bases, grammars, searches, etc.). Thus the usefulness of a system greatly increases when individual researchers can easily tailor it to their specific needs and requirements, as is the case with the ISI Grapher.

Innovations. The ISI Grapher incorporates several novel features. Chief among those is the linear-time layout algorithm, as well as the "continuous-update" scheme utilized by the global scrolling mode. The latter is designed to sharpen the user's awareness and sense of direction and location while "navigating" through a large graph.

6 OTHER GRAPHERS AND RELATED WORK

A notable effort to produce a graph browser called Grab was put forth in [6] and is further developed in [7], where a system to visually display graphs was

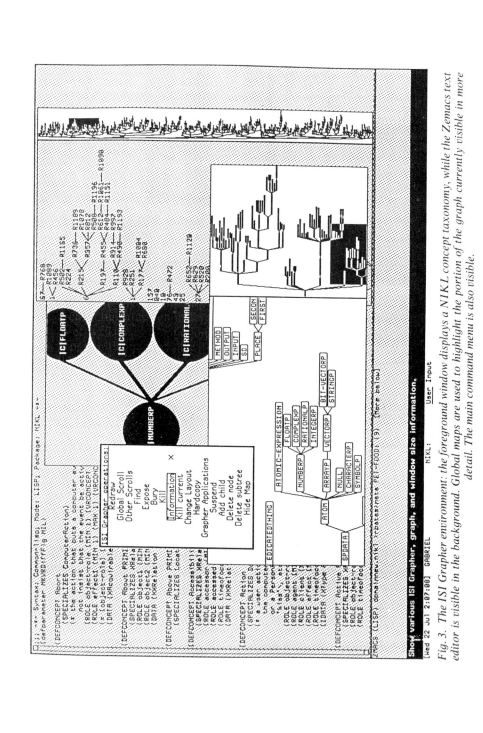

Fig. 3. The ISI Grapher environment: the foreground window displays a NIKL concept taxonomy, while the Zemacs text editor is visible in the background. Global maps are used to highlight the portion of the graph currently visible in more detail. The main command menu is also visible.

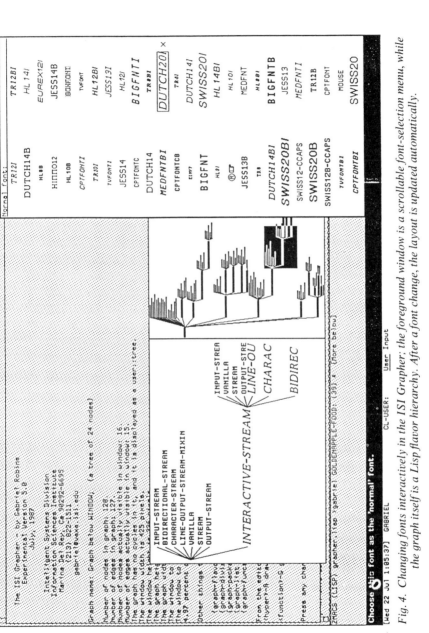

Fig. 4. Changing fonts interactively in the ISI Grapher: the foreground window is a scrollable font-selection menu, while the graph itself is a Lisp flavor hierarchy. After a font change, the layout is updated automatically.

implemented. Unfortunately for AI researchers, the language originally used was C. Secondly, numerous time-consuming heuristics (to optimize edge-crossings, for example), rendering the system so slow, almost to the point of uselessness on large graphs. For example, Grab requires almost 7 minutes to layout a small graph containing 150 nodes and 160 edges; compare this with the speed of the ISI Grapher as discussed above.

Another scheme for drawing graphs is proposed by [8]. To draw a graph, this scheme entails detecting and exploring various properties of the given graph with respect to symmetry and the induced automorphism group. While possessing some mathematical elegance, such a scheme can hardly be expected to yield an efficient implementation. It is recognized that systems which run very slowly but optimize layouts to some degree have their applications, but for our purposes, we regard speed as having paramount importance: users are not likely to tolerate layout times measured in hours.

An experimental graph-layout system was produced by the Symbolics Corporation in the spring of 1985, for internal use. However, the heavy dependence of this package on flavors and other Symbolics features, has rendered this system completely non-portable. In addition, this system used so much space, that attempting to use it on a graph with more than a couple of hundred nodes would typically lead to hopeless disk thrashing (due to massive swapping). In contrast, the ISI Grapher has been successfully used on graphs of up to 25,000 nodes without incident.

7 INVOKING THE ISI GRAPHER

The ISI Grapher is invoked at the top-level by calling the function graph-lattice with a list of roots/options and a *sons-function*. This provides a means for the ISI Grapher to deduce the complete description of the graph by recursively calling the sons-function on the roots and their descendents. Next, a reasonable graphical layout is computed for the graph, and is drawn on the display. Various mouse sensitivity and functions are automatically provided, creating a versatile and user-friendly browsing environment.

7.1 An example

For example, if our graph is {(a, b), (a, c), (b, d)}, our root is {a}, and our sons-function is:

```
(defun sons (x)
   (cond ((eq x 'a) (list 'b 'c))
         ((eq x 'b) (list 'd))
         (t nil)))
```

Note that the sons-function returns NIL if and only if the given node is a leaf in the graph (that is, the given node has no children). Now, the call (graph-lattice 'a 'sons) would produce the picture of the graph:

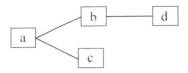

Directed cycles in the graph will be "broken" for displaying purposes by the introduction of "stub" nodes. For example, the graph {(a, b), (b, c), (c, a)} which looks like this:

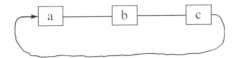

will be actually displayed as follows:

where "A" represents the same graph node as does "a", so in a sense the graph node represented by "a" is displayed twice (with an obvious indication that this has occurred, such as the usage of a bolder font; this is automatically provided by the ISI Grapher). All directed edges are displayed with the direction implicitly going from left to right. The first argument to graph-lattice may in fact be a command list with a special syntax, allowing selective pruning of the graph; this facility may also be used interactively in various ways.

The cycle-breaking may be viewed as a pre-processing pass on the graph, and operates as follows: a topological sort is initiated, beginning at the roots (the parentless nodes, or else an arbitrary user-specified set of nodes). A topological sort is an ordering of the nodes of a directed graph so that all the parents of a given node in the ordering appear before that node in the ordering. It is well-known that it is possible to topologically sort the nodes of a directed graph if and only if the graph does not contain any directed cycles, and moreover there are numerous linear-time algorithms to achieve such an ordering when one exists (or detect that none exist if that is the case).

When the topological sort becomes "stuck" and cannot "proceed" any further on any given node, we have detected a cycle. We now "break" the cycle via the introduction of a "stub" node as discussed above, and continue with the topological sort. We repeat this process until all the nodes in the graph have been processed, thus eliminating all cycles. If one is a little careful in the implementation of this scheme, as the author has been in the case of the ISI Grapher, the total amount of computation required is linear in the size of the graph.

Once a graph has been laid out and is displayed in a window, various commands are available from the main command menu. This menu is activated by clicking the mouse anywhere inside the currently active Grapher window. If the mouse cursor was pointing to a particular graph node during the mouse click, additional commands (tailored for and directed towards that particular node) shall become available on the main command menu. Appropriate documentation/explanation lines are available at the bottom of the display when the corresponding menu entry is highlighted, and a mechanism is provided that allows the user to customize the menus.

8 PERFORMANCE AND EFFICIENCY

The time required by the ISI Grapher to lay-out a graph is linearly proportional to the size of the graph. More formally, the asymptotic time (and space) complexity of the ISI Grapher for a graph $G = (V, E)$ is $O(|V| + |E|)$, where $|V|$ is the size of the node set, and $|E|$ is the size of the edge set. Moreover, the constant of proportionality in this linear relation is relatively small, yielding both a theoretical optimum, as well as practical efficiency. In benchmark runs, speeds of up to 2,500 nodes per real-time minute have been achieved by the ISI Grapher when running on a Symbolics workstation.

It is worth noting that the computational time bottleneck of most graph-layout systems tends to be embedded in the layout algorithm which finds the X and Y positions for nodes on the display. It is further noted that there are numerous algorithms and heuristics to discretely lay-out graphs on the lattice-plane; however, the esthetic criterion that dictates what is a "nice" or "pleasing" layout varies greatly over users, and is very subjective. It can even be shown that under some simple esthetic assumptions, "optimal" layout becomes NP-hard (which in plane language means that polynomial-time algorithms for such layouts are not likely to exist). See, for example, [2].

The author does not advocate his layout scheme as the final word on such algorithms: he came into the belief (after considerable thought and experimentation with alternate layout schemes) that the scheme employed here yields very high returns in terms of esthetic appeal per unit computation time, and is also quite simple to describe. For other layout schemes see, for example, [9].

9 THE LAYOUT ALGORITHM

The layout algorithm employed by the ISI Grapher has several novel aspects. First, as mentioned before, the asymptotic time and space performance of the layout algorithm is linear in the size of the graph being processed; this situation is clearly optimal. Secondly, the layout algorithm employed by the ISI Grapher exhibits an interesting symmetry: layout is performed independently in the X and Y directions. That is, first all the X coordinates (of the nodes in the layout) are computed, and then all the Y coordinates are computed without referring to the value of any of the X coordinates. This property implies a certain logical "orthogonality" in the treatment of the two planar dimensions, and is the source of the simplicity of the layout algorithm (the heart of the layout algorithm is only about two pages of code).

The Y coordinate of a node N is computed as follows: if N is a leaf node (that is, if N has no children in the graph) its Y coordinate is selected so that it is as close as possible to, but not overlapping any node previously layed out. If N has any children, their Y coordinates are computed first, and then N's Y coordinate is set to be the arithmetic average of the Y coordinates of N's children. Note that the second rule implies depth-first recursion. which is indeed how the algorithm is implemented. The Y-direction layout is sensitive to the heights of the objects being displayed. On the other hand, the Y-direction layout is completely oblivious to the X-coordinate values.

Similarly, the X coordinate of a node N is computed as follows: if N is a root node (that is, if N has no parents in the graph) its X coordinate is set to zero. If N has any parents, their X coordinates are computed first, and then N's X coordinate is set to be some fixed amount larger than the maximum of the X coordinates of N's parents. Again, note that this implies depth-first recursion. The X-direction layout is sensitive to the lengths of the objects being displayed, and is completely oblivious to the Y-coordinate values.

For the sake of completeness, we specify the X and Y layout algorithms more formally. The layout algorithm for the Y coordinates is specified as follows:

```
For N in Nodes do Y[N] := 0;
Last-y := 0;
For N in Roots(G) do Layout-Y(N);

Procedure Layout-Y(N);
begin
if Y[N] = 0 then       /* N was not yet layed-out */
   If N has any unlayed-out children then
      begin              /* layout the children first */
      for C in Children(N) do Layout-Y(C);
      Y[N] := average-Y(Children(N));
      end
   else begin            /* layout a leaf. */
      Y[N] := Last-y + Height(N);
      Last-Y := Y[N];
      end;
end;                     /* of procedure Layout-Y */
```

The layout algorithm for the X coordinates is specified as follows:

```
For N in Nodes do X[N] := 0;
For N in Leaves(G) do Layout-X (N);
```

```
Procedure Layout-X(N);
begin
if X[N] = 0 then      /* N was not yet layed-out. */
   If N has parents then
      begin              /* layout the parents first. */
      for C in Parents(N) do Layout-X (C);
      X[N] := Max{X[i] + Width(i) | i in Parents(N)} + constant;
      end
end;                     /* of procedure Layout-X */
```

From the recursive layout scheme specified above, it should be clear that each node gets processed only once during the independent passes (one for each of the two planar axes). What is not so obvious from this discussion however, is whether such layouts actually appear pleasant given real graphs. This question is best answered via inspection of some examples, such as the ones in Figs. 3 and 4.

10 PORTABILITY AND CODE ORGANIZATION

In trying to keep the ISI Grapher as portable as possible, the code is divided into two main modules. The first and by far the largest module consists of pure Common-Lisp code; this code is responsible for all the layout, control, and data-structure manipulation algorithms. The second module is substantially smaller, and consists of numerous low-level primitive calls which are quite likely to be implementation-dependent. The intent here is that when the Grapher is to be ported to another (Common-Lisp) environment, only the second module should require modification. In order to further minimize porting efforts, the calls from code in the first module to functions in the second module were designed to be as generic as possible.

In summary, if a new environment has a window-system which supports a reasonable set of window and graphics primitives (such as open-window, draw-line, print-string, etc), then porting the ISI Grapher to this new environment or machine should require a minimal coding effort, probably all of which would be confined to the second section of the ISI Grapher code.

11 EXISTING APPLICATIONS

As examples of how easily other applications may be built on top of the ISI Grapher, several such applications have already been built and are provided alongside the ISI Grapher. We now describe some of these applications:

The List Grapher. This application displays the natural correspondence between lists and trees. For example, the call

(graph-list '(alpha(beta (epsilon theta))
                     (gamma epsilon)
                     (delta zeta)))

would produce the following picture

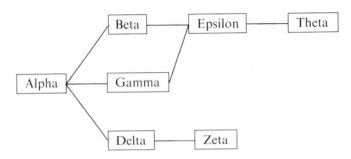

This provides an easy means of quickly obtaining large or complex graphs.

The Flavor Grapher. This application displays the interdependencies between Lisp "flavors," where nodes are flavor names, and edges mean "depends on." This type of a diagram could be quite useful in system development. For example, the call (graph-flavor 'tv:window) would graph all the flavors that depend on the tv:window flavor.

The Package Grapher. This application produces a picture of the package interdependencies between a Common-Lisp package and all packages which use it. An example of a call is (graph-package "global").

The Divisors Grapher. This application displays the divisibility graph of a given integer; that is, all the divisors of an integer are represented as nodes, where an edge between two nodes means "is divisible by." This is also a quick method to produce large graphs. An example of such a call would be (graph-divisors 360).

   To illustrate how easily such tools may be built on top of the ISI Grapher, we note in passing that coding and testing the above 3 tools (the Flavor Grapher, the Package Grapher, and the Divisibility Grapher) took only half an hour of coding.

The NIKL Browser. This application is a browsing tool for NIKL networks and graphs a concept taxonomy below a given concept list. Concepts are fundamental objects in NIKL, and are partially ordered by subsumption (i.e. set inclusion). NIKL is a knowledge representation environment development at ISI and is a popular tool in artificial intelligence research [10, 11].

Other applications include the Function Grapher which draws function-call hierarchies based on lexical scoping, and the Loom Grapher (Loom is the successor to NIKL).

12 EXTENDIBILITY AND OVERRIDING DEFAULT OPERATIONS

Several basic Grapher operations may be controlled via the specification of alternate functions for performing these tasks. These operations include the drawing of nodes and edges, the selection of fonts, the determination of print-names, pretty-printing, and highlighting operations. Standard definitions are already provided for these operations and are used by default if an application-builder does not override them by specifying his own functions for performing these tasks.

For example, the default method of highlighting a graph node when the cursor points to it on the screen, is to invert a solid rectangle of bits over the node. Suppose that the user is not satisfied with this mode of highlighting and would like to have thin boxes drawn around highlighted nodes instead. He may then write a highlighting function that does exactly that, and tell the Grapher to use that function whenever a node needs to be highlighted. The details and semantics of this process are fully described in [12].

As another example, suppose the user is not happy with the way nodes are displayed on the screen; ordinarily nodes are displayed on the screen by printing their ASCII print-names at their corresponding screen location, but the user would prefer that some specialized icon be displayed instead. The user may then specify his icon-displaying function as the normal node-painting function and from then on, whenever a node needs to be displayed on the screen, that function will be called upon (along with arguments corresponding to the node, its screen location, and the relevant window) thus achieving the desired effect.

In particular, the following basic Grapher operations may be overridden by the user:

(a) Deciding which font should be used to display an object's print-name. Different fonts may thus be used to distinguish various types of objects.
(b) Determining the dimensions (width and height) of an object. This information is used by the other grapher functions, such as the layout algorithm (as placement of objects is sensitive to their sizes) and highlighting operations (as the size of the highlight-box depends on the size of the object being highlighted).
(c) Determining the ASCII print-name of an object.
(d) Highlighting and unhighlighting an object. This operation is most often performed when the mouse points to a given object.
(e) Describing or explaining an object. This is the function that gets

executed when the corresponding explain (or pp) command is selected from the main menu.

For each one of the categories above, the Grapher keeps a *function precedence list*, consisting of a primary function, a secondary function, a thirdary function, and so on, for as many functions as are currently available to perform the task associated with that particular category. Whenever a new function is introduced to perform a certain task, each function is "demoted" one "notch" in precedence. In addition, each category also is associated with a default function, which is initially the only function associated with that category. The default function for a particular category has the least precedence relative to any other functions in that category.

When a certain task needs to be performed during the normal operation of the Grapher, the corresponding primary function is called with a graph node object, a complex structure from which a lot of other information may be extracted, and a window. It is then up to the called function to perform the given task and return non-nil if it indeed performed the said task, or nil if it did not (or could not or chose not to) perform the said task. In the former case the Grapher merrily goes about its business, while in the latter case, the secondary function is similarly called, with this process repeating until some function has successfully performed the given task (this event being signaled by the return of non-nil by that function), or until all the available functions have been exhausted and the task has not yet been performed. In the latter case the default function is called, the default function being guaranteed to perform the associated task successfully.

This mechanism gives the user great flexibility in displaying and highlighting graph objects. These operations may depend heavily on the type and size of the object being displayed or highlighted, and so different functions may be used to handle each type of object. It should be noted that this discussion implies the ability to mix various types of objects in the same graph (each having unique size, appearance, and highlighting characteristics) with relative ease and uniformity. In summary, this scheme is reminiscent of a primitive *flavor* mechanism, where "inheritance" has a non-standard semantics.

In summary, many of the basic Grapher operations are parametrized by a set of default methods. This set may be extended by the application-builder in order to make the ISI Grapher behave in ways not provided for by the author. Any operations left unspecified by the application-builder will default to some reasonable pre-defined method. This scheme results in a portable, flexible, and extendible system.

13 ICON DISPLAYS

There are numerous ways to make ISI Grapher displays even more visually striking. For example, the user could utilize icons to display nodes, whereupon the BBN Naval Model (a NIKL network depicting a naval scenario) could take on the style of the following diagram:

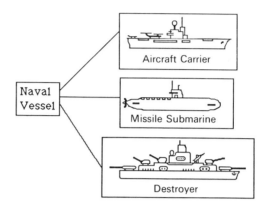

Fig. 5. An example of an icon-based ISI Grapher display.

This may be accomplished by using a font-editor to create a specialized font which would include the above icons as special characters. As the ISI Grapher is capable of working with arbitrary fonts, the above display would readily result from the addition of the proper (trivial) node-paint function.

13 HARDCOPYING

Hardcopying is system and device-dependent, but the ISI Grapher does provide a mechanism which automatically scrolls the current window incrementally in the X and Y directions and calls the proper system function (that is responsible for the actual hardcopying of that portion of the graph which is currently visible in the current window). The idea here is that since most hardcopying devices are capable of producing an image of only a small (page-sized) bitmap, in order to obtain a hardcopy of a large graph (say, several square meters in area), it is necessary to hardcopy small sections of it one at a time, and then cut-and-paste the resulting "jigsaw-puzzle" together to obtain the final wall-sized diagram. The automatic scrolling also provides a small overlap margin between adjacent panes which has proved to be quite handy during the final cutting-and-pasting process. In summary, the ISI Grapher does provide an automatic means of scrolling in order to hardcopy a graph in small sections, but the environment is responsible for providing a hardcopying function which can properly hardcopy each section.

14 CONCLUSION AND FURTHER RESEARCH

In summary, the fundamental motivation which gave birth to the ISI Grapher is the observation that graphs are very basic and common structures, and the belief that the ability to quickly display, manipulate, and browse through graphs may greatly enhance the productivity of a researcher, both quantitatively and qualitatively.

We have shown that various applications can benefit greatly from an interactive grapher-like facility, and then we described an implementation of a prototype, the ISI grapher. Some of the novel features of the ISI Grapher include its linear-time layout algorithm, its portability, and its extensibility. Although our implementation is in a high-level programming language (Common-Lisp), in future user interface design for personal-workstations, it would be preferable to have a Grapher facility at the window-system level, alongside the other primitives of the environment. We believe that the usefulness and applicability of such a graphing facility merits this commitment.

Further research may concentrate on using some heuristics in order to optimize the layout a little, although it is certainly not clear how much of an improvement in the layout can really be achieved while preserving the linear-time complexity of the layout algorithm. It would also be interesting to port the ISI Grapher to other machines and environments. Several such ports are currently in progress; the ISI Grapher already runs on several versions of Texas Instruments Explorers and Symbolics workstations. Finally, numerous extensions to the ISI Grapher are possible, and it is encouraged that applications begin to use the ISI Grapher, or other grapher-like tools, as a building-block in their user interface.

15 OBTAINING THE SOURCES

Further documentation [12], as well as the source code for the ISI Grapher may be obtained by contacting the author: Gabriel Robins, Information Sciences Institute, 4676 Admiralty Way, Marina Del Rey, Ca, 90292-6695, USA; ARPAnet address: "gabriel©VAXA.isi.edu". The author has already received and responded to a large number of requests for the source code and for the full documentation/manual.

16 ACKNOWLEDGEMENTS

The author is grateful to the Intelligent Systems Division Director Ron Ohlander, for providing excellent leadership, as well as interproject support funds for further development effort. The supervision and advice of Larry Miller is greatly appreciated. In addition, the following individuals deserve credit for various suggestions and comments: Bob MacGregor, Bob Kasper,

Ray Bates, Norm Sondheimer, Robert Albano, Tom Galloway, Steve Smoliar, Neil Goldman, and Eli Messinger. The patient help of Leslie Ladd and Larry Friedman with tedious photocopying, binding, and pasting is gratefully acknowledged. Ching Tsun Chou carefully proofread his paper, and made numerous valuable suggestions; further thanks for proofreading go to Tom Galloway and Victor Brown. Finally, the author is especially indebted to Tom Kaczmarek, under who's leadership the ISI Grapher was initially born.

REFERENCES

[1] Kaczmarek, T., Mark, W. and Wilczynski, D. (1983). The CUE Project. *Proceedings of Soft Fair*, July 1983.

[2] Supowit, K. and Reingold, E. (1983). The Complexity of Drawing Trees Nicely. *Acta Informatica*, **18**, 1983, pp. 377–392.

[3] Vaucher, J. (1980). Pretty-Printing of Trees. *Software—Practice and Experience*, **10**, 1980, pp. 553–561.

[4] Reingold, E. and Tilford, J. (1981). Tidier Drawing of Trees. *IEEE Transactions on Software Engineering*, **SE-7**, no. 2, March 1981, pp. 223–28.

[5] Papadimitriou, C. and Steiglitz, K. (1982). *Combinatorial Optimization, Algorithms and Complexity*, Prentice-Hall, New Jersey, p. 327.

[6] Meyer, C. A Browser for Directed Graphs. *Technical Report*, Department of Electrical Engineering and Computer Science, University of California, Berkeley.

[7] Rowe, L., Davis, M., Messinger, E., Meyer, C., Spirakis, C. and Tuam, A. (1987). *A Browser for Directed Graphs. Software—Practice and Experience*, **17(1)**, January 1987, pp. 61–76.

[8] Lipton, R., North, S. and Sandberg, J. (1985). A method for drawing Graphs. *ACM Computational Geometry Conference Proceedings*, June 1985, pp. 153–160.

[9] Wetherell, C. and Shannon, A. (1979). Tidy Drawing of Trees. *IEEE Transaction on Software Engineering*, **5**, September 1979, pp. 514–520.

[10] Robins, G. (1986). The NIKL Manual. *Internal ISI Report*, April 1986.

[11] Kaczmarek, T., Bates, R. and Robins, G. (1986). Recent Development in NIKL. *AAAI, Proceedings of the Fifth National Conference on Artificial Intelligence*, August 1986.

[12] Robins, G. (1987). The ISI Grapher. *Internal ISI Report*, June 1987.

Index

Abingdon Cross, 65
AIS-5000, 131–140
  parallel array, 135–137
  parallel memory organization, 140
  processing element, 137–140
  system components, 134
Associative Processing Elements (APEs), 76–78
  activation functions, 79
  active procedures, 80
Associative String Processor (ASP), 76–83
  evaluating architecture for VLSI, 80–81
  information processing, 81–83
  operations, 79
  software, 80
Atomic Lock Memories (ALM), 118, 120–121
Augmented hybrid systems, 57
Autonomous Land Vehicle (ALV) project, 63
  task categorizing, 64

Base tail points, 26
Bimodality analysis, 1–7
Bimodality detection, 2–4
Binary N-cubes, 56

Cellular arrays, 171
Cellular Logic Processor (CLP), 164–166
Cellular operations, 153–155
Cellular processors, memory design, 171–183
Centipede, 140–147
  accumulators, 141
  applications, 143–147
  indirect addressing, 142
  transpose, 142–143
CLIP4 system, 162–166
Clusters of clusters, 56
Communication protocols, 106
Compounding operations, 56
Computer vision, 97–110
  associative approach to, 75–95
  high level, 109–110
  intermediate level, 108–109
  low level, 107–108
  operations, 107–110
Conditional execution, 111–112
Convolutions, 144

Data partitioning, 122
Dense graphs, 56
Direct addressing virtual memory, 175–178
Distribution functions, 111

Dynamic allocation, 123
Dynix operating system, 120–121

'End concept', 23–34
End regions, 26
  algorithm results, 29–31
  extraction procedure, 26–29
Euler Characteristic Number, 25, 29
Expert systems, heuristics, 46–49
Externally realized memory, 172

Fast Fourier transform (FFT), 108
Fast Hough Transform (FHT) algorithm, 11, 16, 19
Feature extraction, 145–146
Fortran, 110
Frame Store Module, 91
Function partitioning, 122

GAM Pyramid, 23
Generic architectures, 61
Grab graph browser, 189

Hough transform, 9–21
  parallelization, 10–12
    in feature point and parameter space, 12
    in feature point space, 12
    in image space, 11
    in parameter space, 12
  Polymorphic-Torus architecture, 15–19
    parallelization, 15–18
      in feature point and parameter space, 18
      in feature point space, 16
      in image space, 15–16
      in parameter space, 16–17
Hypercubes, 97–110

Ideal memory, 173–174
Image features, 24–34
Image processing, 117–130, 151
Image Processing Module (IPM), 89–93
Image Understanding System (IUS), 37
  database, 41–44
Image Understanding Task, 35–51
  algorithm database, 39–50
  algorithm library, 40
  use of system, 49–50
In-chip memory, 172–173
Indirect addressing virtual memory, 178–182
Information processing, ASP, 81–83
Instruction parallel architecture, 151

Intelligent Operating System (IOS), 37, 46
    database, 44–49
ISI Grapher, 185–202
    applications, 196–198
    code organization, 196
    extendibility, 198
    hardcopying, 200
    icon displays, 199–200
    invoking, 192–194
    layout algorithm, 194–196
    overriding default operations, 198
    performance and efficiency, 194
    pictorial display vs. syntactical display,
        187–188
    portability, 196
    salient features of, 189
Iterative schemes, 4–6

Lines (pipelines, and 1-dimensional arrays),
    55
Lisp, 109–110
List manipulation, 176–178
Look-up-table transforms, 144–145

Mesh Connected Computers (MCC), 10
Meshes, 97–110
Message addressing, 105
Message protocols, 105
MIMD languages, 112–113
MIMD systems, 98, 103–104, 109, 117–130
MPP processing element, 102–103
Multicomputer architectures, topologies and
    specifications, 55–57

NlogN reconfiguring network-based systems,
    56

One-dimensional array, 132–133

Parallel architectures, 98–107
    assigning costs to nodes and links, 58–59
    basic topologies, 61
    categorizing topologies, 60
    combining topology description with esti-
        mates, 59–60
    complexity and cost estimates, 61
    coordinated evaluation, 53–73
    for perceptual tasks, 53–73
    performance evaluation on different algor-
        ithms, 66–69
    representing multi-computer topologies,
        57–58
    results to be expected, 69–70
    specifications and cost estimates, 69
    system for describing, and assigning costs
        to, 57
    task selection, 62–66
    test set, 62
Parallel data declaration, 111

Parallel expressions, 110
Parallel Pascal, 110–112
Parallel programming, 120–121
Partitionable parallel processing system, 36
Patch Buffer Module, 89–91
Perceptual tasks, parallel architectures for,
    53–73
Performance modeling and evaluation, 113
Permutation functions, 111
Pipeline architectures, 10
Pipelines, 152, 159–162
Pixel parallel architecture, 151
Polygons, 55
Polymorphic-Torus architecture, 12–19
    composite physical and internal network,
        13–14
Principal Control Unit (PCU), 91, 92
Process management, 104
Processing elements (PE), 11–12, 100, 151–155
Processor arrays (PA), 151–152, 155–159
Prolog, 109–110
Pyramid computers, 2–7
Pyramids, 56

Reduction functions, 111
Rings, 55
Root cell, 4

Scalar Buffer Unit (SBU), 91
Scalar Processor (SP), 91
SCAPE (Single Chip Array Processing Ele-
    ment) chip, 83–85, 93
    chain controller, 91–92
    Image Processing Module (IPM), 89–93
    image representation, 85–89
    performance, 93–94
Sequent Balance 8000, 117–130
    algorithm parallelization, 121–124
    benchmarks design, 128–129
    measuring applications performance, 124–
        126
    performance analysis, 121
    system overview, 118–120
SHORTPORT switch function, 14–15
SIMD languages, 110–112
SIMD systems, 98, 100, 108, 109, 124
    see also AIS-5000
SLIC bus, 119
Slightly augmented trees, 56
Stars (bus-based systems), 55
Static allocation, 123
Sub-array selection, 111

Tail points, 26
Thresholding, 4–6
Trees, 56
Two-dimensional arrays, 56